FROM CHARACTER BUILDING
TO SOCIAL TREATMENT

FROM CHARACTER BUILDING TO SOCIAL TREATMENT

The History of the Use of Groups in Social Work

Kenneth E. Reid

Greenwood Press
Westport, Connecticut • London, England

Library of Congress Cataloging in Publication Data

Reid, Kenneth E
From character building to social treatment.

Bibliography: p.
Includes index.
1. Social group work—History. 2. Social service—
United States—History. I. Title.
HV45.R44   361.4'0973   79-6567
ISBN 0-313-22016-6

Library of Congress Catalog Card Number: 79-6567
ISBN: 0-313-22016-6

First published in 1981

Greenwood Press
A division of Congressional Information Service, Inc.
88 Post Road West, Westport, Connecticut 06881

Printed in the United States of America

10 9 8 7 6 5 4 3 2 1

*Behold the past, the many changes
of dynasties; the future too you are able to foresee for it will be of like fashion,
and it is impossible for the future to escape from the rhythm of the present.*

MARCUS AURELIUS

CONTENTS

ILLUSTRATIONS

ACKNOWLEDGMENTS

While there may be a single name on the title page of a book, seldom does one person write a book of this nature by himself. Certainly a large number of individuals have contributed ideas, information, direction, and helpful criticism, and I wish to acknowledge their assistance. Gratitude goes to the faculty of the School of Social Work at Western Michigan who gracefully absorbed my teaching responsibilities and assignments while I was on sabbatical leave. Of particular assistance were Mary Burns, Bob Barstow, and Leslie Leighninger who read several of the early drafts of the manuscript and gave encouragement and guidance. Appreciation goes also to the faculty of the University of Bath and the National Institute for Social Work in London, England who opened their offices and libraries to me and provided a home while I was collecting data for the first chapter. Several teachers, who became good friends, also contributed; they include Lucille Barber, Gordon Aldridge, and Minnie Harlow. Appreciation is given to the staff of the Archives of Case Western Reserve University and the Social Welfare Archives of the University of Minnesota, who assisted me in tracking down lost and forgotten information. In addition, I wish to acknowledge the Rockefeller Foundation, which provided me with a grant to do research at the University of Minnesota.

Special appreciation is extended to Gertrude Wilson, Gladys Ryland, Paul Glasser, and William Schwartz who raised important issues and provided invaluable insights. Finally, I want to thank my wife, Eve, and my two children, David and Heather, who were most patient, understanding, and supportive in making this book a reality.

INTRODUCTION

The history of social group work, one of the three major
methods of social work along with social casework and community organization, is the history of social agencies in a
changing society. With roots in such diverse areas as the
settlement movement, the recreation movement, education,
social reform, and the social sciences, social group work has
evolved into an effective means of service for the purposes of
enhancing the social functioning, growth, and change of individuals, and of achieving ends desirable in a political and social
democracy. Social group workers are employed in a variety of
settings such as schools, recreation centers, hospitals, residential treatment centers, and family service agencies, to mention
only a few.

This book examines the use of groups in social work from
a historical perspective. While much has been written about the
evolution of social casework, charity, and social welfare, relatively little has been written about the development of the use
of groups. The intent is, therefore, to fill a gap in the literature
of social work and to contribute a historical analysis of the
growth of this modality from its early beginnings in mid-
Victorian England to its present status within the profession
of social work.

Initially, groups were a means of dealing with the many
social problems that resulted from the Industrial Revolution
in England, such as the migration of uneducated workers from
rural areas to the cities, inadequate housing, and an increase in
crime and delinquency. Underlying these and other problems
was a general disregard for human life and the human condition.

Organizations such as the social settlements, YMCA, YWCA,
Scouts, and Sunday schools evolved as positive ways of saving
souls, strengthening character, reinforcing patriotism, and
rescuing those in need.
Groups were also used for less altruistic purposes. For example, they represented a cheap and effective way of averting
social discontent and protecting property. This is best exemplified in the Sunday school movement of the late 1700s, which
was ostensibly established to teach religion and to "train the
lower classes to habits of industry and virtue." On a more
covert and perhaps more practical level, the movement reflected the community leaders' desire to reduce vandalism on
Sundays, the one day children were not expected to work in
the factories, and one time when there was an inordinate
amount of property damage.[1] As America went through its
own version of the Industrial Revolution, many of the same
organizations that had been conceived in England were adapted
to meet the particular needs and unique aspects of American
life.
In many ways, America was fertile ground for these organizations. In the 1830s, Alexis de Tocqueville observed that Americans tended to form associations.

The political associations that exist in the United States are only a single
feature in the midst of the immense assemblage of associations in that
country. Americans of all ages, all conditions, and all dispositions, constantly form associations. They have not only commercial and manufacturing companies in which all take part, but associations of a thousand
other kinds—religious, moral, serious, futile, extensive or restricted,
enormous or diminutive. The Americans make associations to give entertainments, to found establishments for education, to build inns, to construct churches, to diffuse books, to send missionaries to the antipodes;
and in this manner they found hospitals, prisons, and schools. If it be
proposed to advance some truth or to foster some feeling by the encouragement of a great example, they form a society.[2]

It was Tocqueville's contention that the desire to form associations was closely associated with the principle of equality, a
theme he saw as fundamental to a democracy. Without this

ability to combine in the pursuit of common ends, a democratic and equalitarian society must either fragment and thereby stagnate, or give way to some authoritarian form.

The roots of the early group service organizations lay in
religion and humanism. There was a belief in the dignity and
worth of each individual and the right of each person to achieve
to the utmost of their capacity. There was a belief in individuals
contributing to the common welfare and the responsibility of
each person not to harm or misuse others. There was a belief
in the importance of cooperation and the necessity of learning
to work together.

The pioneers in group work shared a basic concern about the
wretched conditions under which people lived. They fought
against political corruption, poverty, inadequate sanitation,
low wages, exploitation of children, and social injustice. In
addition to providing direct service in the form of clubs,
classes, and recreation facilities, they took on the task of eliminating the social conditions that created many of these problems. Most important, they challenged the prevailing doctrine
which viewed poverty as the result of a character defect. In its
place they posited the notion that many of the causes of poverty
and social problems were in the environment.

As social settlements, the Ys, and the Scouts began to spring
up in the larger cities, early workers were given titles that were
linked to their program organizations such as "settlement
worker," and "Y" or Scout leader. Few of these early workers
would have designated themselves as social workers as this
title meant charity workers—a form of help much different
from that offered by the pioneer workers utilizing groups. The
people who were served in the early groups were "normal,"
and only much later was serious attention given to those defined
as maladjusted or abnormal.

Over the years, attempts to establish a conceptual frame of
reference for the practice of social group work were hindered
by the variety of usages of the term *group work*. To some it has
been a label for a catchall of functions rather than a term to
designate professional service with definite, discrete meaning.
It has also been used to describe a job classification of workers,

a field of work, a classification of agencies, a philosophy or movement. The word "social" eventually was added to indicate that social group work was a method used by social workers, who were professionally educated to use it as a specialized social service in a variety of settings.

Three basic ideas regarding the usage of groups have persisted over the years. The first has to do with the value of the small group as a means of maintaining a democratic society. By involving individuals in group action and decision-making within their neighborhood and larger community, they can become more knowledgeable and skilled citizens. The second idea highlights the importance of the group as a means of socialization. Through the small group experience, an individual's development can be enhanced and the members can learn both the social skills and values of the larger society. The third, and historically the most recent, idea underscores the potential of the group as a vehicle for ameliorating maladaptive behavior. Through the small group, individuals can be assisted to change behaviors that are both self-defeating and classified as "deviant" by society.

Four different approaches based on these ideas can now be identified. Each has its own philosophical and value considerations, conception of the role of the worker, objectives, and type of client served. These approaches (or models) are the social change approach, which has as its focus the use of groups as a way of maintaining a democratic society; the reciprocal approach, which is directed toward the partnership of the worker and clients as in interacting social systems whose aims are mutually determined; the developmental approach, which views the group as a microcosm of society in which people help each other to grow and to develop; and the remedial model, which seeks to adjust and ameliorate maladaptive behavior.

This book begins with the use of groups in England and follows their adoption in the United States. The focus is on those factors both inside and outside social work that influenced the development of group work; these factors include the contributions of its pioneers, significant concepts, and knowledge from other disciplines such as psychology and sociology. Attention is also given to the various methods of group work that are most visible within the literature and in practice. Because of the fragmentary nature of group work's early roots, ideas and themes that cover a wide span of years are presented in one chapter and subsequent information is summarized in later chapters.

The first six chapters of the book have been divided into blocks of time of 16 to a 115 years. Chapter 1 deals with the Industrial Revolution in nineteenth-century England, major social problems, and the numerous youth movements and organizations that were formed to alleviate the problems. Chapter 2, which covers the period 1850-1899, centers on America's transition from a rural to an industrial society. The Charity Organization Society and the shift in the nation's attitude toward the poor are reviewed as a background requisite to tracing the development of the settlement movement, recreation movement, and the youth service agencies. Chapter 3, focusing on the years 1900-1919, when the United States entered World War I, discusses the influence of progressive education and adult education on group work. Chapters 4 and 5 consider the effects of social science and of the federal government's assumption of social welfare services, on group work. Chapter 6 reflects on the years between 1955 and the present, with a description of various modes and approaches presently being utilized in social group work. The final chapter is a summary of the roots and branches of social group work.

Because of the importance of social, political, and economic factors in the development of group work and social work, a brief statement regarding the national scene at the time is presented at the beginning of each chapter to convey a sense and flavor of the period. These statements cannot, however, reflect the extent of the sweeping changes that took place during the various periods. It must be borne in mind that in a 120-year span in America alone, there were three major depressions, several recessions, the end of a civil war, two world wars, a "police action," and the loss of a war in Asia—all of which created heavy social stress. It was also a period in which the United States moved from being an agrarian society to the most industrialized nation in the world.

NOTES

1. W. Roberts, *Memories of Life of Hannah More*, vol. 2 (1834), p. 30, referred to by A. F. Young and E. T. Ashton, *British Social Work in the Nineteenth Century*, (London: Routledge and Kegan Paul, 1956), p. 239.

2. Alexis de Tocqueville, *Democracy in America*, Henry Reeve (trans.), Henry Steele Commanger (ed.), (New York: Oxford University Press, 1947), p. 319.

FROM CHARACTER BUILDING
TO SOCIAL TREATMENT

Chapter 1

THE AGE OF UNCERTAINTY, 1800-1915

Until the nineteenth century, the social and economic history of England was a retreading of the path which the Roman state had traveled two thousand years earlier. The power of the old world was human power, dependent primarily upon the driving force of human strength. When a weight had to be lifted, man lifted it, when a rock had to be quarried, man chipped it out, when a field had to be plowed, man and oxen did the plowing.

In 1760 when George III came to the throne, the old world system of economics and social life, while not dependable, was reasonably predictable. The farmer working in his field and the craftsman working in his cottage accepted their lives, whether easy or hard, as part of the order of things. It did not occur to them to question the framework of society or the oligarchy under which they lived.

The Industrial Revolution in England brought about the substitution of mechanical power for human exertion. A long series of mechanical inventions and improved technical processes rendered the application of human energy more efficient. It made possible the use of water or steam power to perform labor formerly done by hand. A result was the growth of the factory system, which completely altered the lives of industrial workers, developed a new group of industrial capitalists who became influential in politics and society, and affected the living conditions of almost all classes of society.

The mechanization of industry began and was developed most fully in the textile trades. Prior to the 1760s, a family employed in the production of cloth typically worked as an economic unit. The father, most likely a weaver, was assisted by his oldest son whom he apprenticed to the trade. The mother, with the help of the younger children, spun flax or wool. With the advent of the power loom, weaving, which had been primarily a cottage industry, moved from mills on country streams to factories in population centers such as Manchester. The owner usually allowed the skilled weaver to have his own assistants, and this usually meant the owner hired the weaver's wife and children. So, within the anonymous city and impersonal factory an anchor of tradition persisted, and the working-class family, at least in this part of industry, was not under pressure to relinquish a major portion of its traditional functions of apprenticeship and economic cooperation.

With the introduction of the power loom in the 1820s, the weaver's wages decreased, and parents began to feel increasing pressure to send their children to factories for employment. The power loom factories, different from their predecessors, did not permit parental supervision of children at work. Children in one part of the factory, and perhaps their mothers in another part, worked from twelve to fifteen hours a day in unsanitary conditions, without the comforts of life that had relieved the tedium of work in the cottage. The discipline of the early factories was similar to the discipline of early prisons. Small children were often cruelly treated to keep them awake during the long work hours that shortened their lives or undermined their health.

The factory system greatly increased the number of laborers who were completely dependent upon their employers economically. As workers no longer owned the means of production, they were selling only their labor and were totally dependent upon their employers for wages. If the wages were too low, or if employment ceased, they could not fall back upon any other resource. Early in the eighteenth century, combinations of workers similar to trade unions were being formed in the domestic industries, and in the second half of the century strikes for better wages were common.

The change in industry caused a notable change in the distribution of population. Coal, necessary for heat and power, was mainly in the north and west, and the new factories were located largely in the same regions. These industrial centers drew their laborers initially from the surrounding countryside. By 1820 there had been a shift in population from the more densely populated southern counties of England, other than London and its neighborhoods, to the north. Many of the small towns of that region grew large; mere villages became busy manufacturing towns.

The sudden concentration of large numbers of people in towns produced serious problems of housing, sanitation, paving, and lighting with which the existing municipalities were unprepared to cope. Early in the 1800s cities such as London, Birmingham, Bristol, and Manchester could best be described as brutal and violent. A large portion of the working population in these cities lived in overcrowded, unsanitary tenements with an inadequate supply of pure water and an improper sewage disposal system. Discomfort, disease, and misery came to be a part of the life of those working in factories. The congestion of population in the towns increased the dangers arising from the lack of proper sanitation and added to the dreariness of the workers' lives.

In reaction to these conditions, the reform movement mobilized. It included major literary figures such as Charles Dickens (1812-1870) and Thomas Carlyle (1795-1881) who, through their writings, touched people's hearts and consciences. Coming out of a poor background, Dickens painted a vivid, sympathetic picture of the working class whose poverty could be seen not as a punishment or penalty from heaven, but as a product of bad social conditions and of man's inhumanity. Through his writings, Dickens drew attention to the problems of the period: in *Oliver Twist* (1836), the new workhouses recently established under the Poor Law Amendment Act: in *Nicholas Nickleby* (1838), and *David Copperfield* (1850), "profiteering" public schools; in *The Old Curiosity Shop* (1841), cruelty to children; in *Dombey and Son* (1848), the pomp and pride of capitalism; and in *Little Dorrit* (1857), the debtors prison and the red tape as symbolized by the circumlocution office.

Thomas Carlyle, like Dickens, was a social critic deeply concerned with the living conditions of the poor. Carlyle and Dickens, however, differed in their approaches. Dickens stirred his readers through realistic fiction and sympathy with his characters. Carlyle challenged and antagonized his readers through his interpretation of such historical periods as the French Revolution. In his book *Sartor Resartus* (1833), he described England as being separated into two rival sects, the "Dandies and the Drudges," that is the rich and the poor. Carlyle envisioned a time when Great Britain would be completely divided into two camps with no one left in the middle. He distrusted material progress and attacked the principle of laissez-faire. Throughout his writings, he insisted that meaningful progress was dependent ultimately upon the energy, fortitude, and heroism of individuals unwilling to turn their lives over to those who were in power.

Charles Kingsley (1819-1875) was another writer who had serious impact on the attitude of the more educated public toward issues such as worker rights, sanitation, and poverty. Trained as a minister, Kingsley used fiction and his remarkable power of description to reveal the problems of the poor and the exploitation of the working class. In his books *Yeast* (1848) and *Alton Locke* (1850), he was able to awaken members of the middle and upper classes to their responsibility for the plight of the worker. Kingsley became a leader in the Christian Socialist Movement that had as its aim the victory of the "Kingdom of Christ" over industry and trade. The group, greatly stirred by the suffering of the poor, vigorously criticized conservative christianity and lassez-faire industrialization. They fought against self-interest and competition while extolling the biblical principles of self-sacrifice and cooperation. Kingsley and the other Christian Socialists encouraged producer and consumer cooperation, worker education, and profit sharing in industry.

The conditions of the working class were altered in the 1830s with the passage of new legislation to protect the worker. The Factory Act of 1833 prohibited the employment in spinning and weaving factories of children below nine years of age, and restricted the labor of those between nine and thirteen to eight hours a day, and of those between thirteen and eighteen to twelve hours a day. Factory inspectors were appointed to oversee the enforcement of this law. More than 150,000 children came under the general supervision of these factory inspectors.

As factories expanded, a need arose for new processes to be learned, new materials handled, and new skills developed. This meant that workers would have to gain basic skills in reading and writing. The desire for greater literacy as well as educational reform was reinforced by evangelical churchmen who saw it as a way to promote the working classes' personal study of the Bible. By and large, this effort was met with apathy by the public and with resistance by the factory owners, who feared that a learned peasantry would become Jacobinic and drawn to revolutionary activities. In 1815, the most common method of education in Great Britain was one in which older children in schools taught the younger children. The method was cheap and reduced the cost of educating a child to a few shillings a year.

State aid to schools and compulsory education were viewed by the upper class as attacks on the liberty of the individual. By 1870, however, the major political parties embraced these concepts. Rival religious groups fought compulsory education, fearful that opposing groups might be given an advantage. Eventually, a compromise was reached that excluded any catechism or religious formulary distinctive of any particular denomination. Legislation was passed that compelled children under thirteen years of age to attend school and that established locally elected school boards. All parents except those who could not afford payment were expected to pay fees. From 1870 on, at least in theory, no areas in England would be without schools and no children would be deprived of an elementary education merely because their parents were poor.

England, now an industrial state, depended for its prosperity on manufacturing raw materials—many of which came from abroad—and on exporting a large proportion of the finished products.

In the 1840s and 1850s, trade unions began forming in the search for effective protection of the worker's rights and welfare. One of the most noteworthy of these unions was the

Guild Socialists, which attempted to adapt democratic doctrines to the realities of modern industrial conditions. Other working-class movements gained strength, including the cooperative movement and the Workers Educational Association. Taken together, they served as the base for the Labour party, which was formed around 1900 to promote the interests and welfare of the working classes. It directed trade union strength and hopes into constitutional and parliamentary channels, and offered some definite promise that in time the social welfare and security of the masses would be made matters of specific and systematic legislation.

The workingman's living conditions improved greatly by the end of the nineteenth century. Beginning with the Public Health Act of 1848, steadily expanding legislation and an increasing knowledge of public sanitation eliminated many of the causes of death in the industrial towns and rural districts that had existed in earlier years. Proper paving, sewage, and water supply, effective disposal of garbage, and the removal of trades dangerous to the public well-being were common throughout England by the end of the century.

The last quarter of the nineteenth century appeared to be years of prosperity for the British people. Industry was still expanding, and jobs were plentiful. Food and raw materials could be imported at lower prices because of new techniques in shipping. From 1880 onwards, refrigeration and cold-storage methods were used to bring in cheap meats and dairy products. Earlier, the development of railways and steamships made possible the transportation of grain from the United States, Canada, and Eastern Europe. By 1895 the average worker had a better standard of living than his parents. Wages had risen steadily between 1850 and 1895, as much as 50 percent for most of the chief occupations. Shorter hours, better education, street paving, gas lighting, and better housing were gradually improving the living standards of the workers.

In this atmosphere of generally improving living standards, some of the real facts about poverty became known. Charles Booth (1840-1916), a ship owner who decided to finance an enquiry into the living conditions of the poor in London, aided by Beatrice Webb and a number of research workers spent twenty years completing seventeen volumes of material on all aspects of life, including crime statistics, street occupations, and descriptions of the life styles of such groups as scavengers and chimney sweeps. The result was *Life and Labour of the People in London* (1891-1903) in which he showed that one third of the population of London was living in poverty. A survey conducted in York at about the same time by Benjamin Seebohm Rowntree (*Poverty: A Study of Town Life*, 1903), showed similar findings. Both reports used the level at which families could not provide enough food and clothes to keep their members healthy as a standard of poverty. These figures and the information that came out of the surveys shocked people, and the knowledge gained from them set the pattern for social reform.

THE HUMANITARIAN IMPULSE AND THE PROTECTION OF PROPERTY

An important ingredient of the second half of the century was the attention given to religious faith and observance. Evangelicalism, which placed emphasis on moral conduct as the test of the good Christian, was prevalent. Its basis was biblical and its highest virtue was self-improvement. Rather than highlighting ritual or the sacraments as was typical of both the Roman Catholic Church and the Church of England, it encouraged organized prayer and preaching, and the strict observance of the Sabbath.

Linked to this evangelical spirit was a generous humanitarian impulse. The Victorians regarded as intolerable many of the things their parents and grandparents had considered unchangeable. Evils felt to be humanly remediable were dealt with as promptly and, on the whole, as completely as the means at their disposal allowed. The organized improvement of working-class housing, factory conditions, public health, and education came quickly once appropriate devices and scientific knowledge became available.

The importance of humanitarian and philanthropic activities grew out of the religious conviction that a man's future reward or punishment was determined, in part, by his faith, but above all by his conduct. Duty, self-restraint, concern for others, and self-improvement were regarded as outstanding virtues. Pleasure was not banned, but it was not to be pursued as an end in itself, nor should it occupy too large a place in the scheme of a person's life. It was important to be serious, make good use of time, abstain from gambling, keep holy the Sabbath day, and do all things in moderation.

A majority of those drawn to social welfare activities were well-educated men and women who were products of wealthy families, expensive schools, and religious upbringing. They sincerely viewed themselves as their brother's keeper and as having a responsibility for making God's world a better place to live. According to Eager:

The young men [and women] who spent their spare time in mean streets and squalid homes were under no temptation to justify the system which made their voluntary activities necessary and in some ways unpleasant; they did not have even a subconscious desire to prove the necessity of the job they were doing. The attitude with which they entered the work disposed them to sympathize with the victims of the degrading conditions; their detachment, to say nothing of their wider education, impelled them to consider causes, to provide constructive remedies, and to criticize angrily any person who seemed to be making paid jobs for themselves out of the squalor and general beastliness of the slums.[1]

While one can safely presume that not all of those who volunteered to work with poor people and young people were as altruistic as Eager suggests, there was a sense of mission and spirit about the tasks they assumed.[2]

These individuals grew up in a stratum of society that was facing economic and social uncertainty. The anxiety of a growing middle class and an apprehensive upper class, struggling to strengthen its somewhat shaky status against forces both inside and outside the country, was characteristic of the period. From abroad came concern of expanding naval power, considered to be a direct threat to the sea routes upon which Britain's imperialism depended. At home uncertainty was engendered by the growth of socialism, the expansion of organized labor, and an increasing interest in the Labour party, which was seen as encouraging class conflict. The war in South Africa, which revealed the poor physical condition of England's military and the inefficiency of the military commanders, did little to inspire confidence in England's ability to maintain the Empire. Another pervasive fear related to the rising rate of crime, especially by children and adolescents. Delinquency in the form of robbery, vandalism, shoplifting, pick-pocketing, and arson were major social problems during the period.

Late in the eighteenth century many charity and subscription societies had been founded on the principle that the poor could be reformed and kept in their place in society by instruction in the Bible and cathechism. A major reason for the development of Sunday schools was to protect the public and make youth less dangerous. In August 1786, the Salford Hundred of Lancashire passed a resolution deploring what would now be called a crime wave. They recited how "idle, disorderly and dangerous persons of all descriptions" were wandering about and how the "commission of offenses hath increased to an alarming degree." The group asked for more vigilance in the reporting of crime and closer control of public houses and "houses of evil fame." They viewed the Sunday schools as one way of dealing with wayward youth:

Where Sunday Schools have been opened, their good effects have been plainly perceived in the orderly and decent Comportment of the Youth who are instructed therein. That is, therefore, most earnestly to be wished that those virtuous Citizens who have begun this good work, would continue their efforts to forward it with that Zeal and Perseverance that its great Importance requires; and that if these Institutions should become established throughout the Kingdom, there is good reason to hope they will produce a happy change in the general Morals of the People, and thereby render the Severities of Justice less frequently necessary.[3]

The magistrates and community leaders did not view Sunday schools as religious institutions, branches of church organization, or fields for devoted personal Christian service. Rather, they thought of them in more practical terms as rescue agencies and as means of reforming the lives and character of the uneducated masses, the main source of crime and threats to property. Because most children worked the other six days, problems tended to occur on Sundays. In 1783, Robert Raikes published the following in the *Gloucester Journal:*

Some of the clergy in different parts of this country, bent upon attempting a reform among the children of the lower class, are establishing Sunday Schools, for rendering the Lord's day subservient to the ends of instruction, which has hitherto been prostituted to bad purposes. Farmers, and other inhabitants of the towns and villages complain that they receive more injury to their property on the Sabbath than all the week besides: this, in a great measure, proceeds from the lawless state of the younger class, who are allowed to run wild on that day, free from every restraint.[4]

Promoters of the schools most often sought support on the ground that the schools were a form of social insurance. In other words, Sunday schools were an easy and cheap way to civilize the poor and make them less dangerous to society, to render them more useful as workers, and incidentally, to save their souls.

The actual workings of an early Sunday School varied according to the particular teacher. Hannah More, an early leader in the Sunday School movement used teaching techniques which, in the twentieth century, would be called behavior modification. She encouraged children to memorize scriptural passages by giving them a "bribe" of a penny a chapter.

When they seem to get a little tired we change the scene; and by standing up and singing a hymn their attention is relieved. . . . Those who attend four Sundays without intermission, and come in time for morning prayer receive a penny every fourth Sunday, but if they fail once, the other three Sundays go for nothing. Once in every six weeks I give a little gingerbread. Once a year I distribute little books according to merit— those who deserve most get a Bible; second rate merit gets a Prayer Book; the rest Cheap Repository Tracts.[5]

Youth movements in particular developed as an instrument of social conformity. They provided institutional expression to the need for safeguarding legitimate middle-class interests while at the same time making sufficient provisions for working-class leisure. They also offered a potential mechanism for the maintenance of class stability modeled on the elite private schools, which had already proved an effective instrument of social integration for the mid-Victorian business classes and the gentry.[6]

Taken together, the humanitarian impulse and the desire to protect property served as powerful influences in the development and proliferation of the various group service organizations that came into existance during the nineteenth century. The humanitarian impulse served as the catalyst for individuals to want to become involved and give of their time, and the desire to protect property and safeguard middle-class interests brought about support from the community at large.

Charity and Social Casework

From the seventeenth to the early part of the nineteenth century, the Poor Law of Elizabeth (1601) set the standards for who was to receive aid and the specific form of assistance they were to receive. The law confirmed the responsibility of the parish or local community for the maintenance of those poor who were not supported by their relatives. This responsibility to aid the needy was limited to persons who had been born in the community or who had lived there for at least three years. If the individual's relatives were able to give support, the community did not have responsibility. The law distinguished three classes of the poor: the *able-bodied* (paupers and beggars who were forced to work in the "house of corrections"), the *impotent* (the old, the blind, and mothers with young children who were to be placed in the almshouse), and *dependent children* (orphans and deserted children who were to be placed with any citizen who was willing to take them without charge). Certain people were allowed to remain in their own home and receive "outdoor relief" in the form of food, clothes, and fuel. An "overseer of the poor" appointed by the justice of the peace was to investigate the application of the poor person, investigate his condition, and determine eligibility.

The overseer also had the responsibility of collecting the poor tax passed upon land, houses, and tithes of all inhabitants.

In 1834, the Poor Law of 1601 was finally repealed, and a new law was passed in its place. The new law was harsh, for it put a stop to many forms of relief which had long been given to the very poor. At the same time, it aroused a greater feeling of independence in the laboring classes and encouraged them to make a more earnest effort to support themselves. Prior to this time, the poor who moved from one place to another were liable to be returned by the authorities to the place from which they came, for fear their support would fall on the parish in which they wanted to settle. The new law made it possible for them to go freely wherever they wished and wherever they could find work. Able-bodied poor were to receive no relief except for employment in workhouses, and outdoor relief was reduced to an absolute minimum. The new bill also provided for a more centralized administration of the poor laws under a national board, which resulted in a reduction in the payments made for the support of paupers and, in some degree at least, increased the independence of the lower classes.

Besides the assistance made possible through the local governments, the public was both blessed and burdened by the charity societies, which offered easy, immediate, short-term solutions to those in need. Many of these organizations had developed in response to the gaps left in the provisions of the poor law. Despite the fact that there were greater means available to assist the needy, pauperism and human suffering did not vanish, but seemed to increase. Charitable and relief organizations generally originated in order to meet local needs. One of the earliest of these organizations, the Strangers' Friend Society, began in London in 1785 as a means of assisting strangers from rural communities, Ireland, and Europe, who arrived friendless and often destitute. The Jews, especially those in London, were conscious of the influx of their brethren from abroad. In 1859, they organized the Metropolitan Board of Guardians, which provided burial assistance, hospital accommodations for the sick, and general relief for the impoverished in both cash and kind. Money was raised to support these services by assessing all the Jewish families living in London.

Most of the charitable organizations required a complete investigation of anyone who applied for help, as a means of preventing the "undeserving" from obtaining relief and at the same time of assuring that the "deserving" received what they genuinely needed. Not all organizations, however, were structured in this fashion. Some distributed money and food without any thought to whether it was really necessary; nor did they consider the implications the "gifts" would have on the receiver. Other organizations had such rigid standards as to what was "deserving" and "worthy" that many applicants, in order to receive anything, were forced to lie about themselves. One charity, for example, would only give aged individuals pensions if they could prove "purity of character."

Not infrequently, a charity society would be created in order to suppress social evils or protect decent citizens from those who would prey upon them, and it would evolve into a constructive casework organization. One such organization, the Bath Society for the Suppression of Common Vagrants and Imposters, the Relief of Occasional Distress and Encouragement of the Industrious Poor (the title in itself suggests its progression of thought), was established to reduce the number of beggars who frequented the town of Bath during the summer months. Wealthy visitors were being accosted by these individuals, and local merchants, concerned that their presence would affect business, hired an overseer to apprehend these vagrants and place them under arrest. Interestingly, while the organization was repressive, it also began to tell beggars where they could receive help, and it created employment for men who were out of work. Some were loaned money to establish their own businesses, and businessmen were subsidized to hire the jobless.[7]

Several religious groups such as the Congregationalists, Presbyterians, and the Church of England sponsored visiting societies that combined moral reformation efforts with financial help. The visitors usually met with the family twice a month, and, besides inquiring whether they attended church and possessed a Bible, they were interested in their need for medical treatment, whether they had financial resources, or belonged to a benefit society. The volunteers were prohibited from using their own money to relieve the distress of those they visited.

London in the 1840s had thousands of laymen who served as friendly visitors. To recruit more visitors and to ensure that they would get to know those really in need, the Metropolitan Visiting and Relief Association was established. It was hoped that this organization could also serve as a link between the "haves" and the "have nots" in the community. The visitors were expected to keep records of their work in the form of a journal, noting the facts of the cases they were working with, their impressions, and the help given. These journals were turned over to the association in order to monitor and document the work that was being done.

While the charity societies had many strengths, their weaknesses and defects were also apparent. One of the most frustrating problems they had to deal with was the overlapping of services in some areas and the lack of services in others. Another weakness was that the charity organizations, rather than develop a network of cooperation among themselves, developed open competition leading to indiscriminate giving. Although an organization would generally conduct a social investigation of the applicant, it gave little thought to the types and amounts of aid given by other organizations. As a result, some families would make the rounds from one society to another, manipulating to get everything they could, while others received nothing. According to Young and Ashton, it was the human weakness of the social workers that was often to blame for the overlap of services:

Without training and often without adequate preparation regarding the aims and purposes of the society they served, these good-hearted, somewhat sentimental workers all too often were so taken in by apparent distress that they tended to give relief as a matter of course. This was to put the best view on lack of discrimination, but less worthy motives were sometimes ascribed to them. It was said, for instance, that some churches competed with each other in gifts of soup and food tickets, in order to increase their congregations; that such was the competition among the relief societies working with the homeless, that John Burns decided to clear the Thames embankment of all charitable societies distributing relief there.[8]

Another weakness had to do with the effect the charity had on the receiver. Canon Barnett, warden of Toynbee Hall, argued that the working class and the poor were too willing to lay down their tools at the slightest hint of easy money. Hence, rather than the individual putting his energy into improving his lot through work, his energy went into exaggerating his distress and poverty for the purpose of gaining public sympathy and help.[9]

Because of such concerns, it came to be accepted that charity work needed to be better organized so as to avoid duplication and improve the help that was given. Accordingly, the Charity Organization Society (COS) was formed in 1869, not to provide aid, but to supply existing charities and their workers with the machinery that would enable them to disperse relief more effectively. It was to be a means to an end, the end being to raise the standard of charity or "casework,"[10] as it was newly termed.

District committees, organized by COS leaders in 1870, allowed members of the charitable organizations to gather together to discuss cases and make decisions as to the help that was necessary. The essence of this approach was a thorough investigation of the applicant's circumstances, determination of the actual need, and assessment of the resources already available. One result was the "case paper," which in later years was called the face sheet. This form provided space for the family members' names, ages, work history, income, and expenditures. Another result was the recognition that follow through was a necessity and not something that could or should be left to chance. The follow through was done not only to ensure that the individual or family was successfully helped but also to learn which methods were likely to succeed and which to fail.

The COS did not contribute anything fundamentally new to the methods of social work; all of its methods had been advocated and experimented with by many organizations at an earlier date. Its contribution, rather, lay in its utilization of various methods, its codification of these methods, and its passing them on from worker to worker and from charity to charity. The COS established a foundation for modern-day social work, with its own discipline and code of ethics. Part of this contribution resulted from COS's insistence on the scientific approach to help rather than the emotionally based indiscriminate distribution of aid, with little consideration of actual facts.

The COS was not without flaws. One criticism was that it did not promote genuine personal relationships between workers and the recipients of their help. Because of the society's emphasis on administration, the investigation of applicants, collection of funds, or stimulation of aid took precedence over the development of friendly relations between the visitor and the destitute. The visitors were to know the individuals and their circumstances and were to help whenever possible, but they were to guard against any emotional dependency on the part of the recipients.

The charity organization movement in general had little sentiment for the poor as a class. For them, the present system of society was right, and they did not consider the poor the victims of injustice. In fact, the charity movement and society were considered the righteous, and the poor the malefactors.

Housing reform for working families also became popular in the latter half of the nineteenth century. Most notable was the work of Octavia Hill (1838-1912), who was instrumental in developing and managing low cost, adequate housing in London. Born into a family active in social reform and philanthropy, she first showed her interest in the field when she was fourteen years old as the leader of a group of Ragged School children who were engaged in toymaking to earn money. In 1869 she worked with the COS. Octavia Hill had been strongly influenced by the Christian Socialist movement and drawn to its objective of brotherhood between men and better relations between social classes. Using money borrowed from John Ruskin, her former art teacher and a leading Christian Socialist, she purchased a small lodging house with the goal of repairing, improving, and managing it for working-class families in a way that earned a profit.

Her venture was successful, which allowed her to purchase and manage more property. Unlike other housing programs

for the poor, her program did not involve the construction of
new buildings but rather the purchase of dilapidated dwellings
that could be repaired. It was her belief that good management
of the property would lead to an improved way of life for the
tenant. To prevent overcrowding, for example, she refused to
allow families to live in one room of a flat and sublet the remaining room to other families—a common practice in many
areas. Her row houses and tenaments had special rooms set
aside as club rooms. Tenants were encouraged to think of themselves as a community, and to make reasonable rules that would
allow them to live together in a peaceful manner. Nearby vacant
property under Hill's control was used for gardens and playgrounds. To assist her with her work, she trained a corps of
women volunteers to collect rent, establish friendly relations
with tenants, and determine ways in which they could be helped
to greater self-respect and independence.

When one considers the actual philosophy, goals, and principles of the English social welfare organizations, particularly
those related to groups, certain themes become identifiable.
(For the approximate beginning dates of group service movements in England, see Appendix A.) These include the pursuit
of knowledge, spiritual awakening, patriotic duty, self-help
and mutual aid, and recreation for boys. Certainly not all
organizations highlighted the same themes in the same way;
rather, they emphasized one or two while at the same time
utilizing some permutation of the others. The final product was
to be men and women who were God-fearing, intelligent, hard
working, patriotic, and of good character.

THE PURSUIT OF USEFUL KNOWLEDGE

One result of the Industrial Revolution was the recognition
that education should not be a luxury for just a few but a necessity for all. Generations were to pass, however, before the state
acted on this philosophy. One reason for the long resistance
was the widely held belief that education, especially for the
masses, was bad because it would make people dissatisfied with

their station in life. In an 1807 debate in the House of Commons, a Mr. Giddy, who later became president of the Royal Society, said:

However spurious in theory the project might be of giving education to the labouring classes or the poor, it would be prejudicial to their morals and happiness; it would teach them to despise their lot in life, instead of making them good servants in agriculture or other laborious employments; instead of teaching them subordination, it would render them fractious and refractory, as was evident in the manufacturing counties; it would enable them to read seditious pamphlets, vicious books, and publications against Christianity; it would render them insolent to the superiors; and in a few years the legislature would find it necessary to direct the strong arm of power towards them.[11]

This attitude was typically held by the farmers throughout England. There was a genuine fear that educational reform would lead to a revolution similar to the French Revolution almost two decades earlier.

Mechanics Institutes

In spite of this attitude toward educating the masses, by 1820 schools supported by voluntary funds began to be established. The earliest of these schools were the mechanics institutes, which were formed spontaneously by workingmen in various towns or urban areas as a way of improving themselves. One of the originators of the concept was George Birkbeck, who, while a professor at Glasgow University, was touched by the ignorance as well as by the interest of a group of men examining a centrifugal pump. In 1823, he instituted a series of lectures for mechanics in London on usable industrial knowledge. These lectures served as the foundation of the London Mechanics' Institution. By 1850, there were more than 600 mechanics institutes in Great Britain with more than 100,000 members. A difficult problem that many of the institutes had to overcome was the men's lack of basic education. While the men had the desire for knowledge, they did not have the basic foundation on which to build. The more specialized regular courses were too much for them, and they could tolerate only occasional lectures. As a result, discussion groups, entertainment, and dancing were introduced to hold the membership together and attract new members.

An offshoot of the mechanics institute was the People's and Working Men's Colleges. The People's College in Sheffield was founded to enable the youth of the working class to gain culture and knowledge through the study of language, history, mathematics, logic, elocution and drawing. A similar organization in Nottingham evolved from a mechanics institute to a university college and eventually became Nottingham University. By 1850, many of the institutes were phased out as public libraries and reading rooms were set up.

Ragged Schools

Schools that were maintained by the British and Foreign Society and the National Society (two of the major supporters of public education) refused to accept children who were habitually dirty and ill clothed. In response to this restriction, which meant that thousands of children living in the streets would probably never see the inside of a classroom, schools that would accept all children, including those in disreputable conditions, were founded. These schools, the so-called Ragged Schools, were located wherever the children were located, for example, in warehouses, barns, unused storerooms, and even a railway arch.

The origin of the Ragged School is attributed to John Pound, (1766-1838), a crippled cobbler of Portsmouth. He is said to have gathered together in the 1830s a number of the poorest children to educate them in reading, writing, and religion, as well well as nature study, cobbling, cooking, toymaking, and clothes mending. This school was followed by similar schools in London, all of them located in slum areas. The adjective "ragged" was chosen not as an insult but as a way to encourage the participation of impoverished children.

An early supporter of the Ragged School was Lord Shaftesbury who volunteered to be a teacher and subsequently was

invited to become the president of the newly formed Ragged
School Union, designed to encourage and assist those who
teach in Ragged Schools, promote new schools, plan for greater
efficiency, to encourage teachers' meetings and Bible classes,
and to assist the old as well as the young in the study of the
Bible. Shaftesbury made Ragged School philanthropy respectable and even fashionable. In 1867, he was able to report that
the 226 Sunday Ragged Schools, the 204 day schools, and the
207 evening schools had an average attendance of 26,000
children.

Another important figure closely associated with the Ragged
Schools was Charles Dickens who, during a walk in one of
London's most dangerous neighborhoods, came across a group
of children being taught. Located among the very scenes described in *Oliver Twist*, the school, he said, was "an awful
sight." It was:

held in three most wretched rooms on the first floor of a rotten house:
every plank, and timber, and brick, and lath, and piece of plaster in
which shakes as you walk. One room is devoted to the girls; two to the
boys. The former are much the better looking—I cannot say better
dressed, for there is no such thing as dress among the seventy pupils;
certainly not the elements of a whole suit of clothes, among them all.
I have very seldom seen, in all the strange and dreadful things I have seen
in London and elsewhere anything so shocking as the dire neglect of soul
and body exhibited among these children. And although I know; and am
as sure as it is possible for one to be of anything which has not happened,
that in the prodigious misery and ignorance of the swarming masses of
mankind in England, the seeds of its certain ruin are sown, I never saw
that Truth so staring out in hopeless characters, as it does from the walls
of this place. The children in the Jails are almost as common sights to me
as my own; but these are worse, for they have not yet arrived there, but
are as plainly and as certainly traveling there, as they are to their grave.[12]

At first, the teachers were volunteers, and generally the expenses
were met by them and their friends. It was soon realized, however, that unpaid, untrained workers were not achieving the desired results as quickly as was hoped. Gradually, the schools
began to pay their teachers and to use them on a full-time basis.

The Ragged Schools were far from easy places to work. One superintendent, feeling overwhelmed, went to Lord Shaftesbury and complained, "the neighbors are alarmed, the landlord will close the doors, the teachers will flee." "Well," said the Earl, "you cannot have a ragged school without the preliminaries!"[13]

The teachers had to contend with an almost complete absence of parental control. Many of the children were sons and daughters of convicts, thieves, and alcoholics. Some had run away from home because of ill treatment and were living in lodging houses. Others were vagrants living wherever they could and begging for food. A common denominator was their limited experience with cleanliness, discipline, and order. Their concentration level was low and attendance was irregular. It was not unusual for the teachers to be assaulted in class or pelted with mud and stones on their way home.

SPIRITUAL AWAKENING

Closely tied to the theme of the pursuit of knowledge was the goal of spiritual awakening which served as a foundation for nearly all of the early charity and youth service organizations. There was the sincere conviction on the part of charity workers and youth leaders that the Kingdom of God could be created on earth and that Christians had a responsibility to direct their efforts to the relief of suffering and distress.

Settlement Movement

A unique development during the nineteenth century was the settlement movement, an idea that grew out of the writings of John Ruskin (1819-1900). Ruskin, a professor of fine arts at Oxford, believed that all aspects of a society, whether art, religion, or morality, were interrelated, and a corrupt society was unable to produce great art. He hated industrial cities, industrialism, and the division of labor. The industrial process, as he observed it, made some men less than men and separated them from culture and beauty and from those in power. Later, as a teacher in a People's and Working Men's College, Ruskin led groups of students in manual labor projects and encouraged a group of college men to live in a nearby lower class neighborhood.

Of the many who came under Ruskin's influence, Arnold Toynbee (1852-1883) was most profoundly affected. Toynbee, a tutor at Balliol College, Oxford in 1878, was passionately concerned with the lot of the working class and ordinary men and women. He held classes to enable them to share in the delights of learning, and they discussed with him, "sometimes in an atmosphere of bad whiskey, bad tobacco and drains things material and spiritual—the laws of nature and of God." It was his concern that the workingman had been neglected and, rather than the justice they deserved, they had received only charity.

One of Toynbee's friends was Samuel Augusta Barnett (1844-1913) a somber and intense Anglican minister married to Henrietta Rowland, a co-worker of Octavia Hill. In 1873, Barnett became the vicar of St. Jude's in Whitechapel, allegedly described by the Bishop of London as the "worst parish in my diocese." Barnett and his wife met young men from Oxford and Cambridge who were searching for a meaningful and useful existance. The students, like many others of the period, had read the anonymous pamphlet entitled *The Bitter Cry of Outcast London*, which described the horrors of life in the East London slums, and they felt compelled to lend their help.

The pamphlet began on a challenging note:

Wilst we have been building our churches and solacing ourselves with our religion, and dreaming that the millennium was coming, the poor have been growing poorer, the wretched more miserable, and the immoral more corrupt; the gulf has been daily widening which separates the lowest classes of the community from our churches and chapels, and from all decency and civilization.[14]

Shortly after its publication, a committee was established at Oxford to develop and maintain a "University Settlement in East London" and to offer Canon Barnett the wardenship. Before the settlement was established, Arnold Toynbee died, and it was decided that the settlement should be named Toynbee Hall as a permanent tribute to his influence and work. Toynbee Hall was established in 1884.

Plate 1. (*left*) **Canon Barnett.** Originally published in Henrietta Barnett, *Canon Barnett: His Life, Work, and Friends* (London: John Murray, 1918).
Plate 2. (*below*) **Toynbee Hall.** Originally published in Henrietta Barnett, *Canon Barnett: His Life, Work, and Friends* (London: John Murray, 1918).

Barnett believed that man needed every opportunity to attain his own salvation, and should not be given relief and material aid indiscriminately, as was the case with many of the charity organizations. He felt that educated university men living and sharing with people would provide an example of high standards and leadership that would inspire others. Many churchmen of the period shared this philosophy. W. Moore Ede in 1896 suggested the following:

The dwellers in the East End of our towns will not be converted by missionaries and tracts sent by dwellers in the West End. The dwellers in the West End must go to the dwellers in the East themselves, share with the East those pleasures which give interest and delight to the dwellers in the West, and make up the fullness of their life. When the dwellers in the West go thus to the dwellers in the East they will be themselves converted, for they will have turned to Christ and accepted His yoke of personal service, and the dwellers in the East, recognizing true helpfulness of the Christian life will be converted too.[15]

According to Barnett, education was a means not only of edification and pleasure but also of producing social and political change. He felt there was a need to develop leadership in the community and to prick the conscience of England, so that it would take responsibility for the chronic poverty in the midst of plenty. The settlements encouraged the neighbors and the "settlers" to take an active part in the life of the community through committee work and recreational activities.

Many of the activities and programs at Toynbee Hall resembled those of a university. It promoted picture exhibitions, extension classes, and special courses. One American visitor observed that Toynbee Hall was essentially a transplant of a university in Whitechapel. "The quadrangle, the gables, the diamond paned windows, the large general room, especially the dining room with its brilliant frieze of college shields, all make the place seem not so distant from the dreamy walks by the Isis or the Cam."[16]

Toynbee Hall had many critics. Some complained that it had no ecclesiastical connection and stood for no particular religious doctrine. Within weeks of its opening, another group at Oxford, objecting to the nonsectarian aspect, established Oxford House, a settlement linked to a parish and supported by the Anglican Church. Barnett's response was that the only secure foundation for a settlement was "love."

Love strong enough to stand the strain of working with little or no apparent result; broad enough to take in sectarian and secularist; deep enough sink differences in the one common purpose of raising the low, the sick, and the poor to their true life which is not with God.[17]

Another difficulty at Toynbee Hall had to do with the recruitment of committed residents. Barnett felt that every settlement should have at least twelve men of education with broad interests. Toynbee Hall had no trouble attracting workers, but some of the settlements that followed were unable to recruit sufficient residents. Many of those who came because of financial or time constraints were unable to gain much benefit because they did not stay long enough. A criticism linked to recruitment was the refusal by Canon Barnett to utilize women at Toynbee Hall. It was his thinking that social work in the past had been the sphere of women or of elderly men. In the later settlements, however, women were a regular part of the staff, and in the settlements that were subsequently established in America, many of the major jobs, including those of warden or director, were held by women.

With regard to clubs, Barnett did not think they were an effective method of combating hooliganism; they would only do that, he thought, if they offered something better, such as the influence and love of a friend. In consequence, he gave little support to the construction of an elaborate building for boys' clubs or to the gathering of a large number of boys together. He did, however, encourage camping as a healthy activity and as likely to promote good citizenship. Other settlements such as Oxford House did make extensive use of club life for both boys and adults, based on the argument that the service they could offer effectively was a center of political and religious neutrality where all those living in the neighborhood could find warmth and friendship. Some settlements formed penny saving banks for children, clubs for boys, girls, and cripples, and reading programs for the poor.

Boys' Brigade

A problem faced by Sunday school teachers was to make their classes interesting enough so as to attract and retain the interest of working-class boys. In 1880, William Alexander Smith (1854-1914), in response to this need, launched an imaginative experiment using military discipline, organization, and uniforms. He formed a group called the Boys' Brigade whose objective was the "Advancement of Christ's Kingdom Among Boys, and the promotion of habits of Reverence, Discipline, Self-respect and all that tends toward true Christian Manliness."[18] The organization was successful from the outset because of its activities, including summer camping, marching bands, club rooms, and a weekly drill parade. The boys proudly wore their uniforms consisting of military-looking pill box hats, belt, haversack, and dummy rifles which they used for drill. One observer noted:

Amazing and preposterous illusion! Call these boys "boys" which they are, and ask them to sit up in a Sunday class and no power on earth will make them do it; but, put a five penny cap on them and call them soldiers, which they are not, and you can order about until midnight.[19]

The Boys' Brigade was designed for boys over twelve years of age who found traditional Sunday school lacking in excitement and appeal.

When we reached thirteen, most of us felt we were too big for the Sunday School and there was a gap of a few years until we were able to join the YMCA at seventeen. To fill this gap, Captain Smith formed the Boys' Brigade. During that gap period many working class boys ran wild, became hooligans and street-corner loafers. What else was there for them in those days to do?[20]

The composition of the original company founded by Smith in Glasgow in 1880 reflected the nature of its original Sunday school recruitment. It was drawn from the sons of a Mission Church congregation in a predominantly "respectable" working-class area of West Glasgow. A sample of membership in the 1890s taken from early enrollment books demonstrates that sons of skilled manual workers or those with fathers in "white collar" occupations, clearly prevailed over a small number with unskilled or semi-skilled parents.[21]

In spite of its strong religious base, the Boys' Brigade was not tied to any religious faith. Churches of all denominations sponsored brigades, utilizing as leaders Sunday school teachers in their early twenties. While, by modern standards, the original program would appear crude or unimaginative, it held great appeal to boys confined to the drab monotony of urban existence in the late nineteenth century. Discipline, punctuality, and strict obedience orders had definite appeal to the members, because in uniform they were no longer children but young soldiers committed to an ideal and a purpose.

A major problem for the organization arose shortly before World War I when the War Office began to pressure the Boys' Brigade to become part of a national cadet force to be administered by the Territorial Army. The War Office thought the Boys' Brigade and other military-oriented movements could serve as a "second line of defense," and in return would receive government grants and the right to hire army camping equipment. But Smith adamantly refused to forsake the religious aims of the movement to become part of the military machine.

In 1891, the Church of England decided to replicate the Boys' Brigade with an organization it called the Church Lad's Brigade, using the same approach and program as the Boys' Brigade. William Smith had stressed the interdenominationalism of the Boys' Brigade and felt that identification with a single faith, such as the Anglican Church, would defeat its purpose of serving all boys. By the end of the century, a multitude of similar organizations had formed, including the Jewish Lad's Brigade (1895), the Catholic Boys' Brigade (1896) and the Boys' Life Brigade (1899). The last-named was started by a Congregationalist minister.

Young Men's Christian Association

An organization that was to have extensive influence in England and throughout the world was the Young Men's Christian Association (YMCA) whose prime mover was George

Williams (1821-1905), a farm lad from Somerset who was apprenticed to a dry goods merchant at the age of sixteen. During his apprenticeship, he was influenced by the writings of Charles G. Finney (1792-1875), an American revivalist who emphasized the importance of living a moral life, prayer, evangelism, and conversion. Finney encouraged the formation of prayer groups and mutual improvement societies. He had personally experienced a sudden conversion, and his preaching hammered home the idea of social duty and the importance of repenting one's sins.

Upon completion of his apprenticeship, Williams became an assistant in a dry goods firm that specialized in draperies. In this position, he became aware of the plight of thousands of other young men working in similar trades. They generally worked from 7:00 A.M. to 9:00 P.M. and lived in crowded rooms above the store in which they were employed.

Young men in the large houses, for they were worse than the small ones, were herded together, ten or fifteen in a room at night. They were literally driven from the shop to their beds, and from their beds to the shop, by a person called a shopwalker. There was no sitting room, no social comfort, no library; they remained until they were taken ill, then they were discharged at a moment's notice; away they went, many of them to the workhouse, and numbers used to die prematurely.[22]

The only recreation was drinking, smoking, and gambling at local pubs. Employees were given one evening off each week for courting purposes, and two if they attended a prayer meeting regularly. Williams, along with a group of likeminded young men involved in the drapery trade in London, began to meet regularly to pray. In 1841, this group evolved into an organization called the Young Men's Missionary Society, which had as its object "the arousing of converted men in the different drapery establishments in the Metropolis to a sense of their obligation and responsibility as Christians in diffusing religious knowledge to those around them either through the medium of prayer meetings or any other meetings they think proper." The Young Men's Christian Association was born on June 6, 1844. The name, according to Binfield[23] was suggested by C. W.

Smith, a co-worker of Williams and a member of the prayer group.

It was debated in the early Ys whether the predominantly religiously oriented program should have an educational component as well. One of the early founders argued that the YMCA's purpose was to save souls through such activities as devotional meetings and Bible classes. As the organization matured and new members joined, this orientation was challenged. Some felt that if the Ys were to be successful in attracting converted and unconverted young men, it would have to offer diversions such as cards, the theater, and the billiard room. Although the organization did not follow these suggestions, by the mid 1850s, the Ys began to offer courses in German, Latin, French, Hebrew, Greek, English, and arithmatic.

The early leaders of the YMCAs were suspicious of any activities that could be called amusement. This fear was articulated in the 1874 annual report:

while the Theatre flaunts its attractions, and music lends its fascination to the haunts of bad company and to the temptations of strong drink; while the rage for gambling, and betting ruinous as it is absurd, pervades all classes of society; while pleasure is almost universally pursued as an object more than as a recreation; while gluttony, drunkeness, and uncleanness [sic] do their evil work on the bodies and souls of men, and vitiate the tone of our social intercourse; and while the ministers and missionaries of all these forms of evil multiply on every hand and stand up an exceeding great army, leagued against religion and purity, rectitude, temperance and truth—there is urgent need . . .[24]

In 1885 the question was raised as to whether the YMCA should offer and support recreational activities. It was argued that amusement in any form would only detract from the organization's real mission. This time, however, laymen and clergy alike began to question whether a man's Christian character would really be compromised by attending concerts or plays. In 1888, the issue became mute when it was decided to build not only a reading room, quiet room, and library in the London YMCA, but also a gymnasium. Within a year, physical education was firmly entrenched as part of the Y's program of activities.

In recreation, the active member will show that Christ claims the whole man—the body as well as the soul and spirit—that the right use of athletics is necessary for the purity and strengthening of the body, so that there may be a healthy body to contain a healthy mind . . . a manly type of Christianity where men will be only afraid to sin.[25]

The YMCA movement spread throughout England, Scotland, and Ireland. While each association differed from the other, their common interest in the spiritual welfare of young men brought these groups into worldwide alliance. When George Williams was knighted by Queen Victoria in 1894 on the occasion of the London Association's golden jubilee, there were 5,000 associations in twenty-four countries, with half a million members.

Young Women's Christian Association

Quite separate in origin from the YMCA was the Young Women's Christian Association (YWCA) which grew out of a combination of two different organizations. The first was the Prayer Union introduced by Emma Robarts (1818-1877) in 1855. These were collections of women who gathered on a regular basis for prayer. There was no formal organization. The women met in small groups, and these groups, as well as the individuals who composed them, were bound together chiefly by correspondence with Robarts. The members of the Prayer Unions were young Christian women, largely girls of education, and the aim was to win them to a more complete dedication to Christ and to a life of Christian service.

The second organization was the Homes and Institutes of London, a group begun in 1855 by Mrs. Mary Jane Kinnaird (1816-1888), a world traveler and a woman of many interests. Kinnaird was concerned with the welfare of the Protestant churches in Africa and India. She was also interested in the protection of young women and in the 1850s had been instrumental in placing matrons on ships for the protection of women emigrating to British colonies. When young women volunteered to serve as nurses with Florence Nightingale during the Crimean War, she established a home in London to serve as a temporary refuge. From this activity it was but a mere step to the founding of a permanent home in London for young women from the provinces who sought employment in the city. Eventually, other homes were opened, and activities such as Bible classes and religious meetings, educational classes on many subjects, social activities, employment agencies, and clubs were initiated.

In 1876, Mrs. Kinnaird and Mrs. Robarts met to unite the two movements in London. "Evidently no greater formality was needed to bring about this union than the mutual agreement of the two leaders over a cup of tea."[26] Both the Prayer Unions and the Homes and Institutes had, at different times, used the name Young Women's Christian Association, which they borrowed from the YMCA. Thus, the name was a natural choice. The new organization placed emphasis on the members living a Christian life. Practically all the early members were active in the Church of England or in the Free Church, members of which were known as "Evangelicals." They had great faith in the power of the gospel to redeem and save individual lives as well as to provide the cure for the social ills of mankind. They took their responsibility for winning men and women to this faith with great seriousness.[27]

The following statement adopted at the formation of the United Central Council, the central governing body of the YWCA, in 1897 includes phrases taken from earlier statements of both parent organizations.

Basis

A living union with Christ our God and Savior, the only principle of action being the love of God shed abroad in the heart by the Holy Ghost, uniting in prayer and work those who desire to extend his kingdom by all means that are in accordance with the work of God.

Objects

I. Union for prayer for young women.
II. Work amongst young women of all classes by all means that are in accordance with the word of God, namely:
   1. To unite together for prayer, mutual help, sympathy, and instruction in spiritual things young women of all classes who truly love and desire to serve the Lord Jesus Christ.

2. To seek to win to a knowledge of Christ our sisters all around us who are strangers to the joy of his salvation.
3. To draw together for mutual help, sympathy and instruction young women of all classes.
4. To promote the moral, social, and intellectual well-being of all through the various agencies.
5. To provide Christian friends for all young women, especially those who come from the country into the town.
6. To afford protection to those who need it, and thus to help them to avoid the dangers and temptations which they meet.[28]

The early YWCA had voluntary, unsalaried leaders. The association's work, on the whole, was carried out by "Honorary Secretaries" who could write, keep accounts, teach Bible classes, hold evangelistic meetings, and sometimes travel all over the British Isles. The YWCA also had a missionary interest, which was an outgrowth of its strongly evangelical character and emphasis. At the first World's YWCA Conference in London in 1898, it was reported that among their members 496 missionaries were working abroad under various church boards and that the association's branches were supporting fifty or sixty missionaries.[29]

PATRIOTIC DUTY

Another important motive in the formation of many of the youth movements such as the Scouts, Boys' Brigade, and the Girl Guides was the defense of the British Empire against threats of moral and physical decadence. Many of the leaders had served as officers in the military and represented a life of order, discipline, duty, and endurance. By the time of the Boer War, English opinion, including a segment of the previously anti-militaristic working class, had swung behind the drilling and marching. The nation as a whole was aware of the need for military preparedness and for youth who could be depended upon in national crises.

Boy Scouts

Robert Baden-Powell (1857-1941), a lieutenant-general in the British Army, was especially concerned with the problem

of military weakness. During the Boer War, he was highly
decorated for his bravery at the siege of Mafeking. After the
war, with encouragement from his military superiors and with
support from George Williams of the YMCA and William Smith
of the Boys' Brigade, he founded the Boy Scouts in 1907.
Borrowing heavily from his military background, he emphasized uniforms, drilling, and weekly war games. When asked in
1918 what his purpose was in forming the Boy Scouts, he
replied that it was to "counteract, if possible, the deterioration,
moral and physical which shortened our rising generation, and
to train the boys to be more efficient and characterful citizens."[30]

Baden-Powell believed that the threat of national decadence
was evidenced in the physical deterioration and lack of enthusiasm of the English people. He was drawn to Social Darwinism
and the idea of "survival of the fittest" of nations. If the country
did not maintain its vigor, Baden-Powell admonished, it would
face the same decline as Rome had.

And it will largely depend upon you, the youngest generation of Britons
that are now growing up to be the men of the Empire. Don't be disgraced
like the young Romans who lost the Empire of their forefathers by being
wishy-washy slackers without any go or patriotism in them. Play-up!
Each man in his place and play the game![31]

Gillis states that the Boy Scouts tended to come from the
upper class.[32] Baden-Powell, while priding himself on his understanding of "boy spirit," had little understanding of the life-
style of the working class. A majority of poor children could
not afford the outlay of time and money necessary to join the
movement. In addition, scouting chose as its model the separation of adult and youth worlds already established in the elite
private schools. As a single-sex organization, it made virtue of
the postponement of access to adult roles, maintaining that
premature contact with the opposite sex endangered the mascu-
linity of boys and corrupted the domesticized feminity of girls.

The Boy Scout handbook, *Scouting for Boys*, had a far-
reaching effect on youth workers throughout the world. Sub-
titled "A Handbook for Instruction in Good Citizenship
Through Woodcraft," it was divided into chapters on tracking,

woodcraft, endurance, chivalry, lifesaving, and patriotism. Easily understood, it was a blend of practical information, political treatise, and woodcraft training.

Imperialism, Social Darwinism, and the cult of national efficiency, which were part of the scouting ideology prior to 1941, were tested during World War I. The Scouts found themselves giving air raid warnings, helping with the flax harvest, and running mobile canteens in munitions factories. They were also effective in encouraging men to enlist in the services and in guarding reservoirs. Thirty thousand Sea Scouts were organized under the Coast Guard to patrol the beaches, watching for ships, foreign planes, and "suspicious strangers."

Girl Guides

The Girl Guides were an offshoot of the Boy Scouts. After starting the Boy Scouts, Baden-Powell received more than a thousand letters from girls asking that a similar organization be developed for them. Baden-Powell and other Scout leaders at first resisted, but finally, in 1909, decided to start a scouting program for girls based on the principles used by the Boy Scouts. The aim of the organization was to give the girls the ability to be better mothers and guides to the next generation. The November 1909 issue of the *Headquarters Gazette* outlined the reasons for establishing the Girl Guides:

Decadence is going on in the nation, both moral and physical; proofs are only too plentiful. It is preventable if taken in time. Much of this decadence is due to ignorance or supineness of mothers who have never been taught themselves.

Physical defects exist to an enormous extent, a large proportion of which are preventable.

Moral Education is left by the mothers pretty much to the school masters. Girls must be partners and comrades rather than dolls. Their influence in after-life on the actions and quality of the men is very great; they become their "Guides." They therefore need character-training quite as much as boys.

As things are, one sees the streets crowded after business hours and the watering places crammed with girls over-dressed and idling, learning to live aimless, profitless lives; whereas, if an attractive way were shown, their enthusiasm would at once lead them to take up useful work with zeal.

Loafing, trusting to luck, want of thrift, and unstableness are increasing defects among our men. So they are among the women—though possibly not as yet, to so great a degree. Good servants are hard to get, homes are badly kept, children are badly brought up. There is great waste of their life among women of every class.[33]

The name "Guides" was substituted for "Scouts" out of fear that use of "Scouts" would not only prejudice older people against their activities, but would also antagonize the Boy Scouts, who would resent their name being copied. The actual name chosen came from a famous corp of guides in India distinguished for their courage, resourcefulness, and general handiness. The new name was not received with any great enthusiasm by those who had already styled themselves "Girl Scouts," and many felt that the plan proposed, with its substitution of nursing and domestic duties for the more boyish activities, was a watered-down edition of scouting.

The uniform was to be a jersey, neckerchief, skirt, knickers, stockings, and biretta (or large straw hat in summer). In addition, the girls were to have a haversack, cooking billy (pot), lanyard, knife, and walking stick. Badges could be earned for such activities as first aid, nursing, swimming, sailing, and tailoring. The leader was to be called captain and her assistants were to be lieutenants. The Girl Guide organization in each community or area was to be called a "company," which consisted of subunits called "groups" made up of six girls. Similar to the Boy Scouts, each Girl Guide was to do a daily "good turn" which could take the form of helping parents or neighbors.

Agnes Baden-Powell, sister of the chief scout, was chosen president of the new organization. She set out to rewrite the handbook and to interest her friends in the Guides' programs. One of her first problems was to create a positive public image for the group. Many adults were convinced that guiding would turn girls into tomboys and would deprive them of their femininity. Although parents felt it was acceptable for boys to hike, wear uniforms, tie knots, and camp, it was unacceptable for girls to participate in the same activities. Unfortunately for Agnes Baden-Powell, while she struggled to convince parents that girls would not become less ladylike, girls were pressuring her to institute activities similar to those of the Boy Scouts. Eventually, the same activities that were central to the Boy Scouts would become an integral part of the Girl Guides.

As was the case with the Boy Scouts, the threat of war was used to spur the Guides to greater efficiency. In one of the early pieces of Guides literature, girls were given the following advice.

"Girls! Imagine that a battle has taken place and around your town or village . . . what are you going to do? Are you going to sit down and wring your hands and cry, or are you going to be plucky and go out and do something to help your fathers and brothers who are fighting and falling on your behalf?"

The pamphlet went on to suggest that girls should learn tracking in order to search out the wounded; signaling in order to send messages to call and direct the ambulances; first aid to bind up their wounds; cooking in order to make soup and poultices; and foreign languages, "so that we can help the enemy's wounded as well as our own."[34]

SELF-HELP AND MUTUAL AID

In the 1850s, the virtues of industry, honesty, and thrift were extolled not only in Sunday morning sermons but also in weekly classroom instruction. In 1859, a book, *Self Help*, was published by Samuel Smiles (1812-1904), which detailed these virtues and explained the material rewards that one could expect if they became part of one's life. The book sold more than 150,000 copies and became the bible of industrialists and businessmen whose ethics dominated English manners and economic life.[35] *Self Help* was also one of the primary textbooks used in Ragged Schools as a means of developing character in the children.

Cooperative Societies

A method of self-help which Smiles encouraged was that of cooperative societies and friendly societies which cultivated the habit of prudent self-reliance. Organizations of this nature supposedly had links with antiquity. The Loyal Ancient Independent Order of Oddfellows, it was said, had its origins in 55 A.D. during the reign of the Emperor Nero. Early cooperative societies resembled the craft guilds of medieval times where fellow workingmen, living in the same town, formed fraternities for religious, commercial, and social purposes. For example, in 1492 the Drapers in Shrewsbury maintained a school and an almshouse. If one of their members fell on hard times financially, he could count on receiving assistance from a common chest.

Many of the societies owed their origins to the need felt by workingmen to provide themselves with some means of protection against poverty and destitution resulting from sickness and death. One society was formed by Huguenot refugees who escaped to England because of religious and economic persecution. As these immigrants became moderately prosperous, they formed the Norman Society in 1703 to ensure a system of relief for those who were having difficulty supporting their families. A sliding scale arrangement by which benefits rose and fell with the increase and decrease of capital was a feature of the society. The books and accounts were kept in French until 1800, after which English was used.

By the end of the eighteenth century, there were several thousand friendly societies and benefit clubs in England. In a 1843 analysis of seven well-known and established societies in Sheffield in 1840, it was found that members were drawn from seventy-nine different trades.[36] Where a majority of the members of a local society belonged to a single industrial occupation, there was the obvious possibility that the society would become involved in individual disputes. They also tended to develop into trade unions.[37]

The officers of local societies were normally chosen by rotation as in many of the early trade and working-class organizations. The period of office was usually six months and sometimes a year. Management fell upon three or four members who were appointed as stewards. The meeting place tended to be a local tavern or alehouse frequented by the members. The landlord of the alehouse was often the "treasurer," for he kept the box containing the funds. There was usually more than one lock, guaranteeing against any one keyholder gaining access to the funds on his own. The main exception to the principle of universal liability for service and appointment by rotation was for the office of clerk or secretary; this officer had to be able to read and write sufficiently well to keep the club's accounts.

Two financial benefits given to members from the local friendly society were a weekly allowance when they were sick and a funeral payment for widows upon members' deaths. To protect the surviving members from financial collapse, new applicants for membership had to be in good health at the time of joining and could not qualify for benefits until they had paid contributions for a minimum stipulated period of time. If a worker was injured through his own fault or negligence, for example, wrestling or drunkenness, he would be disqualified from receiving benefits.[38]

RECREATION FOR BOYS

The passage of the Ten Hour Act of 1847 made play time available to the industrialized masses. Unfortunately, opportunities and resources were not in abundance, especially for working boys whose needs varied and who often did not fit into the more accepted organizations such as the Scouts and the YMCAs. Nor did they share in the games of the public schools. Their playgrounds were frequently the streets of the city.

Boys' Clubs

In the 1870s there was a felt need to provide recreational activities for working boys. The boys' clubs were the answer to those who required the freer atmosphere of a recreational club where handicrafts, sports, and informal education could be accepted or rejected at will. Clubs of this nature seem to have appeared spontaneously in many of the larger cities beginning in approximately 1850. In London, the first boys' club was started in 1858 in Bayswater by Charles Baker.

Some of the early clubs were called Youths' Institutes. On the whole, these institutes tended to stress education but became increasingly interested in character-training and recreation for boys after they finished work. A split eventually occurred, with some institutes remaining purely educational and others becoming more recreationally oriented. The latter were called boys' clubs.

Until 1880, the working boy was often a boy who had been deprived of the activities proper to his age and who had little opportunity to play the games his middle- and upper-class counterparts played. Some boys' clubs introduced camping holidays, while others sponsored soccer, rugby, and cricket teams. Military drill also figured in the clubs' list of activities.

Two men who contributed to the growth of boys' clubs were T. W. Pelham (1847-1917) and Charles Russell (1847-1916). Pelham, who had been associated with Oxford House, published a *Handbook to Youths' Institutes and Working Boys' Clubs.* Russell, honorary secretary of the Manchester Boys' Brigade, published a manual entitled *Working Lads' Clubs* in 1908, which set out the standards and principles of club work. While both agreed that the clubs should offer a varied program and that the premises where activities were to be held should be as attractive as possible, they disagreed on how the clubs should be organized. Pelham placed stress on small clubs with close interaction between the members and the leader. He favored the boys running their own club, using adult assistance only when necessary. Russell, an efficient businessman, favored large clubs organized by men who knew what they wanted. Leadership would be in the form of a "benevolent despotism," with discipline underscored. Both books were to have a long-term influence on the leadership style in the movement, despite their differences of approach.

By the year 1915 the shock of the Industrial Revolution in England had worn off, and groups such as the boys' clubs, Scouts and the settlements were firmly entrenched as part of the British scene. Organizations of this nature had gained acceptance, and the founders were training others to follow in their footsteps, as a way of perpetuating the programs they had started. While England was going through its struggles, America was struggling with similar problems and social welfare leaders began looking to England for solutions.

NOTES

1. W. McG. Eager, *Making Men: A History of Boys' Clubs and Related Movements in Great Britain* (London: University of London Press, 1953), p. 65.

2. Sidney and Beatrice Webb exemplified the humanitarian impulse of the period. Sidney Webb's father had served on one of London's boards of guardians. As a young man, Sidney became an official with the London City Council and accepted the role of economic analyst with the Fabian Society. His wife, Beatrice, came from a wealthy London family. While a student, she became interested in political and economic theory. She later served as a visitor for the London Charity Organization Society and as a rent collector in a philanthropic housing project erected by Octavia Hill. Through research on the living conditions of the poor, the Webbs were able to document the extent of economics distress and were instrumental in the formation of legislation that provided national pensions for the aged, social insurance for the unemployed, and more humane treatment of the poor. For more information, see Margaret Cole's biography, *Beatrice Webb* (New York: Harcourt, Brace, 1946).

3. *Manchester Mercury*, August 8, 1786.

4. Alfred Gregory, *Robert Raikes, Journalist and Philanthropist* (London, 1880), p. 68.

5. Letter from Hannah More to William Wilberforce quoted in M. G. Jones, *Hannah More* (Cambridge: University Press, 1952).

6. John Springhall, *Youth, Empire and Society: British Youth Movements, 1883-1940* (London: Croom Helm, 1977), p. 123.

7. P. V. Turner, *History of the Monmouth Street Society* (Bath: n.d.).

8. A. F. Young and E. T. T. Ashton, *British Social Work in the Nineteenth Century* (London: Routledge and Kegan Paul, 1956), p. 93.

9. Henrietta Barnett, *Canon Barnett, His Life, Work, and Friends*, Vol. 1 (London: John Murray, 1918), p. 230.

10. The term *casework* was introduced to differentiate charity work from mere giving.

11. Quote by Giddy from George Trevelyan, *British History in the Nineteenth Century and After (1782-1919)*, (London: Longman Green, 1962), p. 162.

12. Edgar Johnson, *Charles Dickens: His Tragedy and Triumph*, Vol. 1 (New York: Simon and Schuster, 1952), p. 461.

13. W. Besant, *The Jubilee of the Ragged School Movement* (1894), p. 18.

14. Anonymous, *The Bitter Cry of Outcast London: An Enquiry into Conditions of the Abject Poor* (London: Congregational Union, 1883), p. 2. The booklet has been attributed to Andrew Mearns.

15. W. Moore Ede, "The Attitude of the Church to Some of the Social Problems of Town Life," quoted in Kathleen Woodroffe, *From Charity to Social Work in England and the United States* (Toronto: University of Toronto Press, 1962), p. 65.

16. Anonymous, Oxford House, p. 9.

17. Henrietta Barnett, *Canon Barnett*, p. 152.

18. Paul Wilkinson, "English Youth Movements, 1908-30," *Journal of Contemporary History* 4 (April 1969): 3-23.

19. Brian Simon, *Education and the Labor Movement, 1870-1920* (London: Lawrence and Wishart, 1965), p. 65.

20. William Wylie, cited in Rushworth Fogg's, "A Scotsman Started It All," in the *Scotsman* (1954), p. 24.

21. 1st Glasgow Company Enrollment Books and Glasgow Electorial Registers, cited in John Springhall, *Youth, Empire and Society* (London: Croom Helm, 1977), p. 25.

22. Young Men's Christian Association, *Occasional Papers*, No. 11, report of speech given by George Hitchcock, September 28, 1954, pp. 15-16.

23. Clyde Binfield, *George Williams and the Y.M.C.A.* (London: Heinemann, 1973), p. 83.

24. Ibid., p. 297.

25. "Report of the Dublin Conference of Young Men's Christian Association, Sept. 3-6, 1889" *Y.M.C.A. Special Bulletin*, p. 22.

26. Mary S. Sims, *The Natural History of a Social Institution--The Young Women's Christian Association* (New York: Woman's Press, 1936), p.3.

27. Anna V. Rice, *A History of the World's Young Women's Christian Association* (New York: Woman's Press, 1947), p. 10.

28. Ibid., p. 10.

29. First World's YWCA Conference 1898 Report.

30. Robert Baden-Powell, "Disposition as to Origins of Scout Movement," affidavit of May 24, 1918: When the Chief Scout appeared at the American Consulate General, as a witness in the case of Boy Scouts of America vs. American Boy Scouts, before Supreme Court, New York County, Scout Archives, London.

31. Robert Baden-Powell, *Scouting for Boys* (London: 1909), p. 267.

32. John R. Gillis, *Youth and History; Tradition and Change in European Age Relations 1770-Present* (New York: Academic Press, 1974), p. 146.

33. Rose Kerr, *Story of the Girl Guides* (London: Girl Guides Association, 1932), p. 73.

34. Ibid., pp. 73-74.

35. Samuel Smiles, *Self Help* (London: 1886).

36. G. C. Holland, *The Vital Statistics of Sheffield, 1843* referred to in P. H. J. H. Gosden *Self Help: Voluntary Associations in the 19th Century* (London: B. T. Balsford, 1973), pp. 211-13.

37. Ibid., p. 16.

38. Francis A. Hibbert, *The Influence and Development of English Gilds* (New York: Augustus M. Kelley, 1970), p. 34. Published originally in 1891 in London by Longman, Brown and Green.

Chapter 2

A PATTERN OF PIECES, 1860-1899

The forces that were responsible for the rapid development of industry in America during the post-Civil War years had been maturing for more than fifty years before the outbreak of the war. By 1860, the United States had entered a period of unprecedented expansion and had become one of the leading manufacturing nations in the world. The sewing machine had revolutionized the clothing industry; Colt revolvers were world famous; reapers were in use throughout the country; New Englanders mass produced guns and watches with standardized parts; and American iron producers utilized the Bessemer process.

Linked to manufacturing were an abundance of raw materials and a favorable market necessary for industrial expansion. Timber stands were still plentiful, and coal and iron ore seemed to exist in limitless quantities. The South produced more than enough cotton to supply the New England textile industry. There were vast deposits of oil to light the nation's lamps and in later years to propel its automobiles. Water power sites, which would eventually be used for generating electricity, dotted the American landscape.

When England entered its period of rapid industrialization some fifty or more years earlier, factory owners had to sell the bulk of their goods abroad. Other European countries moving toward industrialization found that much of the world market had been preempted by the English. But the American manufacturer, located in the midst of an expanding home market, could avoid international competition while he concentrated on fulfilling the needs of the American consumer.

During the last half of the nineteenth century, the population of the United States increased rapidly, mainly because of

immigration. The foreign-born population increased from
4,138,697 in 1860 to 9,249,560 in 1890 and to 13,345,545
in 1910.[1] In the years before 1890, most immigrants came
from Germany, Ireland, Great Britain, and the Scandinavian
countries. After 1890, they came primarily from Poland, Russia,
Hungary, Turkey, Italy, and the Balkans. Between 1890 and
1900, the majority of the immigrants were Jews from Eastern
Europe who had been the victims of widespread discrimination
in czarist Russia.

Unlike many of their predecessors of the antebellum period,
the immigrants after 1860 settled primarily in the cities and
became members of the industrial working class. Most lacked
the attributes necessary for success in American industrial
society except for a willingness to work. Without the skills and
training needed for machine tending of a craft, they were compelled to work at menial jobs with low pay and under poor
working conditions. Many had arrived with only a few cents
in their pocket and the clothes on their back, and had to take
whatever type of work was available. Their inability to understand English made them easy victims of unscrupulous employers, and the strangeness of a new land with new customs made
them too timid to protest when they were victimized. The combination of poverty and limited industrial skills often drove the
immigrant into the most hazardous work in American industry.
A sizable number of immigrants found work in such dangerous
occupations as coal mining and steel making where their inability
to read the warning signs prevented them even from achieving a
minimum of physical security.

Although the immigrant was well received by the industrialist
because of his work potential, he was met with suspicion and
prejudice by American laborers. Native-born workers usually
viewed the immigrant as a threat to their security and so they
refused him even a semblance of economic equality. Jobs that
were thought of as being beneath an American were considered
good enough for an immigrant. Some industries assigned different types of work to separate nationalities, with the most recent
arrivals occupying the least desirable positions.

The philosophy which permeated big business, religion, and education was that of laissez-faire which emphasized individualism. Based on the writings of Adam Smith and Charles Darwin, it was tailored by Herbert Spencer to fit the needs of industrial capitalism. In his articles, lectures, and books, Spencer argued that Darwin's rules of natural selection applied not only to the beasts of the jungle but also to all individuals within society. Life was characterized by an unremitting struggle in which the weak fell by the wayside while the strong inevitably pushed forward. While inhumane and cruel, there was nothing that could be done to alter this pattern, for it was a law of nature that only the fittest survived. In short, only the rich were fit, and their wealth was proof of their fitness.

The easy generalizations of Spencer's theories appealed to businessmen and industrialists, who no doubt wondered why they had been able to accumulate great fortunes in a few short years while others had no more than the clothes on their back. American businessmen, such as Andrew Carnegie and J. Pierpont Morgan, used Social Darwinism as a way of defending their control of American capitalism. Like Spencer, they argued that both economic society and life in the jungle were characterized by a fierce, never-ending struggle for survival and supremacy. Those who were best equipped by nature for the battle invariably emerged as victors.

Carnegie conceded that nature's law at times seemed harsh, but he insisted that all progress depended on the elimination of the unfit because it insured the survival of the fittest. If poverty were to be abolished, according to Carnegie, progress and development would cease. Attempts to organize to help others or form labor unions were futile, for they rested on the false assumption that economic life was controlled by man instead of by natural laws. Although it was true that unions did get an advance in wages, it would have come anyway by the natural laws of competition among the capitalists and without the loss of wages and suffering entailed by a strike or confrontation.[2]

Other businessmen maintained that moral considerations as

well as natural and economic laws determined the distribution of wealth in American economic society. The moral law, similar in many ways to the teachings of John Calvin, placed considerable emphasis on the Calvinistic doctrines of hard work, obedience, and thrift as a means of acquiring wealth. These values were supported by many leaders within the church. The Right Reverend William Lawrence of Massachusetts noted "a certain distrust on the part of the people as to the effect of material prosperity on their morality." He suggested that it would be well to "revise our inferences from history, experience and the Bible" and shed that subtle hypocrisy that earthly riches are wrong but at the same time "work with all his might to earn a competence and a fortune if he can." Once having rid himself of such fake inferences and hypocrisy, man could recognize the great building principles of his life. The first was his "divine nature to conquer nature, open up her resources, and harness them to his service." The second was that only to the man of morality would wealth come, for "Godliness is in league with riches." This being the case, Lawrence added: "we retain with an easier mind and clear conscience the problem of our twenty-five billion dollars in a decade, confident that our material possessions in the long run are favorable to morality."[3]

While the philosophy of laissez-faire generally prevailed throughout the entire period from the end of the Civil War to the close of the nineteenth century, there were strong attacks and eventually a successful assault upon its major tenets. Farmers and industrial workers grew increasingly unwilling to accept a concept of government's role that provided aid and comfort for business and industry while refusing any sort of regulation of their activities. Social and economic critics also argued that a theory of economic development that encouraged both the growth of monopoly and the consequent increase of economic power in the hands of the few was dangerous and destructive to a nation's well-being. In response to such pressure, a number of states enacted regulatory laws. The railways, one of the biggest offenders, challenged their constitutionality on the grounds that such legislation deprived them of their property as guaranteed by the provisions of the Fourteenth Amendment, which stated that no person (a corporation is a person in the eyes of the law) could be deprived of property without due process of law. The Supreme Court upheld the constitutionality of the new laws in the case of *Munn* v. *Illinois* in 1876 and stated that a legislature could in the exercise of its policy power regulate any business "affected with a public interest."

It was soon to become apparent that state regulation of the railroad was ineffective. Local and state governments were too much under the influence of the railroads and other businesses to make enforcement feasible. As a result, Congress felt compelled to act and passed the Interstate Commerce Act in 1887, which set up the Interstate Commerce Commission to pass upon the reasonableness of rates applying to commerce among the states. Concurrently, a comparable movement arose for control of the trust which led in 1890 to passage of the Sherman Anti-Trust Act. It specifically declared that any combinations, trusts, or conspiracies in restraint of trade, so far as applied to commerce among the states, were illegal, and it provided penalties for any infraction of the statute's provisions.[4]

CHARITY ORGANIZATION SOCIETY

During the 1870s, the inadequacy and disorganization of public and private relief increasingly became apparent. Charitable bodies throughout the country incorporated the individualism of the industrial entrepreneur who had grown wealthy in an expanding economy. Not infrequently, a prosperous donor sought to express his particular philanthropy for any relief society that would accept his donation. As a result, there was much overlapping and waste while many needs remained unmet. Coupled with this problem was the strong conviction that pauperism reflected character deficiency and required the maximum of personal influence of the donor upon the recipient. As a means of dealing with the problem, a number of cities decided to develop organizations similar to the Charity Organization Society which had been operating in England since 1869. The COS in America sought to effect the coordination of the existing welfare services and agencies. While the granting of relief would continue to be the function of the existing agencies as it had before, the COS was to develop the machinery and technique whereby relief could be expeditiously and economically administered without duplication and competition.

The first American COS was founded in Buffalo, New York, in 1877 with the specific goal of avoiding waste of funds and of becoming a center of intercommunication between the various charities. The society stressed that there was to be no proselytism on the part of their agents, no interference with any existing societies, no relief given by the organization itself except in emergencies, no sentiment in the matter, and, above all, no exclusion of any person or body of persons on account of religious creed, politics, or nationality. Within ten years, twenty-five similar organizations were formed, all based on the following principles: (1) the cooperation of all local charity agencies under a board of their representatives; and (2) a central "confidential register" and investigation of the social conditions of every applicant by a "friendly visitor" in order to determine the need and individual measures necessary in each case.[5]

The founders of these societies were typically wealthy citizens who felt morally obligated to alleviate the suffering of the poor and to minimize political unrest and strife. The religious and political philosophy of the founders influenced the visitors. Poverty was felt to be caused by personal fault, idleness, mismanagement, drinking, negligence, and vice. It was hoped that by giving friendly advice, by helping in procuring employment, or by giving a loan, they could strengthen the "moral fiber" of the indigent and encourage them to become self-supporting.

America's attitude towards poverty is illustrated by a report of the Massachusetts Board of State Charities in 1866:

In providing for the poor, the dependent and the vicious . . . we must bear in mind that they do not as yet form with us a well marked and persistant class, but a conventional, and perhaps only a temporary one. They do not differ from other men, except that taken as a whole, they inherited less favorable moral tendencies and less original vigor. Care should be taken that we do not, by our treatment, transform the conventional class into a real one and a persistent one.[6]

This attitude was in part based on the traditional religious belief that poverty was a fortunate necessity that led the poor into paths of industry and the rich into acts of charity. There was an equally powerful belief that America was the land of plenty and poverty was an unnecessary misfortune. There was work for all, and any man who wanted work could find it. Therefore, poverty was the punishment meted out to the poor for their indolence, inefficiency, or improvidence; or else it was to be interpreted in terms of heredity or degeneration.

This school of thought which placed such heavy emphasis on individuality and all it implied was certainly not universally accepted. By the last part of the 1800s, there emerged a new trend of thought which highlighted what one of its adherents, Edward T. Devine, called "conscious social action" and which focused on the environment rather than on the individual: "It makes of charity a type of anticipatory justice which deals not only with individuals who suffer but with social conditions that tend to perpetuate crime, pauperism and degeneracy."[7] This philosophy challenged the prevailing doctrine that poverty was due to character defects. As the visitors became intimately acquainted with the conditions of "their families," they too began to question whether unhealthy neighborhoods and housing conditions prevented the maintenance of health and morals. Careful housekeeping and thrift, when wages were low, did not allow for adequate food or housing. In time of sickness or un- employment, families found themselves at the mercy of loan sharks who forced them further into debt by charging high interest rates.

In 1895, a member of the National Conference of Charities and Corrections told his fellow social workers that, although helping individuals one by one was important, Charity Organiza- tion Societies must do all they could "to abolish all conditions which depress, to promote measures which raise men and neighborhoods and communities."[8] The president of the Boston Associated Charities questioned whether the new charity organ- ization movement had not been too interested in relieving single cases of distress without asking whether there were "prolific causes permanently at work" to create want, vice, crime, disease, and death, causes which should be removed. "If such causes of pauperism exist, how vain to waste our energies on single cases of relief when society should aim at removing the prolific sources of all the woe."[9]

Various COS groups began to stress the need for social reform that would fundamentally change living and environmental conditions. Societies began promoting social legislation for the improvement of housing and of penal institutions, the clearing of slums, and the treatment of tuberculosis, a disease that was widespread among poverty-stricken families. The Buffalo Society, for example, very early added to its work the maintenance of employment bureaus, wood yards, laundries, work rooms, special schools, wayfarers' lodges, loan societies, penny banks, fuel societies, creches, district nursing, sick diet kitchens, and an emergency accident hospital.

By the turn of the century, in both England and America, some men and women employed by charitable institutions began to consider their work as a profession in much the same way as other men regarded law, theology, and medicine. Others argued that social work was synonymous with "friendly uplifting" requiring little more than true friendship, sympathy, pity, encouragement, and a warm heart. The fact that many workers accepted payment often incurred the criticism of the rich; the willingness to work for nothing was considered the hallmark of a sincere charity worker. As early as 1893, the Central Council of the New York City COS announced a six weeks "Training School in Practical Charity," warning applicants not to be too interested in money.[10]

In spite of the negativism toward the paid worker, it was becoming obvious that there were not enough well-to-do and leisured individuals who were able to give their time to friendly visiting. In addition, it was found that usually the paid agent did a better job than the volunteer. Mary Richmond (1861-1928), one of the early leaders in social work, discovered that in any unusually delicate or puzzling situation, the paid agent was much more adept and reliable.[11] Near the end of the century, both volunteer and paid visitors began to express the need for deeper understanding of the behavior of individuals and of economic problems and asked for special training for

social work. This request served as a stimulus for the establishment of the Training School for Applied Philanthropy, which
organized the first social work courses in 1898 in New York
City.[12]

As the COS became better established, two conflicting tasks
became apparent. These societies had been formed to achieve
better coordination and organization of existing services and
to improve the health and social resources of the community.
At the same time, vested interests among member agencies
often resented recommendations for change of method of work,
so that some societies were forced to establish divisions for
service to families in need. These divisions conflicted with the
activities of other relief societies, which objected because the
COS had not been founded to set up rival organizations. As a
result, the functions of the COS were separated. The first place
where this separation occurred was Pittsburgh, Pennsylvania,
where the organization split into a family welfare agency and
an an agency for the planned coordination of activities. Other
cities followed this pattern with the development of Councils
of Social Agencies as the coordinating and planning bodies and
Associated Charities as a family welfare societies.[13]

THE SETTLEMENT MOVEMENT

The prototype for settlement houses in America was Toynbee
Hall in England, which was established in 1884. The first American settlement house began in 1886 with the establishment of
the Neighborhood Guild under the leadership of Stanton Coit
(1857-1944) on the east side of New York City. After spending
some time with Canon Barnett in London in 1885, Coit returned home with the goal of developing a similar program in
the United States. Because of a lack of funds and public support, he began meeting with a group of eighteen-year-old boys
in the tenement apartment of an elderly, blind woman who
sold apples. As new members were added, a basement of that
tenement was rented for a club room. Possession of this additional space led to the establishment of a kindergarten and,
within the year in 1886, a girls' club composed of young women

between sixteen and twenty-two years of age. A year later, five different clubs were holding meetings in the basement, and a federation of young people's clubs was organized under the name Neighborhood Guild.

The settlement idea caught on quickly, and a number of other settlement houses opened their doors. In their turn, the Neighborhood Guild, later known as the University Settlement, the College Settlement, and Henry Street Settlement in New York City, and Hull House in Chicago became the models for numerous other settlements in the United States during the 1890s. The idea was so enthusiastically received that within fifteen years after Stanton Coit had organized the Neighborhood Guild in New York, approximately 100 settlement houses were operating in American cities.

The early settlements were located in crowded neighborhoods inhabited by immigrants. Most of the immigrants were forced to live in cluttered, filth-ridden tenements which one observer called a breeding place for vice, crime, and disease. Life in the dark, damp buildings was made worse by overcrowding. Within the two or three rooms of the apartment, there often lived a household composed of a husband, wife, children, plus other relatives and lodgers. Sanitary facilities were limited, and several families used a common sink and toilet. Bathtubs were a luxury which few tenement dwellers had. Even drinking water was scarce, for the pressure was too low to lift the water above the first floor. While most immigrants found life in the New World, even under these conditions, sweeter than what they had known in the Old World, they sometimes concluded, as did one Rumanian immigrant, that America was not the land of milk and honey: "This was the boasted American freedom and opportunity—the freedom for respectable citizens to sell cabbage from hideous carts, the opportunity to live in those monstrous dirty caves [tenements] that shut out the sunshine."[14]

In many ways, the early settlements were extensions of the personalities who started them. The group of "settlers" usually consisted of the head resident, friends, and acquaintances who shared similar interests and a zeal for humanitarian experimentation.[15] Robert H. Bremner points out that the pioneers in the field were all young people who were born too late for Brook Farm and too early for Greenwich Village. Success in conventional business or professional careers and the achievement of assured social position offered less of a challenge to them than to the offspring of less fortunately endowed families. Instead, they found the call to altruistic service irresistible, and they gravitated toward poverty, a condition foreign to their personal experience.[16]

Had they lived in a different age or in a different country, religion, politics, or even revolutionary intrigue might have been their métier. Some of them in fact, had once planned to become missionaries in remote corners of the world and were only deflected from that aim by becoming aware of the opportunities for service in neglected areas of their own communities.[17]

There were differences between the settlements in England and America. The English settlements from the beginning served as an aid and outlet for educated young men and, in many ways, were residences for students located in the slums. The benefits to the neighbors were often a secondary consideration. Support for the settlements came from influential students, professors, and the church. Toynbee Hall, for example, continued to have close links to Oxford University, which has direct ties to the upper class and the established Church of England. In America, the emphasis was more on service to the neighborhood where the settlement was located. University students were utilized, along with a large number of business and professional people and volunteers who helped out but lived somewhere else. Whereas Canon Barnett and other English leaders emphasized changing the individual, American leaders felt that reform needed to be directed to the environment.

Another difference between the two countries was the larger number of women involved in the settlement movement in the United States than in England. Settlements came into being in America at a time when the feminist movement was gathering strength and women were becoming interested in social reform. The typical female settlement leader was single, white, Protestant, and middle class. She was a recent graduate of an eastern or midwestern college for women. Her father was a professional man, and her mother was likely to have been active in the woman suffrage movement and to have urged her daughter to pursue higher education.[18] The settlement served both as a place to work and an intellectual salon, providing an extension of her university training. There intellectuals of many different political persuasions could exchange views on a variety of current problems with their poor neighbors. By 1922, it was estimated that 70 percent of the settlement residents were women.[19]

Of the many pioneers, Jane Addams (1860-1935), the founder of Hull House, best exemplified the total commitment of settlement leaders to the welfare of others. In 1889, she, along with a friend, Ellen Gates Starr, made a pilgrimage to see Toynbee Hall and to meet Canon Barnett. Upon returning home to Chicago several months later, they began searching for a suitable house with a nearby field. They decided upon an old mansion on Halsted Street which had been turned into a lodging house, in a neighborhood populated by Bohemians, Italians, Germans, Greeks, Poles, Russian Jews, and Irish newcomers. From the beginning, they set out to share with their neighbors both their choicest possessions and the knowledge they had gained through experience and intellectual training. Reproductions of paintings were framed and lent to neighbors. Groups were formed to study art, literature, and science. The first specially erected building included an art gallery, a studio, and a library. A series of parties and festivals commemorative of immigrant customs and traditions were arranged, requiring tremendous sensitivity by the settlers because of the deep sense of national loyalty felt by the various groups.

Many of Addams' friends and family questioned why she chose to live on Halsted Street when she could afford to live somewhere else. She felt it was natural that she and the settlement should be there:

. . . it is certainly natural to give pleasure to the young, comfort to the aged, and to minister to the deep-seated craving for social intercourse that all men feel. Whoever does it is rewarded by something which, if not gratitude, is at least spontaneous and vital and lacks that irksome sense of obligation with which a substantial benefit is too often acknowledged.[20]

Plate 3. (*left*) **Jane Addams.** Photo by Moffett, 1924. Courtesy of the Chicago Historical Society. Plate 4. (*below*) **Hull House, circa 1930.** Courtesy of the Chicago Historical Society.

Plate 5. **Jane Addams at Hull House with five children.** Courtesy of the Chicago Historical Society.

Initially, the settlement leaders felt their major work would involve the young men and women of the community. However, they usually found that those most interested in using the facilities were young boys.

Boys approaching adolescence welcomed so eagerly any overture that might be interpreted as friendly, followed up acquaintance with such unwarying persistence and teased with such winning good nature to be included in whatever good times were arranged, that they gained the freedom of the settlement almost against the underlying desires of residents.[21]

As soon as the boys were admitted to the house, they were assigned to groups on an arbitrary basis by the residents. From the beginning, these groups were kept small because it was thought that it was better to know a few children well than many superficially. The advantages of the small group under the guidance of leaders of character and ability had already been demonstrated by Protestant Sunday schools. Another reason, apart from any theory, was that space was limited and

meetings had to be held in the dining room, parlor, or bed-
rooms of the house. This lack of space also resulted in the use
of limited movement activities such as debating, table games,
story-telling, singing, conversation, and the study of parliamentary law.

A question that plagued most of the early settlements was
the desirability of boys bringing their friends to the club meetings. It was generally felt that allowing the members to choose
other members would lead to the formation of gangs. As residents became more secure with their own position, however,
they came to recognize that most boys in the larger cities belonged to gangs, that not all gangs were bad, and that a group
already developed could yield positive results. Resourceful
settlement workers began to recruit clubs and gangs by com-
missioning boys who appeared to have some leadership potential
to begin their own groups or by offering directly the facilities of
the settlement to gangs gathered from neighborhoods and street
corners. It was felt that the movement from "gang to a club"
occurred when the members were able to agree upon rules of
conduct. Woods and Kennedy note that efforts to live up to a
standard written in a constitution and subscribed to set in
motion new and compelling influences.

A little experience makes it evident that distinction within the group de-
pends on effectiveness with one's fellows; that he who serves leads. The
cost of untruthfulness, irresponsibility, and lack of application especially
in others is seen in deeper blackness when silhouetted against group interest. The fact that the club is financially responsible for the actions of
individual members creates a new attitude on the part of the majority
toward wanton destruction. The weak are bolstered, the strong confirmed,
and the rebellious coerced by the most telling force members know, the
publicly expressed judgement of a group of their peers. In the club, the
fact that the moral law represents the sole practicable scheme of human
intercourse finds demonstration in the understood terms of life itself.[22]

Finding qualified leaders for clubs was often a difficult task
for those responsible for club activities. It was generally felt
that volunteers were more desirable as club leaders than paid
workers because they best represented the settlement ideal of
sharing and friendship. Many preferred club leaders who were

"busy" to those with "time on their hands" in that they would have a greater sense of responsibility and would be better equipped to win the respect of the club members. It was also considered important that the leader be fond of people for their own sake, able to generate interest in activities, and capable of dealing resourcefully with new situations.[23]

Before the turn of the century, club directors were usually men who by virtue of their physical strength, personal magnetism, and knowledge of activities were able to keep boys within bounds and to direct their desires. As clubs began to multiply and resources became more adequate, trained individuals in the field of social work were sought. The club director needed to be acquainted with the findings of modern psychological research and pedagogic experiment, able to apply the lessons of these sciences to working with groups for all ages, and to train staff assistants and volunteer associates who would carry out the programs. As part of the job, he had to undertake a neighborhood census of group activities and resources, and know where the various gangs were likely to be found "at almost any hour of the day or night."[24] He had to follow up younger boys who manifested signs of power to direct others and dis-cover the exceptional man who could play games, sing, perform on instruments, tell stories, make speeches, assume responsi-bility, organize group meetings, create public opinion, and induce him to give regular or occasional service in the organized life of the neighborhood.

Girls' and women's clubs at the settlement house differed markedly from those for boys and men. Though called clubs, they were essentially classes with little or no emphasis on self-government, rules of order, and committee work. Attention was instead directed toward training for fundamental domestic activities such as child care, sewing, dressmaking, and cooking. This difference in the program occurred for several reasons. First, it was much more convenient to find teachers than club leaders. To many adults, the club's lack of structure was threatening. Second, girls were much more receptive to a class-like structure. Boys viewed the class structure as being too much like school and rebelled against anything resembling the classroom. Third, the settlement in its early stages was primarily a home and only secondarily a house. Residents found it difficult to tolerate the excessive wear and tear on household furnishings which was inevitable in boys' club work. Finally, some of the early leaders in the settlement movement and the youth service agencies believed that the "instinct" of club loyalty was much weaker in girls than in boys and that their "natural sense of membership is not easily enlarged beyond the family."[25]

Some felt that the girls' and women's groups should be a laboratory for assisting them to learn about business. Bernheimer and Cohen, in their early book on boys' clubs, argued that the fact that girls often lacked business sense was a reason for cultivating it through a club.

The girls who have acquired this business sense in their contact with the business world show ability in their clubs to run the clubs. The school girl and the girl in other walks of life are somewhat at a disadvantage as compared with the "business girl"; much more when compared with the brother who imbibes ideas of organization from the associationships from early boyhood to which he naturally gravitates.[26]

Another reason for the establishment of social clubs for adults and children in the neighborhood was to provide opportunities for recreation that were safe and moral. Addams, Coit, and other leaders became concerned with the commercial dance halls, "five cent theaters," houses of prostitution, and neighborhood saloons which were seen as vicious and corrupting influences on youth. The settlements' answer to this situation was to offer decent and safe recreation programs. Playgrounds, gymnasiums, and game rooms were opened, while at the same time social action was undertaken to clean up commercial recreation and to provide public facilities.

The social club often provided the impetus for vocational and educational ambition and helped many of the members learn the ways of an American community, which were often alien to their immigrant parents. At the same time, clubs helped the foreign-born parents find the social life they missed after coming to America. The social clubs were a halfway point between the Old and New World. Here they could speak their native language with individuals of a similar background and also could share the experiences and problems that they faced daily in their new country. The settlement house workers did not treat them as foreigners but as human beings dealing with painful and complicated problems in adjusting to a new and different world.[27]

In addition to the social clubs, a number of other interest groups flourished. These were of several kinds, including classes in drama, music, and the arts. Lecture and discussion groups were also formed and dealt with such topics as John Dewey's lectures on social psychology, Plato, politics, and the poems of Robert Browning. One means of stimulating the interests of members was the reading of plays. Once the play was finished, the worker would direct a discussion of the themes with which the play dealt.

Although groups were not used as a means of treatment in settlement houses until the mid-1940s, there is evidence to suggest that some leaders recognized the pressure of group dynamics on deviant behavior much earlier. Jane Addams wrote about how the settlement house worker worked with a group of young boys who were drug addicts:

It is doubtful whether these boys could ever have pulled through unless they had been allowed to keep together through the hospital and convalescing period, unless we had been able to utilize the gang spirit and to turn its collective forces towards overcoming the desire for the drugs.[28]

THE YOUTH SERVICE AGENCIES

During the years between 1850 and 1900, "character-building" organizations for boys and girls increased rapidly. They developed as a result of the growing mechanization of industry which made necessary new interests to fill leisure time and to provide a means of protection against the problems created by city life in a rising industrial society. Some organizations focused on the multiple problems of immigrant families adjusting to a new world, while others concentrated on the working and living conditions of youth. These organizations included the Boy Scouts, Girl Scouts, Catholic Boys' Brigade, Young Women's Christian Association, Young Men's Christian Association, Young Women's Hebrew Association, Young Men's Hebrew Association, and Boys' Clubs. Among the activities usually provided by character-building agencies were active sports (football, volleyball, golf); outdoor life (camping, hiking, nature study); social contacts and group experiences (dances, parties, social club activities); training in new skills, (hand crafts, cooking, homemaking); community service projects (first aid, cultural improvement); and vocational classes and individual help (lectures, personal counseling).

These organizations generally began as local endeavors by a small number of middle-class, educated citizens to deal with a particular group of children, and subsequently evolved into national or international organizations. Stone has summarized the tendencies in boys' work:

The changes from local efforts at boys' work by a few interested men to nationalization and standardization of boy organizations, from social saving to boy guidance in method, from the church to the school as an organizing center; the growing use of equipment whenever available for boys' groups and the growing reliance on neighborhood and interest groups using the life situation of boys as the basis for program building; the efforts to eliminate friction, the growing interest of civic clubs in boys' work as a method of reducing the cost of crime in American life, and the growing interest in informal leisure time education for boys . . . and experimentation in the private practice of boys' work, summarizes the major trends in boys' work.[29]

Once an interest in an activity was stimulated, the organizations used it to develop specific behavior patterns. Some stressed the development of loyalty, honor, physical fitness, social and racial consciousness, love of country, class, party, or sect; others had as a primary goal intellectual development or increasing appreciation of art, aesthetics, and nature. These aims were often expressed in such generalizations as "character building," "development of personality," "good citizenship," and "control over nature."

One of the earliest organizations for youth was the Woodcraft Indians, introduced by Ernest Thompson Seton (1860-1946). Seton, born in England and reared in Canada, was a well-known artist and writer of nature stories and an ardent disciple of the outdoor life. It was his belief that America's shift to an urban way of life would result in physical and social decay for both children and adults. As a remedy, he decided to work through the young, and he devised the "science of woodcraft," which was a blend of the prose of Henry Thoreau, the philosophy of Emerson, and the fiction of James Fenimore Cooper. As a symbol of the organization, he chose the American Indian. In spite of a residue of prejudice which held that the only good Indian was a dead Indian, he was able to build the Indian to heroic proportions in the eyes of children. The "noble red man" was presented in a romanticized setting of tepees, tom toms, feathered war bonnets, and campfires, with an infinity of high principles. Seton detailed Indian ceremonies, dances, sign language, tracking, and the secrets of smoke signaling. Rules were stated in somewhat negative terms, such as "do not make a dirty camp," "no smoking," "no fire water," and "do not rebel."

Seton announced his new organization, the Woodcraft Indians, in 1902, and immediately the first lodge was formed in New York State. Other lodges sprang up throughout the country. Baden-Powell included some of the ceremony developed by Seton into the program of the Boy Scouts. In 1910, Seton became the chief scout of the Boy Scouts of America, but five years later he resigned because of conflict with Baden-Powell. He felt that the Scouts placed too much emphasis on what he called "city scouting," on the modern, and on training in subjects that seemed to him to have little to do with the outdoors and nature. The Woodcraft Indians lost its influence as a movement when organizations such as the Scouts, the Chautauquas, and the Ys adopted many of the rituals and traditions that once had been part of Seton's philosophy.

Generally, boys' and girls' clubs evolved into two general types, the mass club and the small group. The mass club was a larger grouping of integral units in which a variety of activities could be undertaken simultaneously by different leaders. The club as a whole met frequently on the basis of some common interest which may have been nothing more than age grouping, time of meeting, or a purpose set by the sponsoring organization. The second type, the small group club, carried on activities in which all of the members could participate in comparatively close association with one another.

Some organizations, such as the YMCA, started as mass clubs but expanded into the extensive use of small groups when the departmentalized-styled programs failed to give recognition to the life of the individual member as a part of a school, church, and community. In short, all members were seen as being alike with no differentiation for different life-styles. McCaskill, reflecting on this issue, felt that there was little carryover of what was learned in the YMCA building to other parts of the boys' life and that the departmentalized organization made democracy and self-government for boys a very difficult procedure. Often a small group of members, usually about fifty, "capture[d] the leadership" of the organization and conducted it as a benevolent oligarchy in which the members had little or no voice.[30]

Of the many youth service agencies, the Young Men's and Young Women's Christian Associations, Boy and Girl Scouts, the Boys' Clubs, and the Young Men's and Young Women's Hebrew Associations had the most influence on the development of what was to become social group work.

Young Men's Christian Association

The first of the group service agencies in the United States was the Boston YMCA established in 1851 by a converted Baptist sea captain, Thomas V. Sullivan, who, while visiting London, had been impressed by the London YMCA. Sullivan, with the help of the Protestant community, established a similar organization for young men who had come to Boston to work. Eventually, it added the aim of helping boys meet the problems and conditions of present-day life through groups organized within their own environment and neighborhood.

These included Bible study classes, hobby and interest clubs, teams, school clubs (notably Hi-Y and Junior Hi-Y), church clubs, employed boys' clubs, and gang and neighborhood clubs.

The YMCA clubs sought to achieve social redirection from a Christian viewpoint among boys as well as self-development in desirable skills and habits of living in a Christian democracy. To a large extent, the work was carried on by employed, trained, boys' work secretaries, along with volunteer group leaders. The evangelical emphasis of some of the local associations frequently involved them in general religious and welfare work. Hopkins in his history of the YMCA movement has noted that in its first decade the organization functioned as a "sort of cooperating agency for the advancement of any good work that any good man thought ought to be prosecuted."[31] As late as 1874, many local associations had committees in charge of relief whose task was to distribute money and clothing to poor families.

While relief work ranked second only to the conversion of young men, the YMCA frequently came under fire by its board for its priorities. After such an attack in 1867, the Chicago YMCA reported that it was fast becoming "a society for the improvement of the condition of the poor, physical[ly] and morally," and wished to impress on all concerned that "our mission is not only to relieve the suffering but to improve the morals of those who are aided by us."[32] Gradually, the YMCA began to limit its activities to work with young men and left the field of general philanthropy to other organizations.[33]

Young Women's Christian Association

The history of the YWCA in America closely parallels that of the YMCA in that it, too, was based on an organization already established in England and was concerned with the mental, spiritual, and physical well-being of female youth. In 1858, the Ladies Christian Association was established in New York City with the goal of holding religious meetings among self-supporting young women employed in mills and factories. The name Young Women's Christian Association was first used by the Boston Association, established in 1866. Like its predecessors in England

and New York City, the YWCA in Boston was concerned with
the plight of young women moving to the city in search of work.
Since there were no agencies that offered protection or advice
of a Christian nature, the Boston YWCA assumed the duty of
seeking out young women who were taking up their residence
in that city. It endeavored to bring them under moral and
religious influences by aiding them in selecting suitable board-
ing places and employment and by encouraging their attendance
at some place of worship.[34]

The early associations emphasized Christian motivation, both
in their organization and in the type of work they did. The
following statement appears in a summary report made in 1876:

But above all, the great aim of the Associations is to win souls for Christ,
and it is this object which occupies the best thoughts and noblest efforts
of those engaged in the work. Yet, of this part of the work, the results
cannot be counted up. They will be known only on that day when the
Searcher of all hearts shall say to those who have been faithful in the dis-
charge of this duty, "Inasmuch as ye have done it unto one of the least
of these my brethren, ye have done it unto me."[35]

It was only a short time before those women who had had their
attention drawn in the first place to the needs of young working girls realized the value and satisfaction of group organization
as a way of service. By the end of the 1880s, the YWCA had
enlarged its function so that it not only provided a wide range
of programs for girls living under its roof, but also began to
organize Christian women for service within the community.
Local YWCAs organized homes, city prisons, workhouses, jails,
orphan asylums, and hospitals. Religious services were conducted in hospitals, jails, and other institutions. Day nurseries,
orphan asylums, and "retreats for sinful, sorrowing women,"
all made their appearance in various YWCAs.

The overall program, especially in the last half of the 1800s,
was adapted to meet the ever-widening professional and emotional interests of young women. Classes in penmanship, bookkeeping, astronomy, and physiology began in the 1860s, and
in 1872 the YWCA was the first organization in the country to
offer sewing machine lessons. By the 1880s, stenography, china-

painting, domestic science, and cooking were added to the list of instructions offered. To meet the increasing demand for general education, many associations offered classes in a wide variety of subjects, with emphasis on their practical application to everyday living. The education process of the YWCA was to provide for individual development, with emphasis on thinking, working, and acting together.[36]

Boy Scouts of America

The American organization of the Boy Scouts, with roots extending back to before the turn of the century, was officially founded in 1910 by Ernest Thompson Seton (1860-1946), Daniel Carter Beard (1850-1941), and William Boyce (1858-1929). Seton had introduced the Woodcraft Indians movement in 1902, and Beard had started the Sons of Daniel Boone, a nature oriented organization for youth in 1905. Boyce was a Chicago publisher interested in club work for boys.[37] The goal of the Boy Scouts was to supplement existing institutions, such as the home, the school, and the church by engaging boys in outdoor games and activities of cultural value. Borrowing from the British Boy Scout movement and the writings of Baden-Powell, it stressed such romantic activities as camping, outdoor cookery, and trail-blazing. Uniforms, distinctive symbols, and insignias added dash and color to the organization. From its very beginnings, prominent businessmen and government officials composed its leadership. President Taft, for example, within the first year, accepted the honorary presidency of the Boy Scouts and established a precedent that has continued.

From its inception the purpose of the Boy Scouts has been to develop character and to train boys for citizenship by help-ing them do things for themselves, by training them in scout craft, by teaching them patriotism, courage, self-reliance, and by developing in them strong bodies and physical fitness. This purpose is epitomized in the "Scout Oath" in which the Scout promises on his honor to do his duty to God and his country, to obey the Scout law, to help others at all times, and to keep himself physically strong, mentally awake, and morally straight.

Over the years, the Scout program received considerable criticism for being too militaristic and nationalistic. Since the founder and some of the early leaders were army officers, military regimentation was stressed. Others maintained that belonging to the Scouts was too expensive. Though uniforms were not required, if the boy wanted to participate in all of the activities he was encouraged to have full equipment. Another criticism of the Scouts was its lack of flexibility. Members advanced from one rank to another by passing a series of tests. The program was prearranged, and there was little opportunity for individualism in the initial ranks. In sharp contrast, the boys' program of the YMCA was based on the interests of the boys as determined through discussion and counseling.

Girl Scouts of America

The Girl Scouts of America was a replica of the Girl Guides founded in England in 1909. Juliette Low (1860-1927) of Savannah, Georgia, met Baden-Powell while visiting England and became enthusiastic with the idea of scouting. She subsequently gathered a group of girls together in Genlyon, Scotland, in 1910 and began a company of Girl Guides. The girls were taught the history of the British flag, first aid, cooking, and how to tie knots. They were also taught map reading and signaling by military officers living in Genlyon. Upon returning to Georgia in 1912, she began two patrols of Girl Guides using the English handbook as a guideline. As scouting spread throughout the United States, leaders began to refer to the Girl Guides as Girl Scouts and called companies "troops." When the first American-oriented handbook, entitled *How Girls Can Help Their Country* was published in 1913, the promise and laws sections read "Girl Scouts" instead of Girl Guides.

Low and the other early leaders felt that the organization should provide a constructive group experience flexible enough to meet the needs and desires of the members and at the same time foster self-reliance, consideration of others, and a sense of social responsibility. Programs included homemaking, outdoor activities, international friendship, arts and crafts, community life, dramatics, music, and dancing. The members were placed in small groups called patrols, much as the Boy Scouts were, and progress was made through the levels of tenderfoot, second-class and first-class rank. Girls were encouraged to try new experiences so that they would broaden their interests. A number of proficiency projects were part of the program, allowing for the development of special talents.

Many of the early paid professionals who directed the Girl Scouts had backgrounds in social work. One of the most noteworthy was Jane Detter Rippin (1882-1953), who became national director in 1919. She had been chief probation officer of Philadelphia and had rendered distinguished service to the War and Navy departments in Washington during World War I. In girl scouting, she saw a chance to institute preventative programs against delinquency.[38] Rippen was also instrumental in developing Girl Scouts from local units set up on an informal framework into a nationwide movement. She developed standard scouting procedures for the whole country, established close coordination between local units and national headquarters, and provided for ongoing training of Girl Scout leaders. During her leadership, she added new activities such as community and political studies, to the outdoor pursuits and homemaking studies traditionally associated with the movement, so as to prepare girls for active and informal participation in community life.

Boys' Clubs

The earliest Boys' Clubs were established as independent units by individuals or groups who were often unaware of similar undertakings in other communities. The first club for boys that left a record of its work was established in Hartford in 1860 by three young women who, for a number of years, supervised a self-governing group of boys known as the Dashaway Club. The members participated in such activities as games, music, dramatics, and dancing. Atkinson and Vincent in their history of the Boys' Clubs note that the Dashaway

Club was financially secure. When it disbanded during the Civil War, it had a library fund of $1,000 which was donated to the Free Public Library in Hartford.[39]

The oldest Boys' Club is the Salem Fraternity, which was begun in 1869 in Salem, Massachusetts, and has maintained uninterrupted service. A report on its operation, dated 1881, lists the following characteristics: (1) The club was centrally located. (2) Its equipment was practical and relatively inexpensive, emphasizing light, warmth, and an atmosphere of cheerfulness and genial friendship. (3) The organization was nonsectarian. Its founders recognized the church and the religious life, but they set themselves the task of doing the things "commonly left outside of church work." (5) They recognized that their task was distinctly a personality job, dependent for its success upon the attitudes and the character of its workers. (6) The organization was devoted entirely to boys.[40] These same principles, with variations, became part of Boys' Clubs that were to follow.

Although the early leaders of the various Boys' Clubs had the same humanitarian motives as other youth leaders, the founders of the early Boys' Clubs were in one respect ahead of the thinking of their day. While they were as zealous as any other youth workers in their care for society's victims, they were even more eager to learn and to put into operation the preventative and constructive measures that have come to be a part of social planning and community organization. The idea of keeping boys off the streets, of protecting youth, of preventing mischief by giving boys something to do, and many other similar expressions of purpose indicate their constructive approach to the problem.

Jewish Youth Agencies

It is estimated that the Jewish population in the United States grew from 50,000 in the mid-nineteenth century to approximately 250,000 in 1880. The earlier German-Jewish immigrants followed the Orthodox tradition, but by the middle of the nineteenth century, new liberal interpretations of Judaism began to attract increasing numbers, marked simultaneously by the growth in the number of reform congregations. During this period, the principal Jewish organizations other than the synagogues and the charitable agencies were social clubs and benefit organizations. Jewish social clubs first appeared in America during colonial times and by 1850 were well established in many communities.

In the early 1840s, a spontaneous Jewish youth movement arose, taking the form of literary societies. These groups usually limited their memberships, and sometimes several existed in the same city. They eventually adopted the name Young Men's Hebrew Literary Association (YMHLA). The first of these organizations was the Young Men's Hebrew Literary Association of Philadelphia, organized in 1850 under the guidance of Reverend Isaac Leeser, a noted rabbi and author. Within five years, similar groups were organized in New York City, Baltimore, and New Orleans. Many of the new associations dropped the word "literary" and became known as the Young Men's Hebrew Association (YMHA). The program of these associations consisted of lectures, debates, dramatics, and social activities. The larger associations maintained permanent quarters, which usually included libraries, reading rooms, and assembly halls. Both the literary societies and the early Young Men's Hebrew Associations drew a sharp distinction in function between social clubs of the period and the literary associations. Wherever facilities were acquired, a ban was usually placed against card playing, gambling, and drinking.

Many of the Jewish literary associations eventually changed their purpose and program to conform to those of the YMHA, with greater emphasis on social activities. In general, the American Jewish community made little distinction between the Young Men's Hebrew Literary Association and the Young Men's Hebrew Association. In 1880, the American Hebrew Association was formed, which was to serve as the national organization of the YMHAs. The first facilities established by the early YMHA (and the YMCAs) were libraries and reading rooms, and often the librarian was the first professional employee.[41] The Young Women's Hebrew Association (YWHA) was established in 1902 in New York City to provide leisure-time activities and to strengthen Jewish life. The YWHAs sponsored religious services, libraries, club work, cultural, educational, and social activities, and camping.

By the end of the century, the settlements and youth serving movements were established in most of the larger cities throughout America. Programs and activities were viewed by the early founders of group serving agencies as a means of assisting individuals to make constructive use of their leisure time, develop character, solve common problems, and adjust to a new culture. There was the basic belief that the individual could bring about constructive changes in his life if he joined together with others and worked toward common goals. Although mass activities were a part of settlements and youth organizations, there was a growing conviction that it was better to work intimately with a few rather than superficially with many.

NOTES

1. U.S. Department of Commerce, Bureau of the Census, "Historical Statistics of the United States, Colonial Times to 1957" (Washington, D.C.: 1960), pp. 56-59.

2. Louis M. Hacker, *The World of Andrew Carnegie 1865-1901* (Philadelphia: J. B. Lippincott, 1968), Ch. 3.

3. Sidney E. Mead, "American Protestantism Since the Civil War," *Journal of Religion* vol. 37, January 1956, pp. 1-15.

4. Samuel P. Hayes, *The Response to Industrialism 1885-1914* (Chicago: University of Chicago Press, 1957), pp. 137-39.

5. Frank D. Watson, *The Charity Organization Movement in the United States* (New York: Macmillan Co., 1922).

6. Second Annual Report of Massachusetts Board of State Charities, January 1866, in Sophonisba P. Breckinridge, *Public Welfare Administration in the United States,* Select Documents (Chicago: 1938), p. 305.

7. Edward T. Devine, *When Social Work Was Young* (New York: Macmillan Co., 1939), p. 4.

8. Jeffrey R. Brackett, "The Charity Organization Movement: Its Tendency and Its Duty," *Proceedings, 22nd National Conference of Charities and Correction* (Boston: 1895), p. 84.

9. Robert Treat Paine, "Pauperism in Great Cities: Its Four Chief Causes," *The Public Treatment of Pauperism,* being a Report of the First Section of the International Congress of Charities, Corrections and Philanthropy, June 1893 (Baltimore: 1894), p. 35.

10. S. E. Tenney, "The Class for Study of the Friendly Visitors' Work," *Charities Review*, II (November 1892-June 1893), pp. 58-64.

11. Mary Richmond, "The Training of Charity Workers," *Charities Review* 6 (June 1897): 308-15.

12. Sponsored by the New York Charity Organization Society, this pioneer course consisted of lectures, visits to agencies and institutions, and field work. In 1904, it became the first full-fledged school of philanthropy in America. In 1919 it took the name the New York School of Social Work and became part of Columbia University.

13. In Pittsburgh, the Associated Charities was created in 1908 as a means of coordinating philanthropic endeavors. An offshoot of the organization was the Social Services Exchange in 1910 established to produce better service for the client. In 1922, the Federation of Social Agencies was formed to enhance the provision of services. This organization was followed in 1928 by the Welfare Fund as an effort to coordinate voluntary social work by means of joint financing. For a more detailed account, see Philip Klein, *Social Study of Pittsburgh* (New York: Columbia University Press, 1938), p. 405.

14. Walter Trattner, *From Poor Law to Welfare State: A History of Social Welfare in America* (New York: The Free Press, 1974), p. 139.

15. Kenneth E. Boulding, "Alienation and Economic Development," *Neighborhood Goals* (New York: National Federation of Settlements, 1958), pp. 61-71.

16. Robert H. Bremner, *From the Depths: The Discovery of Poverty in the United States* (New York: New York University Press, 1964), p. 61.

17. Alice Hamilton, *Exploring the Dangerous Trades: The Autobiography of Alice Hamilton, M.D.* (Boston: Little, Brown and Co., 1943), p. 27.

18. Dorothy G. Becker, "Social Welfare Leaders as Spokesmen for the Poor," *Who Spoke for the Poor? 1880-1914* (New York: Family Service Association of America, 1968), pp. 10-11.

19. Robert A. Woods and Albert J. Kennedy, *The Settlement Horizon: A National Estimate* (New York: Russell Sage Foundation, 1922), pp. 430-31.

20. Jane Addams, *Twenty Years at Hull House* (New York: Macmillan Co., 1926), p. 109.

21. Woods and Kennedy, *The Settlement Horizon*, p. 73.

22. Ibid., p. 75.

23. Arthur Holden, *The Settlement Idea: A Vision of Social Justice* (New York: Macmillan Co., 1922), p. 67.

24. The term *director* was used to designate the resident responsible for organized club work, while *leader* indicated the volunteer, resident, or paid associate who met regularly with the club.

25. Joseph Lee, *Constructive and Preventive Philanthropy* (New York: Macmillan Co., 1906), p. 25.

26. Charles S. Bernheimer and Jacob M. Cohen, *Boys' Clubs* (Baltimore: Lord Baltimore Press, 1914), p. 83.

27. Addams, *Twenty Years*, pp. 231-55.

28. Jane Addams, *The Spirit of Youth and the City Streets* (New York: Macmillan Co., 1909), p. 66.

29. Walter L. Stone, *The Development of Boys' Work in the United States* (n.p., 1835), p. 75. Quotation by Informal Education Service, cited by Martin H. Neumeyer and Esther S. Neumeyer, *Leisure and Recreation* (New York: A. S. Barnes and Co., 1936), p. 331.

30. Joseph C. McCaskill, *Theory and Practice of Group Work* (New York: Association Press, 1930), p. 4.

31. Charles H. Hopkins, *The History of the Y.M.C.A. in North America* (New York: Association Press, 1951), pp. 189-90.

32. Ibid.

33. As early as 1885, the YMCA had its own training program for leaders. The School for Christian Workers at Springfield, Massachusetts (later called Springfield College) offered instruction for those young men interested in becoming Y secretaries. In 1890, the YMCA Institute and Training School was opened in Chicago for the training of leaders; the name was subsequently changed to George Williams College. Those who went into YMCA work were expected to view it as a calling and something to which they would commit their total life.

34. Elizabeth Wilson, *Fifty Years of Association Work Among Young Women, 1866-1916* (New York: National Board of the YWCA, 1916), p. 31.

35. J. P. Cattell, "Women's Christian Associations in America—Their Work and Its Results," *Faith and Works*, I (August 1876), p. 4. Cited by Mary S. Sims, *The Natural History of a Social Institution—The Young Women's Christian Association* (New York: Woman's Press, 1936), p. 8.

36. In later years, the YWCA was to have major impact on social group work through the provision of scholarships, field instructors, and field placements. In addition, five of the more prominent leaders in the field—Grace Coyle, Ann Elizabeth Neely, Clara Kaiser, Gladys Ryland, and Gertrude Wilson—had been employed by the YWCA.

37. According to legend, William Boyce, a Chicago publisher, was visiting London and became lost in a foggy street on the way to an appointment. Out of the darkness a boy emerged who "saluted smartly" and offered to guide Boyce to his destination. Upon arrival, he offered the boy a shilling, but the youth refused, explaining he was a Boy Scout and could not take a tip for services to someone else. The following day Boyce visited Baden-Powell and subsequently carried information on the Boy Scouts back to the United States. For more detail, see Will Oursler, *The Boy Scout Story* (Garden City, N.Y.: Doubleday and Co., 1955).

38. Ely List, *Juliette Low and the Girl Scouts* (New York: Girl Scouts of America, 1960), pp. 37-52.

39. R. K. Atkinson and George E. Vincent, *The Boys' Club* (New York: Association Press, 1939), p. 23.

40. Ibid.

41. Benjamin Rabinowitz, *The Young Men's Hebrew Association, 1854-1913* (New York: National Jewish Welfare Board, 1948).

Chapter 3

CONSOLIDATION OF THE PATTERN, 1900-1919

In the nineteen-year period between the turn of the century and the end of World War I, Americans continued to experience, at an even more rapid rate, the social and economic changes that had begun at the end of the nineteenth century. Population concentration in the urban areas was fed by the persistence of the movement from farm to the city, augmented by the arrival of fourteen million immigrants from Europe, most of whom came between 1900 and 1914. The social problems of the earlier period continued in ever-growing proportions: problems of poverty, disease, unemployment, child labor, slum housing, and dangerous working conditions. Economic problems were multiplying, and the need to regulate financing and banking and to curb abusive monopolies was becoming apparent.

The number of people employed in manufacturing, mining, and construction doubled in the years between 1900 and 1914, a rate higher than for the population as a whole. But the growing demand for workers did not bring a corresponding improvement in the lives of the workers. Employers continued to economize on payrolls, viewing labor as the most manageable cost of production. The work week remained between fifty and sixty hours, and the ten-hour day was normal. Furthermore, long layoffs were common, so only the very fortunate worked every week of the year. Salaries were very low; the annual earnings for factory workers, for example, averaged $400. More and more Americans began to discover the extent of poverty in their midst, and with this discovery came the recognition that wages of labor were inadequate to sustain a decent level of existence. Families often compensated by drawing on the labor of other family members. Children took jobs as soon as they could, and women who were willing to accept lower wages than men could sometimes get jobs in factories when men could not. Some girls found a growing number of openings as typists in offices and behind the counters of shops, but the largest demand for them was in factories.

Child labor presented a serious social problem, for the conditions under which the children worked were generally destructive to their health and well-being. James Carey commented on child labor in 1904:

Hundreds of small boys work for Mr. Borden, and many of them toil ten hours a day without a thread of clothing on their bodies. No one except employees is allowed to enter the works, and therefore when it was stated before a women's club in New York last week that naked babies were at work in the Fall River mills, much interest was aroused. . . . They worked in the big tanks called "lime keer," in the bleach house, packing the cloth into the vats. This lime keer holds 750 pieces of cloth, and it requires one hour and twenty minutes to fill it. During that time the lad must work inside, while his body is being soaked with whatever there is of chemicals which enter into the process of bleaching, of which lime is a prominent factor. The naked bodies of the children are never dry, and the same chemicals which effect the bleaching process of the gray cloth naturally bleach the skin of the operator, and after coming out of the vats the boys show the effects in the whiteness of their skins which rivals the cotton cloth.[1]

Working conditions for both children and women represented a serious problem throughout the country. In 1900, nearly two million children between ten and fifteen years of age were part of the labor force, and at that time approximately half of the states had adopted some legal protection for children. By 1914, through the concerted effort of such organizations as the Child Labor Committee, the National Consumers' League, the General Federation of Women's Clubs, and the YWCA almost all the states had laws covering hours and conditions of child labor in factories, mills, and workshops, and setting minimum ages for leaving schools.

Many of the most flagrant abuses took place in industries that were engaged in interstate trade. The first formal attempt to bring child labor under the control of the federal government

was made in 1906 with the introduction in Congress of legislation prohibiting the shipment from one state to another of
articles produced in mines or factories employing children.
While the bill failed to get through Congress, soon thereafter,
in 1912, the Children's Bureau was formed. Among the Bureau's
many responsibilities was that of reporting on dangerous occupations, accidents, and diseases of children.

The problems of the 1900-1919 period were similar to those of
the previous forty years, but now a stronger desire for social, economic and political reform was evinced. The reform movement
burst into full flower after the turn of the century and continued until the United States entered World War I. This movement, known as the Progressive movement, was a many-sided
attack on the various social abuses that had become glaring in
the decades following the Civil War. While there was never a
national organization to direct and coordinate the numerous
reform campaigns, they nevertheless were bound together by a
contagious enthusiasm for reform and an all-out, pervasive
optimism. The Progressives believed in political democracy,
individual initiative, competitive capitalism, and property rights,
and felt that a moderate increase in the power of government
provided the only means for preserving individual freedom. The
growth of governmental authority was thought to be a means
to an end and not an end in itself.

According to the Progressives, man was a rational creature
who knew his own best interests. If given all the pertinent information regarding a problem, he was capable of weighing the
facts and reaching a correct decision that would be in his own
and society's best interest. In short, man was inherently progressive, and barriers to progress were man-made obstacles that
were capable of being removed by man. This faith in the judgment of the individual led the Progressives to a reaffirmation
of the tenets of Jeffersonian democracy. Man was capable of
governing himself, and any alleged defects of democratic
government were corruptions rather than weaknesses of the
democratic process. The Progressives urged that all be allowed
to participate directly in government and that the differences
between leaders and followers be eliminated so that the group

would be essentially the same. They pressed for such reforms as the direct election of senators, referendum, and recall, with the expectation that a government would evolve which was not influenced by wealth and that political machines would be reduced to a minimum.

The Progressives had considerable impact on the corrupt political machines that controlled many of the large urban areas. By the turn of the century, every major city had at least one reform group that was attempting to control the corrupt alliance between wealth and politics. In return for the votes of the poor, the machine distributed favors that ranged from an occasional bag of coal or turkey at Christmas to getting someone out of jail. It obtained its funds from selling street railway and lighting franchises, building contracts, police protection, and special privileges to businessmen who were willing to pay the price.[2]

The enactment of social reform measures was in large part the work of a group of writers nicknamed the muckrakers, who sought to ferret out business and political corruption, bringing it to the public's attention through articles and books. These men and women devoted their talents to exposing what they thought were the outstanding evils of American political and economic life. Among these crusaders were Ida Tarbell, Ray Stannard Baker, Upton Sinclair, and Lincoln Steffens. In 1902, Tarbell published a series of articles in *McClure's* on the Standard Oil Corporation and exposed its inner workings. She challenged the ethical costs of a monopoly and the sanctification of business success. In 1903 Baker uncovered the malpractices of the railroads and labor unions and later examined the status of the Negro in American society. Also in 1903, Upton Sinclair wrote on the revolting conditions in Chicago's meat packing industry in his book, *The Jungle*, a novel written to promote socialism. In it Sinclair used as background the meat packing industry, and detailed the life of an immigrant family employed as meat packers. In 1906, three years after the book was published, the Pure Food and Drug Law was passed, primarily due to the sense of outrage felt by citizens who had read Sinclair's book. Lincoln Steffens reported on municipal corruption in a series of articles that later appeared

in 1904 in the book *Shame of the Cities.* It was Steffens conclusion that the American businessman, whom he described as
a "self-righteous fraud," was bound together with corrupt
political bosses. Steffens believed that the system rather than
the individual was at fault; the officeholder had favors to
bestow, and the businessman had money with which to
purchase these favors.

SOCIAL WORK IN THE AGE OF REFORM

Social work had an effective role in the protest against the
social evils of the period. Daily contact with human suffering
placed social workers in a uniquely strategic position, for they
knew the facts and recorded them. Their repeated experience
with poverty had slowly forced them to change their earlier
conviction that poverty was the result of a defect within the
individual, and they now were persuaded that man's socioeconomic environment could offer or deny opportunity for
secure, healthy, social living and general well-being. For its part,
the Charity Organization Society movement was shifting from
its earlier concentration on individual economic dependency
and pauperism to a concern with the total family and its relationships.

Along with this new focus, social work had begun to develop
its methods, with investigation as the core of the methodology.
The technique was not new, but it was now being utilized with
a new set of objectives and values. The goal was no longer to
determine the worthiness or unworthiness of the individual to
receive benefits but rather to gather information about all
facets of the family's condition so that the social agencies could
render more effective help. With the needs more scientifically
determined, it was then possible to utilize the necessary resources, including those of other agencies. As a result of this
shift in attitudes, services for children and other dependents
developed. At the urging of the National Child Labor Committee, the National Consumers' League and prominent social
workers, such as Paul Kellogg, Edward Devine, and Florence
Kelley, President Theodore Roosevelt in 1909, invited repre-

sentatives of child welfare agencies from throughout America to the White House for a Conference on the Care of Dependent Children. The conference adopted a platform that normal children who had to be removed from their own families should be placed in foster homes rather than in institutions. Children should not be removed from their own homes because of poverty. Children's agencies should be licensed for their work and inspected by state authorities. States should enact laws to enable widows and deserted women to keep their children; and the Federal government should establish a Federal children's agency. Most important was the general reaffirmation of the importance of home life to the child, and the need for strengthening family life. "Home life is the highest and finest product of civilization. It is the great molding force of mind and character. Children should not be deprived of it except for urgent and compelling reasons." With this principle as a guide, the states responded quickly to the recommendation of the conference, and beginning in 1911, they enacted legislation providing the administration of "mother's aid" under local auspices. This concept was later supported by the Children's Bureau.[3]

An important development of the period was the increase in the number of training schools for social workers and the parallel development of professional self-consciousness. The term *agent*, which had been replaced around the turn of the century by *charity worker*, was beginning to give way to the generic term *social worker*. In 1910, the term *social worker* fell into disuse as special fields of social endeavor strove for identity, adopting such titles as *case worker*, *family worker*, *children's worker*, and *settlement worker*.

Before 1900, social workers worked primarily in child welfare and charity organizations; after 1900, they moved into other settings such as hospitals and schools. In 1905, Massachusetts General Hospital introduced medical social work, and a year later a social worker was hired for the psychopathic wards at Bellevue. The use of social workers in hospitals grew out of the recognition that understanding the patient's personal and social condition was essential for accurate diagnosis and effective treatment. A more formalized social service department was initiated at the Psychopathic Hospital in Boston in 1913, under the leadership of Mary C. Jarrett, wherein the role of social worker in a psychiatric setting became clearly defined. It was her task to gather information on the patient's family background and life experiences, and to act as an intermediary between the patient and his family. Between 1906 and 1907, programs of school social work were introduced in Boston, Hartford, and New York under private agencies. In 1909, the first child guidance clinic, known as the Juvenile Psychopathic Institute (renamed the Institute for Juvenile Research in 1917), was organized in Chicago. Members of the staff studied wards of the court and suggested methods for their mental and social adjustment.

In 1917, Mary Richmond published *Social Diagnosis* which was to serve as a framework for the diagnostic activities of the caseworker.[4] Richmond presented a set of principles that defined the parameters of casework practice and the specific responsibilities of the social worker within them. She elevated the importance of interviewing, which had been carried out formerly by social workers in a mechanized way. She described the influences that affected the nature of the interview, including the origin of the request, the setting of the kind of task at hand, and what was known about the client. Transcending the methodological importance of Richmond's work was her emphasis on a more humanistic "doing with" in contrast with the former style of "doing for."

One of social work's most significant contributions to social reform during the era was the utilization of research as a tool for supporting social legislation. Social workers such as Paul Kellogg, Florence Kelley, and Robert Woods were instrumental in introducing systematic social surveys to the study of social problems. These surveys, such as the ones done in Pittsburgh between 1907 and 1908, covered wages, hours, working conditions, housing, schooling, health, taxation, fire and police protection, recreation and land values. Not only did the results of the research serve as a factual base for social action, but they also caught the interest of the public when the findings were quoted in newspapers and in popular magazines.

Some caseworkers, along with settlement leaders and YWCA

leaders, in 1909 began working with Progressive leaders such as Robert La Follette, Jacob Riis, and Theodore Roosevelt in bringing about changes in government. Among other things, they advocated strict regulation or prohibition of child labor; they lobbied for the regulation of sanitation and housing; they pushed for the government to assume responsibility for the care of dependent citizens; they urged the establishment of industrial standards for decent wages; and they supported the right of labor to organize and bargain effectively.

IMPACT OF THE SOCIAL SCIENCES

The last decade of the nineteenth century and the first decade of the twentieth were marked by the growth of universities and an increased interest in research in the physical and natural sciences. European institutions such as those at Heidelberg, Berlin, and Leipzig with their emphasis on the scientific method of research, served as models for the American universities. There was little room for the man of broad interests, either in European or American institutions, for the pursuit of knowledge was deemed to be so arduous a business that only the specialized could hope to master even a segment of a particular field.

The accomplishments of the natural scientists in their studies of the physical universe convinced many scholars that the scientific method would prove equally fruitful in the study of man. With the influence of Darwin, psychologists, sociologists, and philosophers began to change their conception of the mind as being a static entity to a means by which the organism adjusts to its environment. They felt that natural laws governed the behavior of man and that it was the social scientist's task to scientifically determine the invariant natural laws of human behavior. Social scientists shared a belief and faith in progressive social change. Based on the writings of such early thinkers as St. Augustine, Henri de Saint-Simon and Auguste Comte; and the English exponents of this view, John Stuart Mill and Lester Ward, it was felt that the naturalistic accumulation and application of knowledge would lead to an improved society. This faith in progressive social change was compatible with

Christian notions of utopia and was consistent with the Darwinian theory of natural evolution. It also supplied an explanation
of the social upheavals resulting from urbanization and industrialization. As a consequence, many social scientists were easily
able to accept this faith.

Besides determining the natural laws of human nature, social
scientists felt they had a responsibility for developing and applying scientific knowledge about social organizations and social
evolution, thereby assisting in the achievement of ideal social
conditions. Urbanization was seen as a necessary and irreversible
part of evolution, and realistic amelioration of its undesirable
conditions required modifications progressing in the same direction as the main process of change. Such reform would be
fundamentally sound only if it attacked the basic difficulty
which rested in the patterned behavior and moral character of
individuals. The best remedy for urban problems such as crime,
poverty, suicide, illegitimacy, and racism was the education of
the young. This training was to be based on the norms and behavior which sociologists and other social scientists would dis-
cover as most adequate to the new urban way of life.

Psychology

The influence of psychology on social work was foreshadowed
by early articles in the Proceedings of the National Conference
on Charities and Corrections which demonstrated the importance
of the social worker studying the personality of the client. In
1888, Peter Bryce pleaded for a more humane treatment of
what he called "moral imbeciles," stressed the need for study
of the mind along with the body, and came to the conclusion
that all the actions of man—physical, intellectual, and moral—
were the inevitable consequences of prior circumstances and
conditions that absolutely controlled and dominated him.[5]

After 1910, new influences from psychology resulted in a
swing away from socioeconomic determinism to the psychological determinism of the 1920s. The child guidance movement in the United States, with its emphasis on psychotherapy
for children, as a means of minimizing serious problems in

later life, had taught social workers to recognize the importance of the family in molding the infant years, and even though there were times when this knowledge was not adequate for complete understanding, it did form a base from which later psychologists were to work.

Psychology, which by 1920 was to supplant sociology and anthropology in feeding social work, in 1925 began to be differentiated into special areas such as educational, experimental, social, and abnormal psychology. The work of the French psychologist Alfred Binet (1857-1911) on mental tests in the first decade of the twentieth century found warm reception among American psychologists. Binet advanced testing in psychology and demonstrated the superiority of objective measurement over clinical diagnosis carried on without such instruments. He also contributed a more personal approach toward the study of psychology. Rather than viewing the subjects as objects to learn something from, he perceived them as individuals, not only to be studied but also to be helped.

One of the most important influences in psychology in the early twentieth century was William James (1842-1910), a physician turned psychologist. His theory of pragmatism, which emerged partly as a protest against the more classical and religious philosophies, defined truth as that which works or functions well. Reality was not static but the result of the individual's experiences that occur through such processes as problem-solving and searching. Neither the mind nor the "self" according to James were rigidly fixed structures but forever expanding and changing in tune with new experiences.[6] The writings of William James served as the foundation for the social psychology of Charles Horton Cooley, Thorstein Veblen, and George Herbert Mead, and for role theory that was to develop much later.

Another major force in psychology in the early 1900s was John Dewey (1859-1952) at the University of Chicago. Deeply interested in the application of psychology to human relations and learning, Dewey argued that individuals learned only through the process of experience. Strongly influenced by the theory of evolution, Dewey's philosophy was based on the notion of social change. He was against things remaining static, and for progress gained through the struggle of man's intellect with reality. Dewey was greatly concerned with the welfare of man and his physical, social, and moral adjustment. He considered man's psychological processes, such as thinking and learning to be of paramount importance to his adjustment to life. More than anyone else of the period, Dewey was responsible for the application of a pragmatic spirit to education. He believed strongly that education was equivalent to life itself, and that teaching should be oriented toward the student rather than the subject matter.

At approximately the same time, G. Stanley Hall (1844-1924), at Clark University, began to work on genetic psychology and human development. This interest was to lead him to the recognition of individual differences and of the influence of early childhood on later life. This new psychology began to provide a methodology for studying and dealing with problems of the individual.

Until 1908, psychoanalysis was virtually unknown in the United States. Through the writings of A. A. Brill, however, the work of Sigmund Freud (1856-1939), became part of American life. Brill had studied with Freud in Vienna and began to publicize Freud's writings to American audiences in 1908. In 1909, Freud gave five lectures at Clark University at the invitation of its president, G. Stanley Hall. Whereas Freud's ideas were met with suspicion and skepticism in Europe, they generally elicited interest in America. This difference Freud attributed to the absence of any deep-rooted scientific tradition and a less stringent rule of official authority in America.

In spite of its appeal, the merits of Freudian theory were hotly debated both in the intellectual community and at the popular level. Some argued that Freud's approach to the study of man took away his goodness and rationality; others felt it was a rationale for lust and sin. It was especially painful for American intellectuals to admit that intelligence had as little importance as Freud suggested. Freud and his followers generated a popular interest in psychology which extended far beyond its use as a means of treatment. Originally an esoteric branch of medical knowledge, psychology was broadened and diluted to the point of becoming a popular fad. Oversimplification and sensationalism followed, especially with reference to Freud's ideas. Dozens of condensed "summaries" of Freudian theory appeared, as did books such as the *Psychology of Jesus* and the *Psychology of Golf.* The popular song "Yes, We Have No Bananas" was explained in an article in the *New York Times* as a symbol of a national inferiority complex.[7]

The focus of much of the early writing on groups was on the phenomenon of large groups. In his book *The Crowd,* LeBon described the dynamics of the collective mind and the transformation of thinking one way as an isolated individual to thinking another way when part of a crowd.[8] William McDougall produced a similar theory: he felt that groups had unique characteristics and qualities that could be observed and understood. These qualities were different from those of the individuals who composed the group and the society in which the group existed. In short, the group was more than the sum of its parts.[9]

In one of his last works, *Group Psychology and the Analysis of the Ego* (1922), Freud began a theoretical formulation of groups. Noting that group psychology was the oldest form of human psychology, he posited that the behavior of members in a group was similar to the dynamics that take place in a family. In a somewhat childlike way, the individual members resent having to share the leader (parent) with the other members (siblings). Group spirit, bond, contagion, and development of the capacity for empathy developed through the affectional ties of each member to the leader. One of Freud's major contributions to group theory is his systematic analysis of the powerful and irrational way group members view the leader. At one level the members wish to be controlled and governed by him. At another level, according to Freud, there may be resistance directed at the leader and anger expressed when they perceive that restrictions are being placed upon them.[10]

Sociology

By 1900, sociologists were preoccupied mainly with the problems of human behavior and social causation. Edward A. Ross became interested in the "social pressures" which operate within society to make the individual conform to the group norm.[11] Charles Horton Cooley, (1864-1929) making the most significant contribution to the early development of small group theory, created the concept of the "primary group," which he felt was responsible for the initial development of values and standards of behavior.[12] Cooley saw small informal groups, such as families and play groups as primary in that they gave the members a sense of solidarity and mutual identification. He hypothesized that socialization in childhood, which continues into adulthood, takes place in primary group associations and that small groups influence the behavior, reinforcing and stabilizing it in wider relationships in adulthood.

Robert MacIver (1882-1970), a Scotish-born sociologist who taught at Toronto University in 1920 and later at Columbia University, wrote both in the field of political science and sociology. His strong interest in intergroup relations, social development, and social action theory drew the attention of social workers and those working with groups. He wrote on the vital problems of associations and their relation to political power, the nature of the state, which he viewed as an interest association, and the community as a form of association encompassing many spheres of culture. MacIver felt that social work had something to learn from sociology and also that sociology had something to learn from social work. Of special importance for the sociologist was the acquisition of accurate data as to the processes of individual and group life.

One of the hardest and one of the most essential tasks of sociology is to understand the cohesive and the disruptive forces that make and mar social harmonies, to understand them not merely in their results but in their operation. They can be seen most intimately in the near group, the primary group that is the unit of every social structure. Sociologists have done comparatively little to study it. They lack the opportunity to do so which the social workers possess. . . . It is significant that those who have recently advanced the study of group process are writers who themselves have been associated with social work in one way or another. I might illustrate by reference to the various studies made by Lindeman, Professor Sheffield and Lasker, or to the recently published volume of Grace Coyle's entitled *The Social Process in Organized Groups*. These studies suggest the potentialities of this largely unexplored field.[13]

George Herbert Mead (1863-1931), a contemporary of John Dewey, was interested in the genesis of the self through gradually developing ability in childhood to take the role of the other and to visualize his own performance from the point of view of others.[14] According to Mead, the child passes through two broad stages in the development of self. First is the play stage in which he takes the role of one other person at a time. Here self-image is not well organized or stable, and the child moves from one specific act of role-taking to another in disparate fashion. By serially taking and playing roles of significant others, the child is able to get a better outside view of himself and thus contribute to the organization of self. At approximately the time he starts school, the child enters the second stage, the game stage, in which the more complex task of simultaneously taking the roles of several other persons is encountered. Games involving two or three others, according to Mead, are important in that they require the child to anticipate the moves of others and to fit them into his plan. Without this complex form of role-taking, the person would be apt to interpret the action of others as irrational or hostile when there was no such intention.[15]

In Europe, in the first quarter of the 1900s, several social scientists began to question the processes that occurred in groups. Heretofore, it was felt that only individuals were real and that groups and institutions were abstractions from individual organisms. Emile Durkheim (1858-1917) and Georg Simmel (1885-1918) were the most influential leaders of this new group. Durkheim, a French sociologist, was concerned with the characteristics of groups as well as those social and historical forces that brought them together and allowed them to operate. He believed that understanding of a group required one to go beyond the personal attributes of the individual actors and to look at the characteristics and structure of the group as a whole. Durkheim focused on such problems as the cohesion or lack of cohesion of specific religious groups, and not the traits of individual believers. He showed that such group properties were independent of individual traits and must therefore be studied in their own right.[16]

Simmel, a German scientist, developed theoretical formulations regarding group size and the significance of numbers for group life. His conceptualization, including the nature of power alliances and the effect on interaction of various sizes of groups, increased knowledge of the nature of the interacting process within the small group and the different nature of interaction resulting from change in group size. Simmel highlighted the sterility of psychological reductionism by demonstrating the influence of adding various new members to a group.[17]

THE RECREATION MOVEMENT

The event that is generally accepted as marking the beginning of the recreation movement in the United States was the opening of the Sand Garden in Boston in 1885. There were a number of important antecedents, however, including the initiation of organized sports, the formation of kindergartens, and the provision of parks by local governments. The movement for organized athletics, gymnastics, and sports began with the establishment of an outdoor gymnasium in the Salem, Massachusetts, Latin School in 1821. A year later, a gymnastic school was organized in Boston, and Harvard College established a gymnasium. Much of the early impetus came from German gymnastics and from physical education leadership first by German visitors and later by immigrants.[18]

During the 1840s, boating clubs were organized at Yale and Harvard, and college baseball began to make its appearance a decade later. Football can be traced to the 1860s, while at approximately the same time athletic associations began to be organized in various parts of the country.

Friedrich Froebel is credited with establishing the first kindergarten in 1840. Prior to that time, there were few schools or established activities for children too young to enter regular schools. He worked out the principles and methods of the kindergarten and gave the movement a start, placing emphasis on such activities as music, games, storytelling, and play in general. The kindergarten movement did not get fully under way in America until nearly thirty years later.

The purchase of a large tract of land, later known as Central Park, by the city of New York in 1897 was also an important event in the development of the recreation movement.[19] Many cities followed New York's example in acquiring large parks, but for many years these properties were for rest and contemplation rather than for recreational activity, although horseback riding, boating, and picnicking were usually allowed. Most parks were open space and had little provision for athletic fields, water sports, and the like. The "meadow" in Washington Park, Chicago, was opened for team games as early as 1876, but park officials did not provide systematic recreation. No instruction was provided, only police supervision.

The first organized outdoor play center for children was established in Boston in 1885. A large sand pile was placed in the yard of the Children's Mission of Parmenter Street through the efforts of the Massachusetts Emergency and Hygiene Association. This was the direct result of a visit by Dr. Marie Zakrewska, a physician active in charity work, to Berlin where she observed a sand garden which had been established for the children of that city. The sand garden at the Children's Mission averaged fifteen children a day for six weeks during the months of July and August.[20] In addition to playing in the sand, the children sang, listened to stories, and marched about under the guidance of women who lived in the neighborhood, with additional voluntary supervision by interested mothers. This experiment was to continue through succeeding years. It was succesful, for in 1887 ten centers were operating with paid supervision. For many citizens living in Boston, playgrounds were a weapon against the rising tide of juvenile delinquency and gangs, and the problems associated with bad housing and the growth of tenement slum areas. In 1889, the city assumed some of the financial burden of the playgrounds, and three out of twenty-one centers were designated for boys between twelve and fifteen years of age.[21]

The Boston achievement was not to be measured by local consequences in the New England area alone. New York, Philadelphia, and Chicago reacted by building facilities similar to the Children's Mission sand garden. Generally, the initiative and funds were provided by philanthropic individuals or social agencies. The facilities were built on private property and were eventually taken over by the city and transferred to public areas. The early sand gardens were very simple, consisting of sand heaps together with swings, seesaws, and other simple playthings. They were located in densely populated sections of the city, equipped for outdoor activities, and were open a few hours a day during the summer months for small children. The main idea behind them was to keep children off the streets by providing an environment that allowed for free and spontaneous play.

In 1892, Jane Addams established a playground in connection with Hull House. Because it was more comprehensive in its equipment and program of activities than the earlier sand gardens, it was referred to as a model playground. It covered a wider area; provided for handball, baseball, and various other sports; and was supervised by a trained kindergarten leader and a policeman. Older children, as well as those of pre-adolescent age, were admitted, and adults were allowed to come as observers.[22]

Other cities took steps to acquire playgrounds, largely because of the insistence of social workers and influential citizens who were concerned with the influx of immigrants, the increase in the number of factories, accompanied by the perils of child labor, unsanitary, unsafe working conditions, and the spread of commercialized amusement, which was often associated with vice. In New York City, a tract of two and five-eighths acres, covered with five- and six-story tenements, was purchased in 1897 at a cost of $8,000 after a most determined effort led by Jacob Riis. This land was later equipped with apparatus, wading pool, a place for games, a gymnasium, and baths.[23]

The development of recreation and leisure-time activities often came into direct conflict with Calvinistic ideals that glorified hard work and condemned leisure. Some of the more strict protestant groups questioned whether the new interest in playgrounds and play facilities was not the work of the devil. Increasingly, however, both individuals and the churches began to recognize that the spiritual and moral growth of people could be strengthened through a wholesome and satisfying use of leisure. But, to be acceptable, recreation had to strengthen family life and enhance moral qualities, and at the same time, it should not be designed solely for pleasure or diversion or for the individual's social and economic advancement.

By the early 1900s, parks were beginning to be designed to serve persons of all ages with varied interests. In 1903, Chicago passed a bond issue for the acquisition and development of small recreation parks in the crowded neighborhoods of South Chicago and established a new standard in park and playground building. The city provided an assembly hall with stage and dressing rooms, gymnasiums for men and women, shower and locker rooms, clubrooms, and a branch of the public library. Other facilities included outdoor swimming pools, wading pools, and bandstands. The employment of trained leaders under a general director helped to make these playgrounds and neighborhood centers successful.

No concerted action was taken to coordinate these various developments into a national movement until 1906 when the Playground Association of America was organized. It was later changed to the Playground and Recreation Association in America in 1911 and is now called the National Recreation Association. This organization was one of the most important factors in establishing adequate playground systems for cities, towns, and rural communities. The first officers of the association included such leaders as Theodore Roosevelt, Jacob Riis, Luther H. Gulick, and Jane Addams.

Paralleling the development of the parks was the social center movement which stressed the opening of school buildings for social, civic, and recreational use by the citizens. According to the traditional opinion, the school hours were to be used only for formal instruction of children. After the final bell rang, the building was to be locked up and the grounds deserted. The economy of opening these facilities to the public rather than spending money to duplicate them in special recreation buildings was apparent, and many states prior to 1900 had passed laws permitting school buildings to be used as civic or social centers. It was argued by recreation leaders that if the definition of education were broad enough, it could include recreation.

Perry, in listing the various types of activities carried on by community centers, found that a large proportion could be considered recreational in character. These included civic occasions, educational events, entertainments, handicrafts, neighborhood services, physical exercises, social occasions, club and society meetings, and voluntary classes.[24]

The value of recreation was articulated in Joseph Lee's book *Play in Education*, published in 1915. Lee viewed play and leisure-time activities as important dimensions in the prevention and cure of physical and mental illness, and in preparation for citizenship. Through activities such as games, sports, and drama, children learned rules, dealt with reality, and adopted moral values that would be carried into their adult life.[25]

A large number of recreational organizations geared toward youth became popular after the turn of the century, including 4-H, Camp Fire Girls, B'nai B'rith, and the Catholic Boys' Brigade. The 4-H movement began unofficially in 1891 as a way of augmenting the education children were receiving in rural schools. This movement was coupled with a growing sentiment for practical education in agriculture, manual arts, and home-making.[26] Clubs under volunteer leadership conducted such projects as corn growing, soil testing, vegetable garden growing, and collecting of wild flowers, weed seeds, and insects. By 1914, the U.S. Department of Agriculture created a bureau to support youth projects, and 4-H clubs officially came under the sponsorship of department's Cooperative Extension Service. While a majority of the youth were white, black youth were encouraged to take an active role. In 1916, it was estimated that in the southern states, there were 2,551 clubs enrolling 55,871 Negro boys and girls.[27]

The Camp Fire Girls was founded by Luther Gulick and his wife Charlotte in 1910. Gulick (1865-1919), a physician interested in physical education, had served as director of physical training at Springfield College, and while in this role, he designed the body, mind, and spirit triangle of the YMCA. In 1909, while on the staff of the Russell Sage Foundation, he established the Camp Fire Girls program as a means of meeting the physical, spiritual, and emotional needs of girls and of utilizing the new knowledge that was becoming available in the fields of child development, education, and sociology. The purpose of the Camp Fire Girls was to perpetuate the spiritual ideals of the home through the work of girls. Its programs involved home crafts, handicrafts, health crafts, citizenship, and patriotism.[28]

Other organizations such as B'nai B'rith and the Catholic Boys' Brigade carried both a religious and cultural commitment. B'nai B'rith was founded in 1843 as a means of supporting its members in the event of illness. This fraternal self-help organization later adopted the goal of uniting people of the Jewish faith and inculcating the principle of philanthropy, honor, and patriotism. It also set out to assist the victims of persecution.[29]

The Catholic Boys' Brigade, founded in 1916, was designed to promote the spiritual, moral, mental, physical, social, and civic welfare of Catholic boys between the approximate ages of ten and eighteen. Program activities, which included military drills, physical training, first aid, music, and athletics, were carried on chiefly by volunteer leaders selected and supervised by the clergy. In 1930, the Catholic Youth Organization (CYO) was established in Chicago, and eventually in other cities. This program focused on leisure-time activities, particularly athletics for boys and girls of all ages and also coordinated other Catholic youth programs to avoid duplication and overlapping of services. In dioceses where youth programs were highly developed, youth directors were appointed on a fulltime basis.

THE ADULT EDUCATION MOVEMENT

The adult education movement in the United States was an important contributor to the development of group work. The originator of this movement, Josiah Holbrook of Derby, Connecticut, traveled throughout New England giving lectures on the physical and natural sciences. In his travels he became determined to establish an association for the sharing of useful knowledge. In 1826 his ideas appeared in the periodical, the *American Journal of Education*, and in the same year he formed the first lyceum in Millbury, Massachusetts, which was attended by farmers and merchants "for the purpose of self culture, community instruction, and mutual discussion of common public interest."[30]

In 1831, a national organization, the National American Lyceum, was formed whose purpose was the advancement of education and the general diffusion of knowledge. The annual meetings were poorly attended and by 1839 the organization ceased to exist. However, the town and country lyceums continued to operate until about the time of the Civil War. Around 1869, the function of providing popular lectures for literary societies, women's clubs, and other groups began to be taken over by commercial speakers bureaus, often called lyceum bureaus.[31] The lyceum movement left several permanent marks on the mainstream of American culture, particularly adult education.[32] It demonstrated the feasibility of an integrated national system of local groups organized primarily for adult educational purposes, and it developed an educational technique, the lecture forum, which was later adopted by university extension services.

A spinoff of the lyceum movement was the Chautauqua Institution founded on the shore of Chautauqua Lake in New York in 1874 as an interdenominational normal school for Sunday school teachers.[33] The idea became so popular that it attracted other participants and began to broaden its program to include every aspect of culture. In 1878, the first integrated core program of adult education, the Chautauqua Literary and Scientific Circle (CLSC), was organized. The program was made up of a four-year core of home reading in history and literature carried on in connection with local reading circles. Concurrently, Chautauqua developed a series of summer schools in language, liberal arts, speech, music, and other disciplines. A related force was the Chautauqua tent shows that toured the country every year. They featured lectures by speakers such as William Jennings Bryant as well as drama and music.[34]

A controversial issue in the nineteenth century was that of who should be educated. While there was little opposition to the idea of universal education, there was strong opposition to the idea of universal public education supported by taxation. The process by which the battle was won was essentially an adult education process, strongly flavored with social action. Public interest ran high, and individuals were stimulated to study and discuss the issues throughout the activities of hundreds of schools, societies, lyceums, and educational associations. Once elementary and secondary schools were established, evening schools began to be formed. Some were set up for children who could not go to school during the day, while others were distinct schools with separate administrative units. For the most part, they were established for working youth, and the curriculum was a repetition of the regular academic courses given in the daytime.

By the turn of the century, educators began to question the focus of adult education. Should the focus be on helping people to enjoy their leisure through literature, art, drama, music, and interest groups, or should it be on vocational education, with the goal of guiding a person toward a more promising career. By 1915, the majority of the students participating in adult education were seeking some form of self-advancement. These students included persons who had dropped out of school at an early age and found it desirable or necessary to make up school deficiencies, the foreign-born responding to the pressure of Americanization campaigns, and those preparing for entrance or advancement into an occupation.

Adult education had five major functions: remedial, occupational, relational, liberal, and political.[35] The remedial involved study undertaken to give an adult whatever was needed to bring his educational experiences up to the minimum that was necessary for his life-style. It included the ability to read and write, and for immigrants it also included a knowledge of spoken English and participation in American citizenship programs. Training in homemaking and child care on an elementary basis and the simple rules of health were also considered remedial since grown citizens were presumed to have this knowledge. It was hoped that one of the outcomes would be the complete eradication of illiteracy in America.

The occupational function, perceived by many as being in the range of public education activity, prepared individuals for advancement on the job or to another job of a different

nature; provided for the industrial rehabilitation of people who
were unemployed because of mechanization; and gave guidance
in choosing or adjusting to an occupation. Occupational schools
for older students typically included those who wished, by
added labor in their free time, to equip themselves for job promotion or to obtain a more difficult job, and those who were
unemployed because of mechanization.

The relational function included "parent education" and
self-study designed to help persons better understand themselves and those around them. An example of parent education
was the parent-education movement which, through the use of
specialist and lay leaders, attempted to bring the new scientific
knowledge regarding the care and protection of children into
use in the home. In the self-study, it was presumed that through
discussion and lectures one could better one's adjustment in all
contacts of life. Some communities instituted self-improvement
and family study groups.

The liberal function describes those activities undertaken
chiefly for their own sake, for the pleasure inherent in them.
The "liberating" influence was expected to produce results
beyond the satisfaction of achievement. In the pursuit of art
or philosophy or science, the student would find the enjoyment of effort. Much of this philosophy was tied to the recognition that citizens needed to be prepared to make good use of
their increased leisure time.

The political function was predicated on the theory that
direct political education was necessary and covered all those
studies, practices, and experiences which men deliberately
pursued to be better members of a community. Such education included not only the study of politics as a subject but
also all forms of training for political action. Because of the
complication and formidable quantity of public business, the
average individual was seen as being both unequipped and ineffective in influencing government. However, it was felt that
through active discussion of public business in public forums,
using trustworthy information about public questions, the
individual citizen could have some influence.

Of these five functions, the political came closest to the
philosophy of the reform-minded Progressives. It was not

enough for individuals to vote in elections; they should also be involved in the decision-making process at the grass roots level. Mary Parker Follett (1868-1933), one of the most influential political thinkers of the period, wrote that the only way democracy would work was for individuals to organize themselves into neighborhood groups and to bring to the surface the needs, desires, and aspirations of the people.[36] As a recognized political unit, the neighborhood group had many advantages. First, it made possible the association of neighbors, which meant fuller acquaintance and greater understanding among individuals. Second, it provided an opportunity for constant and regular intercourse which would provide the individuals with knowledge of the techniques of association. Third, it would result in a fuller, more varied life in that the participants would be involved with people different from those close to them. Too much congeniality, according to Follett, would result in a narrowness of thinking. A major goal of the neighborhood organization was to dismantle the political party organization as the middle man between the individual and government. This goal would be accomplished by substituting real unity for the pseudo unity of the party, by gaining genuine leaders instead of bosses, and by substituting a responsible government for an irresponsible party.[37]

Two important ingredients of adult education were the use of the group process and the direct participation of the student in the learning experience. The teacher, according to Eduard Lindeman (1855-1955), was the group chairman who kept the discussion going, maintained its direction, enlisted the active participation of all members, and pointed out discrepancies and relations. He was different from the traditional teacher.

He no longer sets problems and then casts about with various kinds of bait until he gets back his preconceived answer; nor is he the oracle who supplied answers which students carry off in their notebooks; his function is not to profess but to evoke—to draw out, not pour in; he performs in various degrees the office of interlocutor (one who questions and interprets), prolocutor (one who brings all expressions before the group), coach (one who trains individuals for team-play), and strategist (one who organizes parts into wholes and keeps the total action aligned with the group's purpose).

Whatever he brought to the group in the form of opinions, facts, and experiences must be open to question and criticism on the same terms as the contributions of other participants.[38]

By the end of the second decade of the twentieth century, leaders in the adult education and recreation movement had a genuine regard for the potential of the small group experience. The group could be used to train people in more effective problem solving, and the development of adaptive social skills that would enhance their social adjustment. The group could be used to help individuals develop their capacity to participate more intelligently in the communities of which they were part. The group also could be used to enrich and support those people whose other primary relations were not proving satisfying. Finally, the group experience, under competent leadership, could be used to prevent delinquency and social maladjustment.

NOTES

1. James F. Carey, "The Child Labor Evil," in Robert Hunter (ed.), *Poverty* (New York: Macmillan Co., 1907), p. 357.

2. Richard Hoftstadter, *The Age of Reform: From Bryan to F.D.R.* (New York: Vintage Books, 1955), pp. 1-22.

3. Nathan E. Cohen, *Social Work in the American Tradition* (New York: Dryden Press, 1958), p. 117.

4. Mary Richmond, *Social Diagnosis* (New York: Russell Sage Foundation, 1917).

5. Peter Bryce, "Moral and Criminal Responsibility," *Proceedings, 15th National Conference on Charities and Corrections* (Buffalo, N.Y.: 1888), p. 88.

6. William James, *Pragmatism: The Will to Believe* (New York: Longman, Green and Co., 1931), p. 23.

7. Nathan Hale, Jr., *Freud and the Americans: Beginnings of Psychoanalysis in the United States 1876-1917* (New York: Oxford University Press, 1971), pp. 225-49.

8. Gustave LeBon, *The Crowd*, (London: T. Fisher Unwin, 1896).

9. William McDougall, *The Group Mind* (New York: G. P. Putnam's, 1920).

10. Sigmund Freud, *Group Psychology and the Analysis of the Ego*, authorized translation by James Starchey (London: Psychoanalytic Press, 1922).

11. Edward A. Ross, *Social Control: A Survey of the Foundation of Order* (New York: Macmillan Co., 1920).

12. Charles Horton Cooley, *Social Organization* (New York: Schocken Books, 1943).

13. Robert MacIver, *Contributions of Sociology to Social Work* (New York: Columbia University Press, 1931), p. 82.

14. Anselm Strauss (ed.), *George Herbert Mead on Social Psychology* (Chicago: University of Chicago Press, 1964), p. 36.

15. Mead was active in the progressive education movement and was closely associated with Hull House in the early 1900s.

16. Lewis A. Coser, *Masters of Sociological Thought, "Emil Durkheim"* (New York: Harcourt, Brace, Jovanovich, 1971), pp. 218-60.

17. Kurt H. Wolff (ed. and trans.), *The Sociology of Georg Simmel* (New York: The Free Press, 1950).

18. George Butler, *Introduction to Community Recreation* (New York, McGraw-Hill, 1940), p. 60.

19. Ibid., p. 63.

20. Ibid., p. 61.

21. Funds for operating the playgrounds were provided by the Massachusetts Emergency and Hygiene Association until 1899 when the city council of Boston appropriated $3,000 toward meeting their cost.

22. Ibid., p. 62.

23. Ibid., p. 63.

24. Aaron Perry, *Recreation in the United States* (New York: Harper and Row, 1937), p. 39.

25. Joseph Lee, *Play in Education* (New York: Macmillan Co., 1915).

26. Franklin M. Reck, *The 4-H Story: A History of 4-H Club Work* (Ames, Iowa: Iowa State College Press, 1951).

27. USDA Misc. Circ. 72, "A Decade of Negro Extension Work, 1914-24."

28. Ethel Rogers, *Sebago-Wohelo* (Battle Creek, Mich.: Good Health Publishing Co., 1915).

29. Edward E. Grusd, *B'nai B'rith: The Story of a Covenant* (New York: Appleton-Century, 1966).

30. Carl Bode, *The American Lyceum: Town Meeting of the Mind,* (New York: Oxford University Press) 1956, p. 10.

31. *Handbook of Adult Education in the United States, 1960* (Chicago: Adult Education of the USA), p. 10.

32. Ibid.

33. Ibid., p. 22.

34. Victoria Case and Robert O. Case, *We Called It Culture; The Story of Chautauqua* (Garden City, N.Y.: Doubleday and Co., 1948).

35. Lyman Bryson, *Adult Education* (New York: American Book Co., 1936), pp. 29-47.

36. Mary Parker Follett, *The New State* (New York: Longmans, Green, 1920), p. 40.

37. Ibid., pp. 227-44.

38. Eduard Lindeman, *The Meaning of Adult Education* (New York: New Republic, 1926), pp. 50-55.

Chapter 4

FORMULATION OF A METHOD, 1920-1936

Perhaps no period in the history of the United States is filled
with as marked contrasts as those years from 1920 to 1936.
A substantial number of Americans came to believe that isola-
tion was the only safe policy for their country. They rejected
any new ties with the outside world and sought to dissolve
existing connections. Yet, the United States had inherited from
the past continuing responsibilities abroad, and actual ties with
the outer world did not simply dissolve. The change in the way
in which Americans appraised their relations with other countries was linked to the spreading discontent within their own
society. In earlier times, they had been confident about the
excellence and durability of their own institutions, and na-
tionalism had been compatible with involvement. Citizens of
the United States had no doubt that their own democratic
form of life was best not only for themselves but also for other
people.

By 1920, city dwellers outnumbered rural inhabitants. Of
the 106 million people in the United States, 54 million lived
in cities, and by 1930, approximately 70 million in a population of more than 138 million were city dwellers. The growth
of the cities during this period can be attributed to the opportunities they provided for acquisition of wealth, but also for
the excitement and freedom that had been traditionally associated with urban living. The city was able to assimilate the
ever-increasing flood of new arrivals, primarily from rural areas,
because of the numerous technological processes that had been
perfected after the Civil War. The expansion of the railroad
system, the refrigeration of meat, and the canning of fruit and
vegetables made it possible to crowd together, in a relatively

small area, a vast number of people who were unable to produce their own food.

With the growing number of people, adequate housing and office space were at a premium. The use of elevators and structural steel permitted cities to grow skyward, while at the same time, subways, elevated railroads, and the automobile made it possible for them to grow horizontally. Each of these developments had been lauded as effective ways of reducing urban congestion, but ironically, each in turn, aggravated rather than eliminated the problem. The lesson that urban congestion feeds on congestion was to be learned and relearned with each successive generation.

The need for adequate living, recreation, and work space was not an easy problem for cities to resolve. Skyscrapers built in the city's most congested sections provided additional office space but at the same time increased the number of people within the area. Factories were located on the cheaper land in the city's outskirts. Pieces of property that were not being used as either factories or office buildings went by default for housing. The indigent lived in slums in structures that had been abandoned years earlier by the well-to-do. Crowded together, lacking adequate sanitary systems, and an easy prey to disease, the poor were living examples of the ruinous results of urban congestion.

Immigration, which had always been a major contributor to America's diversity, was reduced to a trickle in the years following World War I. The Emergency Quota Act of 1921 restricted the number of immigrants to 3 percent of the number from each nationality that had been living in the United States in 1910. This act was followed by the Immigration Quota Act of 1924 which made 1890 the base year and reduced the quota from 3 to 2 percent. Legislation to reduce immigration was the result of pressure from the labor unions and from superpatriots who desired a completely homogeneous America.[1] Many of those who desired greater uniformity within the country felt that drastic steps needed to be taken to chastise those who did not meet their standards. The Red Scare of 1919-1920, when police arrested thousands of political eccentrics and a few communist subversives, served to galvanize the anxieties of those who were fearful of America's decline and "takeover by foreigners." In addition, homegrown fascist organizations such as the Ku Klux Klan organized as instruments of terror against Jews, Catholics, and Negroes.

Another extreme attempt to bring about conformity was the experiment with national prohibition. The Volstead Act, which was enacted in 1919 to reduce drinking, proved that it would take more than legislation to make most Americans change their habits. Citizens from all walks of life, who would not have thought of breaking other laws, cooperated with racketeers to violate the prohibition statute. Bootleggers, speakeasies, and gangsters like Al Capone were the chief beneficiaries of the "noble experiment."

The fear of radicalism had its counterpart in the realm of religion. The fundamentalist feared that a "new" or "liberal" interpretation of the Bible would weaken traditional Protestantism. Reacting against scientific theories of the evolution of man taught by Darwin, the fundamentalist insisted on a literal belief in the Scriptures. Prohibition of the teaching of Darwin's views was enacted into law in many states. In Tennessee, John Scopes, a high school biology teacher, was indicted in 1925 for teaching Darwinism. In the so-called monkey trial, Scopes was found guilty, but the fundamentalist view was held up to ridicule and suffered a drastic decline.

An older order was passing. Industrialism, urbanization, and the mere increase in the numbers involved complicated all human relationships and led to the breakdown of the inherited systems of social control. Progressive reform measures solved some problems but also created new ones. The family, the church, and other community organizations adjusted painfully, and not always adequately, to the shifting needs of their members. The 1920s was the era of the ticker-tapes and jazz, of "flaming youth" and the automobile. In this brittle, somewhat manic period, there was little concern with values other than those symbolized by dollar signs or the resistance to old standards. During the 1920s, the population as a whole enjoyed a higher standard of living, better health, and more education than their parents. To all but the "intellectuals," and those working in settlement houses and with charity organization societies, the mood of the time was one of optimism that the future held nothing but increased health, wealth, happiness, and continued growth.

This optimism came to an abrupt halt as the collapse of the stock market in October 1929 ushered in the depression of the 1930s. The depression revealed the internal contradictions of the existing economic and social order, and created a complex and interlocking set of problems that would occupy the United States for a whole decade. The number of people out of work rose steadily until over fourteen million persons were unemployed; the industrial plant stood idle much of the time; the farm situation deteriorated to the point of anarchy; and the banking system of the country neared collapse. Suffering was acute, as provision for monetary assistance of the unemployed was totally inadequate in responding to the size, intensity, and duration of the crisis.

The need for reform again became a major issue, and the last three years of the period saw the federal government take on major responsibility for public welfare through a multitude of programs designed to protect individuals and the national economy from the impact of this and future depressions. The program devised under the leadership of Franklin D. Roosevelt started the process of reconsideration of the relationship of government to the economy and imbued the people with a sense of hope so that they could pass through the trial of the years after 1933 without succumbing to despair. This achievement was an important one in a decade when other countries were surrendering their faith in democracy.

SOCIAL CASEWORK

The emergence and acceptance of Freudian theory exerted a major influence on social casework in the 1920s. The experience of working with shell-shocked patients in the war period strengthened an enthusiasm for psychiatry which provided

what was needed to understand the inner person. Freudian
psychology, to the average worker, was a welcome substitute
for the sterile laboratory psychology that emphasized diagnosis,
classification, and intelligence tests. Within a short period of
time, the profession made a radical shift from concern with
environmental factors to preoccupation with the intrapsyche.
With this change came the addition of such words as "libido,"
"ego," and "ambivalence" to the social caseworker's vocabulary.
The concept of "relationship" as developed in psychoanalytic
literature became part of the caseworker's stock-in-trade,
while "dynamic passivity" came to be a therapeutic style.

While the new knowledge supported the prior acceptance
and acclamation of Mary Richmond's book *Social Diagnosis,*[2]
it drew attention away from the "social" and redirected it to
the inner self. The focus was now on the individual and his
personal conflicts rather than on the various systems impinging
upon his life.

The Freudian influence reshaped the role of the caseworker.
In accordance with Freudian technique, the social worker de-
parted from the stance of doer, a provider of concrete services,
to that of passive observer. With this change came the concept
of a detached professional attitude, with stress on the worker
keeping his feelings and activities in abeyance. It also meant a
different type of client. Using Freudian technique meant limiting
services to those clients who could respond to the use of a less
active approach and to those problems that did not require
immediate action.

Freudian theory overshadowed all other approaches to social
problems and orientations about behavior. By 1930, casework
teaching staffs in schools of social work taught psychoanalytic
principles as a basis for casework practice, and it was not unusual for both faculty and students to undergo psychoanalytic
therapy as a part of their training. The outlets for this form of
practice were expanded by the emergence of child guidance
clinics and veterans' programs and by the development of
psychiatric social work specialization.

Another milestone in the development of social casework
was the Milford Conference Report released in 1929. Prior to
this time, definitions of social work in general and social case-

work in particular tended to take on the coloring of the specific field in which it was practiced. Rather than workers being referred to as social caseworkers, they were children's caseworkers, hospital social workers, family social workers, psychiatric social workers, and so forth. The Conference Report underscored the generic base of social casework which the participants felt to be much more substantial in content and more significant in its implications than the emphasis on the various casework fields. As the basic aim of social casework, the conference specified not the development of personality, but "the human being whose capacity to organize his own normal social activities may be impaired by one or more social deviations from accepted standards of social life."[3]

SETTLEMENT HOUSES DURING THE DEPRESSION

After World War I, the reform activities of the settlements declined partially because of the Red Scare and a conservative reaction to the war resulting in the discouragement, by boards and councils, of activities that could be interpreted as radical. There were also financial difficulties because of new buildings, expensive equipment, and the growing number of paid workers. In the earlier years, residents could depend upon the donations of philanthropists for support, but, as many of these benefactors died it became harder to attract new ones. Settlements also began to affiliate with the developing community chest campaigns, which resulted in a loss of financial independence and a further restriction in experimental programs.[4]

Another reason for the decline was the inability of the settlements to attract dedicated workers, especially those interested in social reform. The number of settlement scholarships was reduced, which limited the number of young people who could spend a year or two after college working in a settlement. Most of those who chose to become settlement workers in the 1920s thought of themselves as social workers rather than social reformers. They had been trained in recreation or in casework and "scientific" charity, and were critical of the more traditional practices that seemed sentimental and haphazard.

Whereas the early settlement workers viewed their work as a way of life, the newer workers considered their work as a job. As the sentimental and emotional tradition was stripped away, in the process some of the crusading zeal of the Progressive movement was lost.[5]

The stock market crash of 1929, followed by the depression, brought about a renewed interest in social reform which was combined with the task of meeting the material needs of those whom they served. Chicago Commons settlement, for example, was deeply involved in encouraging social action to improve the living conditions of the unemployed workers. Where once, brief months or years earlier, various ethnic groups used the halls of the Chicago Commons settlement for educational or recreational activities such as citizenship classes, dances, and folk celebrations, Italians, Poles, Greeks, and Mexicans began to assemble in 1930 to study the depression. Discussion and debate covered many topics, including the need for work relief through public works, the need for state and federal assistance to cash relief funds, and the need to develop security through old age pensions and unemployment insurance. The outcome of the discussions was a city-wide workers' Committee on Unemployment in 1932, composed of fifty local units, twenty-two of which were settlement-based and -led, with a membership of over 20,000. Lea Taylor, daughter of Chicago Commons director Graham Taylor, reported to the National Federation of Settlements at the end of the year: "The men are developing initiative and responsibility through serving on committees and delegate bodies. They have organized self-help projects and have sought direct contact with legislators interested in relief measures."[6] One of the major accomplishments of this organization was to organize a protest march on Chicago's city hall to make known their problems.

Just as settlements in Chicago were at the vanguard of social protest, settlements elsewhere were moving toward direct political action. They argued to whoever would listen that families were being disrupted by the economic problems and that the social services generally available to help them were breaking down under the impact of overwhelming need. They demanded that an immediate program of public relief be set up for meeting the basic needs of food, clothing, and shelter for the millions of unemployed. They urged that work relief programs be established so that individuals would again be able to be self-supporting. Finally, they pushed for institutionalized assistance programs, sponsored by the federal government, to guard against loss of income because of death or retirement.

The influence of the early settlements was fully felt in the period of the New Deal. As Schlesinger reports:

Hull House, Henry Street, the Consumers' League and the other organizations educated a whole generation in social responsibility. Henry Morgenthau, Jr., Herbert Lehman, and Adolf A. Berle, Jr., all worked at Henry Street; Frances Perkins, Gerard Swope, and Charles A. Beard at Hull House (where John Dewey was an early member of the board of trustees); Sidney Hillman at both Hull House and Henry Street; Joseph Eastman at Robert A. Wood's South End House in Boston; and Iowa boy coming East from Grinnell College in 1912 went to work at Christadora House on the lower East Side of New York; his name Harry Hopkins. Through Belle Moskowitz the social work ethos infected Alfred E. Smith; through Frances Perkins and others, Robert F. Wagner; through Eleanor Roosevelt, active in the Women's Trade Union League and a friend of Florence Kelley's and Lillian Wald's, Franklin Roosevelt.

And for all the appearances of innocence and defenselessness, the social workers apparatus wielded power. "One could not overestimate," observed Wagner, "the central part played by social workers in bringing before their representatives in Congress and state legislatures the present and insistent problems of modern-day life." The subtle and persistent saintliness of the social workers was, in the end, more deadly than all the bluster of business. Theirs was the implacability of gentleness.[7]

By the mid-1930s, the service and reform aspects of the settlements were different than they had been in the past. The New Deal brought aggressive intervention on the part of the government, and social welfare policy and social experimentation ceased to be the prerogatives of private agencies. The times demanded programs quickly and on a large scale that only the resources of the federal government could supply. The settlements in general had lost much of their basic thrust in social reform and increasingly shied away from programs that would draw criticism. More specialized agencies took over some of the settlements' programs. Local governments, for example, commonly provided playgrounds, kindergartens, adult education, and Americanization programs. Often, settlements merely supplemented their former programs in order to maintain their initial investment in building and equipment.

PROGRESSIVE EDUCATION

A significant development in the field of education during the 1920s was the expansion of the average school's curriculum. The first eight grades of public schools, which had at one time taught little beyond the three "R's," enlarged their curricula to such an extent that by 1930 the typical elementary school offering included as many as thirty different subjects. There was a corresponding increase of courses in the high schools. Since large numbers of the children were drawn from every background and represented different degrees of intelligence, considerable emphasis was placed on practical subjects. Boys were taught machine shop practices and woodworking; girls attended classes in sewing and cooking; all could study typing, stenography, and bookkeeping.

Curriculum changes were sometimes accompanied by new teaching methods reflecting the philosophy of progressive education. Learning by rote and complete reliance on textbooks gave way to an emphasis on individual differences among students and an attempt to make learning an exciting experience rather than a series of dreary, unconnected tasks. Severe classroom discipline was abandoned for a more informal attitude based on the assumption that interested pupils seldom present behavior problems. Efforts were also made to integrate subjects, and frequent use was made of available library resources.

The philosophy of progressive education, based on the writings of John Dewey and William Kilpatrick, was received with great interest by those working in leisure-time agencies and settlement houses. They were well aware of the shortcomings of traditional educational methods which they considered outdated. Writing in 1902, Jane Addams attacked educators for their failure to prepare students for social relations:

The educators should certainly conserve the learning and training necessary for the successful individual and family life, but should add to that a preparation for the enlarged social efforts which our increasing democracy requires. The democratic ideal demands of the school that it shall give the child's own activities a social value: that it shall teach him to direct his own activities and adjust them to those of other people. We are not willing that thousands of industrial workers shall put all of their activity and toil into services from which the community as a whole reaps the benefits, while their mental conceptions and code of morals are narrow and untouched by any uplift which the consciousness of social value might give them.[8]

In spite of this concern, the early group work movement inherited traditional educational philosophy and teaching techniques. Most work with group practice was based on the assumption that the elements constituting "character" could be taught in the same way English, arithmetic, and social studies were taught. As schools began to consider critically their methods of educating children, those working with groups also began to question their methods. Some of the practices which came under question were the use of formulas, the emphasis on specific learning, the regimentation of boys' and girls' organizations, many of the traditional club forms in institutions as well as the extensive devotion to competitive athletics, and the faith that play on playgrounds, more than any other significant part of a child's life, prevented delinquency and "built character."

A major factor in group work's new interest in progressive education was the work of Grace L. Coyle, who had been strongly influenced by John Dewey. Coyle, born in 1892 in North Adams, Massachusetts, received her A.B. from Wellesley and a certificate from the New York School of Social Work. After several years as a settlement worker, she joined the staff of the Industrial Women's Department of the YWCA where she was responsible for adult education and recreation. In 1923, she started the first course in group work at the School of Social Work at Western Reserve University.

Coyle's experiences with women in industry through YWCA programs, with groups of children in settlements, and with discussion groups in the adult education movement led to a series

Plate 6. **Grace Coyle.**
Courtesy of the Archives
of Case Western Reserve
University, Cleveland,
Ohio.

of preliminary formulations on group process which were
articulated in her dissertation and published in *Social Process
in Organized Groups* (1930). In discussing the evolution of
structure, Coyle utilized Dewey's definition. She wrote:

The structure of organized groups consists of the agreed upon instruments through which the group puts its purpose into action. They take
the form sometimes of written constitutions and established precedents;
sometimes of unwritten or even unspoken assumptions, commonly
accepted by the organization as a permanent part of the group life. Their
apparent stability is in fact, an illusion produced by the more swiftly
moving processes that go on by and through them. They too change and
shift as the group creates, uses and modifies them for its purposes.[9]

This concept came, as Coyle declared, "directly from John
Dewey's *Experience and Nature.*"[10] Coyle also viewed leadership in light of Dewey's philosophy. In any organization, there
exists the "necessity for the investiture of certain individuals
with a public character, a responsibility for these common

consequences of weal and woe for all participants."[11] Then, quoting Dewey, she wrote: "The ultimate source of authority will determine the direction of its flow. Most of our organizations reflect the common democratic mores." She concluded this discussion by stating that: "[p]sychological reactions of a most complex sort are constantly remaking both leaders and group together by their reciprocal stimulus and response. Out of that interaction group morale and decisions are born and group functions performed."[12]

By the late 1930s, it was recognized that a reformulation of group was necessary and that the methods and philosophy of progressive education were not only most compatible, but also had the most to offer. Bowman prophetically saw the change occurring in four areas:

First, integration. Emphasis in group work will be placed, I believe, more on the relation the work bears to the problem of the individual, his place in society, his combination of interests. . . . Second. . . . A group will get together for as long a period as there is interest and profit in the members remaining together. . . . There will be less competition and fewer inter-institutional athletic contests.

Third, leaders. . . . It will be out of place for a leader to take pride in "being good" to his group in any paternalistic way. Affection for one's charges will be a part of group leadership, but the aim will be to adjust them emotionally to their associates in successive undertakings. The emphasis will be more upon the interaction of the members than upon direct leadership.

Fourth, in the large social implications, the teacher or leader in progressive education lays emphasis on no pattern as such. . . . (It is more important that the individual learns to cooperate with others in various active spontaneous original and adaptable ways for various ends.) Group experience and not a preimposed or preconceived notion of order is the aim.[13]

In 1939, a book entitled *New Trends in Group Work* was published based on the writings of group workers using progressive education methods and of leaders of the progressive education movement.[14] At least half of the chapters dealt specifically with group work as education and a significant number with group work as progressive education. Common to the various authors was the belief that group work had accepted a task that was educational in nature and related to development of personality through group experience.

SMALL GROUP THEORY

Until the mid-1930s, the theoretical orientation of social group work came almost exclusively from progressive education and the social psychology of Cooley. After that, practitioners and faculty who taught group work and recreation skills began to look to other sources for knowledge regarding groups. One such source was the University of Iowa and the work of Kurt Lewin and Ronald Lippitt. They and others had set up a series of experimental studies on the effects of certain types of leadership on group structure and on the member's behavior. The researchers compared three types of leadership—democratic, autocratic, and laissez-faire—by having adult leaders behave in a prescribed fashion. It was their general conclusion that there was more originality, group-mindedness, and friendliness in democratic groups, and more hostility, aggression, scapegoating, and discontent in laissez-faire and autocratic groups.[15] Although the results of their studies influenced the leadership styles of club leaders and youth group leaders, the research was to come under attack by social work leaders for experimenting with human emotions. Had there been more receptivity at the time to experimental methods of research, the results of these studies might have had more influence on the use of groups in social work.[16]

Another source of knowledge came out of the research of J. L. Moreno, an Austrian psychiatrist, and his associate Helen Jennings. During World War I, Moreno had administrative responsibilities for a camp of displaced persons in Austria. It came to his attention that the adjustment of individuals in the camp seemed to be better when they were allowed to form their own groups. Later, while associated with a reform school in the United States, he undertook to check this observation out through more systematic research. With the use of a simple questionnaire, he measured the interpersonal relations of people by the choices they registered of desirable partners for work and play in particular activities.[17] The data concerning "who chooses who" were converted into a "sociogram" or picture in which individuals were represented by circles and choices by lines. It became apparent that through this subjective technique, valuable information about interpersonal attraction and repulsion among collections of people could be learned. Study of such sociograms revealed that some groups were more tightly knit than others, that individuals varied in their social expansiveness and in the choices they received, and that cliques formed on the basis of characteristics such as age, sex, and race. Group workers used sociometry as a means of determining the interpersonal process going on within a group at a given time. In addition, it was used to draw attention to such features of groups as social position, patterns of friendship, subgroup formation, and, more generally, informal group structure.

Those social workers working with delinquents and gang groups were influenced by social psychologists such as Clifford Shaw, Frederic Thrasher, and William Whyte. Shaw, author of *The Jack Rollers*,[18] and Thrasher, who wrote *The Gang*,[19] were employed by the University of Chicago and were associated with the Institute of Juvenile Research to study the internal workings of autonomous street gangs. One result of their work was the modification of professional work with autonomous groups, especially in settlements and youth organizations. Whyte examined the informal and formal social organization of the Italian community of Boston. By spending time with the members as a participant-observer, he was able to gather information on the effects of group life both on the individual participant and the social structure of the community. In his book *Street Corner Society*,[20] Whyte discussed his findings, with special attention to such dynamics as cohesion, interaction, structure, leadership, and status.

Muzafer Sherif pioneered in research on the "autokinetic effect," or the phenomenon of a still light giving the appearance of moving when viewed in a dark room when the viewer has no point of reference for measuring its location.[21] When estimates were made as to the amount of movement in the presence of several people, the judgments of the observers were influenced by each other's opinions and converged toward a mean. Sherif's research revealed that the influence of the group was a powerful force in changing individuals' attitudes and could be utilized in intercultural relations.

It was speculated that the group members would unconsciously adopt the values of the leader and other influential members, particularly around such issues as discrimination. These values would be carried outside the group and incorporated into the participant's relationships with others.

EDUCATION FOR GROUP WORK

The first sequence of graduate courses on group work services was offered by the School of Applied Social Sciences at Western Reserve University in 1923. Before then, those interested in receiving education and experience in group leadership were directed to agencies working with groups such as social settlements, recreation centers, and playgrounds, and to courses offered on playground management and recreation. Schools of social work, while desirous of students with experience with groups, generally considered group work as something that could not or should not be taught in a university setting. This attitude is illustrated in a report on social work education written in 1915.

Of these three general types of clinical activities (case work, group work, and community organization) social work with groups is the most elementary. It demands sufficient skill to justify the requirement of practice work under supervision, but it approximates so closely the non-professional activities in the social work field with which students are usually familiar, that they find little difficulty in adjusting themselves to the groups assigned to them. . . . The experience of schools of social work . . . indicates that group work possesses too little educational value to be given much emphasis. . . . With few exceptions, clinical work with groups will have a very small place in connection with training in community organization (i.e., social settlements, community centers, play ground associations).[22]

In the years before social group work became a course or a curriculum in a school of social work, it was customarily viewed in terms of its setting rather than its methodology or its practice, and those working with groups were identified with the agency in which they were associated. For example, those individuals working in settlement houses were "settlement workers," while those working in YMCAs were "Y" secretaries. With the establishment of the Playground Association of America in 1906, the titles playground director and recreation worker came to have recognition. In the same year, the New York School of Philanthropy offered a course of study that prepared students for positions as head workers and assistants in social settlements and other social and religious organizations. By 1913, a full course of study for playground and recreation workers was instituted.[23] Similarly, the St. Louis School of Social Economy, in 1911, offered a one-semester course entitled "Gymnastics in Athletics, Games and Folk Dances," followed by the course "Neighborhood and Group Work." In the latter, focus was on training students to work with groups in settlements and social centers.[24]

One of the major precursors of social group work education was the recreation curriculum directed by Neva Boyd (1876-1963) at the Chicago School of Civics and Philanthropy.[25] A kindergarten teacher by training, Boyd was thoroughly convinced that the spirit of any group came from the interaction of its members, and it was this spirit that provided substance from which the group derived lasting benefits from their experiences together. If a worker was to be effective, it was essential that he know how to help a group develop its own program rather than to superimpose a series of activities unrelated to the cultural milieu of the members of the group. According to Boyd, the role of the worker was to help the group develop its "natural spirit" rather than fit the members into a predetermined system.

A statement published in 1922 about the functions, qualifications, and training of group workers summarizes the need and opportunities for training which existed just prior to the formal institution of the first group work course.

The group worker must understand the psychology of the group, must be able to conduct the kinds of activities which groups can do and enjoy doing, and must have that identifiable "group leadership" quality which can make an often haphazard collection of individuals a live, coherent group. It is hard to define these qualities, hard to isolate the technique, yet there is a skill which grows with practice, which has been acquired under certain conditions, and without which a successfully, constructively active group cannot be conducted.

As has been suggested, much of the group work lay in the field of leisure-time activities, where it benefits the individuals through recreation, self-expression, physical development, mental improvement and character building. The group worker must, therefore, have special equipment, such as ability to direct activities, teach games, lead group singing, coach dramatics or teach handicrafts. He may, however, only organize clubs and stimulate them to activity; they themselves can conduct. . . .

Training for the group work technique has not yet been well developed. Besides entering the work through study in the training schools for social workers, there is the possibility of apprenticeship training. There are few opportunities in settlements for resident positions which offer definite training and in addition provide board and room. However, because of the small number of these training opportunities and because most of the paid positions in group work require more maturity and life experience than the person just graduated from college possesses, many positions are filled by people from other fields of social work who have demonstrated as volunteers a capacity for group leadership.[26]

The first course on group work offered by Western Reserve University was intended to afford training for positions of playground director. For an academic year, a range of field experiences "under supervision" was offered with students placed in such agencies as social settlements, the Department of Public Welfare, and the Humane Society. In addition to field practice, students were required to take such courses as "Normal Demands of Childhood" and "The Philosophy, History, Theory and Practice of Play."[27]

In 1923, the Cleveland Girls Council, a coordinating agency of girls' organizations, pressed the School of Applied Social Sciences at Western Reserve University to develop a course in group service. The course was to provide training for men and women interested in working with groups in the Cleveland area. In the fall of that year, a training course in group service work was offered. It was designed to:

[t]rain workers in the principles and methods of dealing with groups through club and class leadership, through promotion of activities and administrative work in social settlements, community centers, young men's and young women's organizations whose purposes are to give direction to the lives of their members through their group associations.[28]

A growing concern in the 1920s among practitioners working with groups was how to provide continuity of service when there was staff turnover. Linked to this concern was the desire for teaching records, similar to the ones already in use by case-workers, to teach group work. Under the guidance of Clara Kaiser, a faculty member at Western Reserve, a number of instructors began to meet periodically with several group leaders to develop a system of recording. By 1930, a set of records was published "for the use and criticism of teacher and group workers."[29] The records were samples from recent student social workers in field placement at the University Neighborhood Centers, from 1926 to 1930. Through the records, Kaiser attempted to develop a form of recording that would describe the important facts in the organization and development of a given group.

Concurrent to the study and use of records conducted at the Neighborhood Centers was the research on group behavior, called the Wawokiye Camp Experiment, done in 1929. Fifty-one different boys were given a camping experience. The goal of the experiment was to do research on group work and gain new insights into the special problems of boys. The findings of the research, published by Wilber Newstetter, the director of Camp Wawokiye, Marc Feldstein, and Theodore Newcomb in 1938, dealt with the concepts of bond, interaction, and status, and demonstrated that the needs of individuals could be fulfilled and people could grow individually through group associations.[30] The research focused attention more sharply on the individual in the group, his adjustment to the social situation, and the group worker's role in relation to the individual members. This delineation reinforced the idea that work with small, stable groups was a way of realizing the larger goal of a more democratic, humanitarian society for all people. The major contribution of Newstetter's work was the demonstration that experimental research could be done in "natural settings" and that phenomena of groups could be studied and documented.

Many thought that the introduction of a social group work sequence into the curricula of an increasing number of schools, after the example of Western Reserve University, was premature in view of the prevalent state of knowledge of social group work as a method in social work. As late as 1934, Philip Klein said, without expectation of contradiction, that of the four technological divisions of social work, only social casework had received "reasonably adequate discussion in the professional literature." Group work, preventative and educational work, and community organization on the other hand, "[a]lthough clearly differentiated in practice, in the distribution of personnel in the curriculum provisions of professional schools and in meetings, conferences, special associations and committees, still lack comprehensive formulation."[31] In spite of this concern, there was a steady growth of group work courses in schools of social work. The Committee on Current Practices and Problems in Professional Education of the American Association for the Study of Group Work, which made a study in 1936 of available training programs, found that thirty-three schools were offering at least one or two graduate courses in social group work. In twenty-three of these schools, the courses were taken in conjunction with supervised field work practice.[32]

MOVEMENTS IN SEARCH OF A METHOD

By 1920, the settlement movement was thirty-six years old and, while on the decline, was recognized as part of the urban scene. Public recreation, after the establishment of the first playground in 1885, had won wide recognition during World

War I as an essential service and was making steady progress. The adult education movement was developing into a regular part of the public school system and the public library. Of the youth service agencies, the YMHAs, YWHAs, YMCAs, YWCAs, Campfire Girls, and 4-H were all organized national movements with considerable staff. Although most of the early pioneers had died, their administrators were well established and their staffs were growing.

Volunteers were an important part of the organizations; increasingly, however, agencies began to employ professional workers. Professional and in-service training of some sort was beginning in many agencies; experience was accumulating; national conferences were stimulating technical discussions. The consciousness of common problems and the clarifying of the issues as met in daily practice had created a "felt need" among professional workers. In reflecting on the changing perspectives on groups and the need for better trained workers, Coyle wrote:

It is no accident that when our movements—settlements, public recreation, YMHA's, YWHA's, YMCA's and YWCA's—began to concern themselves with methods, that concern inevitably leads them into questions about human relations. It turns up at that point for the same reason that similar concerns in worker's education, management, education lead to the same questions. The wider reasons for this lie in our social scene. Urban living, mechanized industry, mass commercialized recreation, impersonal education—all the more determining aspects of life—act to squeeze out the essential human response, the intimate relation of one person to his own immediate group. Social relations, natural and inevitable in the small town of our forefathers, must be consciously preserved in our society. The need of human beings for a rich fare of human contacts and responses is a real element in all of our groups, societies and other organizations. It is not enough however merely to open clubrooms and classrooms, recreation centers and playgrounds. The doors of our agencies have stood open now for fifty to sixty years. As we have worked within those clubrooms we have been forced to recognize that, when certain people acted as leaders, the groups were not only more fun for the participants but that more people got more out of them. When others led them, the groups were arid, mechanical, sometimes sentimental, occasionally, actually demoralizing.[33]

Most of the workers had college training, and some of them had training in schools of social work. As these workers came to know each other, there was a ferment of discussion around two major discoveries. First, it was discovered that workers in a variety of agencies had a great deal in common and that the major component of that common experience lay in their experience with groups. Out of this recognition came the widespread use of the term *social group work* and the development of interest groups focusing on work with groups in a number of cities. The second discovery was that what was common to all the groups was that, in addition to the activities in which the group engaged, groups involved a network of relationships between the members and the worker, between the group as a whole and the agency and neighborhood in which the members lived. This combination of relationships was called the group process. This second realization produced a search for deeper insights into these relationships, an attempt to describe them and to understand their dynamics.

It was for those involved in this search a period of excitement and ferment, of social discovery and of deepened insight as we tried to clarify both our philosophy and its aims and values and our methods of dealing with groups. It is perhaps sufficient to say . . . that by 1935 enough people in cities and agencies across the country had become involved that there inevitably began a period of formulation.[34]

Thus, it was no surprise that Margaretta Williamson, in her study the *Social Worker in Group Work*[35] (1929), found that while there was not a clearly defined homogeneous form because of divergence in method and motive, there was

evidence of a growing awareness of common professional ground—a recognition of a similar philosophy, a convergence of training and technique, some interchange of personnel, and a tendency toward exchange of experience. . . .

Workers are seeking the development of the individual to his fullest capacity and encouraging more satisfactory relations between the individual and his environment. . . . Group work concerns itself with service toward individuals in a group, brought together through common interests and guided by means of suitable and congenial activities toward a well rounded life for the individual; and for the group, a cooperative spirit and acceptance of social responsibility.

Group work undertakes to guide the group life . . . maintain[ing] that normal and satisfying group activities tend to develop in the individual a richer personality that is emotionally sound and effective in its adjustment to other people . . . [and] that group life is the means of passing on the social patterns, customs and conventions by which society is organized. The group director is trained in activities and processes thought to be developmental to those with whom he is dealing. He meets leisure-time needs by socially minded leadership. He seeks to direct activity into constructive channels. . . . He desires the individual to experience situations calling for character-forming decisions. . . . He lays a foundation for responsible citizenship by encouraging participation in self-regulatory groups. He cultivates the friendship of the individual and seeks to share his problems and achievements.[36]

Largely as a result of the development of group work curricula in schools of social work, questions began to be raised as to whether the base was in the area of education, recreation, or social work. Social casework had gone through a similar struggle, and many caseworkers felt strongly that anything lacking psychological dynamic grounding was not appropriate for the social work profession. Others, such as Mary Richmond, felt that casework and group work were closely related. At the National Conference of Social Work in 1920, she commented on this relationship:

This brings me to the only point upon which I can attempt to dwell at all, to a tendency in modern casework which I seem to have noted with great pleasure. It is one which is full of promises, I believe, for the future of social treatment. I refer to the new tendency to view our clients from the angle of what might be termed small group psychology . . .

Halfway between the minute analysis of the individual situation with which we are all familiar in casework and the kind of sixth sense of neighborhood standards and backgrounds which is developed in a good social settlement there is a field as yet almost unexplored.[37]

In spite of these remarks, there is little evidence that social caseworkers participated in the process of social change other than on an individual basis. This emphasis on the individual and consequent refusal to face social and economic facts reflected the social worker's new preoccupation with psychiatry and psychoanalysis as well as the conservative and economic climate of the postwar years. The deeply rooted conviction that moral inadequacy lay at the heart of most problems of poverty and dependency was now reinforced by an overemphasis on psychological inadequacy.

Social workers who worked with groups often found greater camaraderie with members of other disciplines, such as recreation and education, than with individuals doing more traditional casework. There was the feeling by many group workers, that caseworkers had lost their commitment to social reform and social action. Even though caseworkers spoke of changing communities and solving problems, such as poverty and unemployment, their real commitment was to working with people on a one-to-one basis. The increasing interest in professionalism of social work in general, was viewed by many group workers as leading to further corruption of the reform tradition. If the social causes of maladjustment, and the broader programs of prevention were neglected, significant changes achieved in social welfare over the previous fifty years would be lost. The common denominator for all who called themselves group workers was their conviction regarding the value of group work as a medium for individual development. Those working with groups felt the need to share ideas, beliefs, and experiences with others working with groups. In approximately 1930, a New York Conference on Group Work in Education was formed. Members included Arthur L. Swift, William H. Kilpatrick, Joshua Lieberman, Le Roy Bowman, and Henry Bush. In 1934 it was instrumental in sponsoring a weekend meeting at Ligonier, Pennsylvania, for the purpose of examining research techniques for group work, evaluating training processes, formulating and assessing standards and recent factors of social change, that had implications for group work. The meeting was attended by group workers from Western Reserve, Ohio State, and the Chicago Committee on Group Work. One important result of this two-day meeting was the initial planning for the National Association for the Study of Group Work which was founded in 1936. This association is discussed in detail in Chapter 5.

THE 1935 NATIONAL CONFERENCE OF
SOCIAL WORK

Before 1935, no formal papers dealing with group work had been presented at the National Conference of Social Work. A number of the individuals who had been present at the Ligonier Conference in 1934, petitioned the Conference to add a social group work section at the 1935 meeting to be held in Montreal. This request was granted, and papers on group work were called for, both from educators and practitioners. The topics of the papers accepted for presentation centered on issues such as the definition of group work, work with those who had special needs, the contribution of research and community studies to group work, and the coordination of group work agencies, especially as they related to public and private agencies. The paper delivered by Grace L. Coyle received the Pugsley Award, given by the Editorial Committee of the National Conference of Social Work, in recognition of its contribution to the subject of social work at the Conference. This honor also reflected credit on social group work and on the School of Applied Social Science at Western Reserve where Coyle was a faculty member.[38]

W. I. Newstetter delivered the first paper to the section with the question, "What Is Social Group Work?," pointing up the necessity of distinguishing between group work as a field, group work as a process, and group work techniques. He defined group work as a "process" that focused on the "development and adjustment of an individual through voluntary group association and the use of this association as a means of furthering desirable social ends."[39] These other social ends included cooperation, social legislation, peace, a planned economy, social attitudes, and love of country.

Newstetter predicted quite accurately that one day curricula in schools of social work would be changed because the goals of casework, group work, and community organization would be nearly identical, and it would be discovered that the techniques of the three models had many similarities. He noted that his definition of group work set it apart from casework, which focused primarily on the individual in a one-to-one relationship.

He called attention to the new experimental efforts in casework, such as dealing with families as a group over a period of time.

The acceptance of group workers into the fraternity of social work bears testimony to the broadening base of social work and an emphasis on generic concepts. It can be partially explained by the need felt by case-workers for more adequate treatment resources. It is being increasingly recognized that both caseworkers and group workers have much to give each other, and that generic social work can only be achieved to the ex-tent that the contributions of both are focused upon problems demand-ing application of both methods.[40]

Roy Sorenson, acknowledging the relatively few differences between group work and casework, predicted their emergence into an integrated method.

The group worker is talking about individualizing the program, recogniz-ing the uniqueness of personality, and understanding more about the social history and family of group members with socialization needs. The concept of "guidance" has developed within group work agencies to the extent that a literature, personnel and conference structure has appeared. The Boston Y.W.C.A., has four trained interviewers, an educational guidance person, a vocational guidance person, and a social psychiatric worker to provide individualized services to those who come for group activity.[41]

According to Sorenson, caseworkers were recognizing the possi-bilities of the group as part of the casework process, with the group used as a means of treating some types of personality adjustment. However, group work was at the stage where it was critically in need of definitions, terminology, record forms, and professional recognition.[42]

Two of the papers dealt with the use of groups as a vehicle for the treatment of physical and mental illness. Anne Smith, reporting on her work with children in a medical hospital, observed that many of the children viewed their illness as punishment for something they had done. Through the use of groups, a climate of trust and reassurance was developed. "Like a stranger in a foreign land who suddenly hears his own language, the child reaches out to play as an assurance of friendliness in a bewildering situation."[43]

The second paper emphasized the importance of play. Neva Boyd, in a paper on the use of groups in the treatment of the mentally ill, delinquent girls, and the retarded, described the goals of these experiments. They centered on helping children and adults experience the opportunity of planning their own leisure time; encouraging initiative rather than superimposing ideas; minimizing rivalry and competition between groups and group members; and selecting "[a]ctivities which hold the greatest possibilities for growth and directing them in such a way that the potentialities of the individual, however limited, are called into action [so that] a fuller utilization of the individual's powers may be accomplished, and a more harmonious, constructive social life achieved."[44]

While the majority of the papers presented stressed that the group workers should direct their efforts toward the same objective as caseworkers, a small minority argued that group work should not align itself with social work. LeRoy Bowman, identifying himself as a social worker, opened his paper with a challenge:

This paper will not be pleasing to those who think that group work is primarily social work; or that it is a new field that needs the techniques the people have previously acquired; or that it opens up areas for social workers in which they can extend their usefulness without laboriously learning new ways; or that it neatly supplements case work and combined with the latter, gives an easy comfortable way of encompassing mentally the whole field of organized effort to serve people.[45]

Bowman also reported that group work was neither a job of rehabilitation, nor a service to those who asked for help, nor a social service like casework. Rather, group work was a social mechanism which perfectly competent people utilized to achieve their own ends. To the extent that it was used by social workers to serve groups of underprivileged persons or those who were physically or mentally ill, it was merely an adaptation.[46]

Arthur Swift, director of field work at Union Seminary, questioned the tendency to think that anyone could lead a club, maintaining that without adequately trained and professionally competent leaders, group work could not come into its own. While recognizing the value of the volunteer leader in certain situations, he believed that professionally competent leaders should carry the major responsibility for group work. The essentials of training in group work according to Swift were:

Field work in the observation and leadership of groups under skilled supervision, supplemented by discussions and lectures dealing with the place of group work in the field of social work and of social history, the underlying philosophy of group work, the contributions to it of sociology and of psychology, educational, social, and individual, the place of group work in a program of social action, and the acquiring of skills in the conduct of group programs.[47]

A recurrent theme of the section was the use of groups as a way of strengthening democracy. This concern would be articulated again and again as events in Europe spread to America, fostering fascist and communist ideologies under the guise of providing a quick solution to complex social problems. Grace Coyle's paper "Group Work and Social Change" best exemplified this position.[48] She urged the participants to examine the quality of the group effort they were providing. Did it allow for democratic participation, or did it instead encourage a dependency upon authoritative leadership. According to Coyle, it was the responsibility of group work to transmit cultural heritage to individuals and to reevaluate this heritage when it became inadequate to meet the new circumstances of a rapidly changing time. The group worker could contribute in several ways.

(1) In the first place he can encourage and develop social interests within his own groups. This takes skill and insight, but it can be done. These will often culminate in the group participating in social action as it sees fit. The educational process in this line cannot stop short of experience in social action if it is to be effective. (2) He can help members of this agency, as they mature, to find their place in the organized life of the community, in those social action groups through which their collective interests are finding expression. (3) He can see that provision is made in the agency for the free discussion of the basic economic and social conflicts which are so crucial to adequate solution of the present crisis.[49]

GROUP WORK FOR THERAPEUTIC ENDS

Neva L. Boyd's paper, presented at the 1935 National Conference of Social Work in Montreal, described the utilization of group work for therapeutic purposes at the Chicago State Hospital for the mentally ill.[50] According to Boyd, the experimental recreation program begun in 1918, was directed by a man trained in Denmark in gymnastics, two women trained in recreation, and a second man trained on the job. The recreation staff, after consultation with the ward physician, determined the choice of activities. Patient wards averaging close to 900 people with a whole range of psychiatric disturbances represented were selected as subjects. The workers found that gymnastic exercises were valuable in working with both excitable and extremely apathetic patients. The patients were brought to an improvised gymnasium in groups of approximately sixty and were given a forty-five minute period of marching to piano music and easily executed exercises. Once the patients were able to handle this type of activity, they were advanced into more complex patterns of activities such as games and group dances. Those with special skills were asked to assist the workers. For example, patients who could play the piano were invited to play for the marching, while the more stable patients were used to set the pattern for those who tended to wander out of line. It was believed that if the severely ill patients watched the worker as well as the more stable patients, they would be influenced to participate. It was reported that no patient was ever coerced to participate but all were encouraged to take part.[51]

Another early experiment in group work was carried out at the Geneva Training School for Girls, a reform school for delinquent girls in Illinois. In 1932, the school employed a group worker to work with the girls in order to give them an opportunity to plan their leisure time.[52] According to Boyd, the program

[a]s ultimately evolved by the girls and the group worker created an unprecedented *esprit de corps* and culminated in a satisfying climax on the last night when all the girls gathered around the campus and entertained

each other with activities especially prepared for the occasion, closing the program by singing in unison songs familiar to them all. Good will and joy prevailed, at least temporarily, throughout the group. The whole project was safeguarded against rivalry and competition; no mention was made of one cottage excelling another, no prizes were offered, and no special privileges given to the "good" girls or withheld from the "bad" ones. This intensive experience in cooperative planning required considerable organization of the cottage groups and made a good beginning in coordinating the girls into working units easily made permanent.[53]

The units evolved into clubs, and the group worker met with the girls regularly for the purpose of facilitating rather than restricting their freedom or superimposing ideas upon them. Although the worker's principal function was the establishment of recreation, the very nature of the activity forced the girls to deal with behavior problems arising among the various members. During one of the meetings, the girls asked the group worker to leave. Another staff member, curious about this, was told that "one of the girls had done something too bad for her [the group worker] to know about it, and they were taking it up in the club to see what ought to be done."[54]

During the summer of 1929, the Illinois Institute for Juvenile Research introduced an experimental group work program into the Lincoln Illinois State School and Colony, an institution for the retarded, to create happier conditions for the children and to conduct research on the treatment of the mentally retarded. Groups were established with a membership of up to twenty children who were taught dancing, sports, and games. The leaders observed that if the activities such as basketball and square dancing, were taught as a whole rather than as separated actions, the children learned faster. It was concluded by the researchers that recreation for mentally retarded children did more than merely occupy their time. They maintained that by selecting activities that held the greatest possibility for growth and by so directing them that the optimum potential of the individual would be called into action, a fuller development of the individual's powers could be accomplished, and a more harmonious, constructive social life achieved. The researchers found that the children quarreled less, played more happily and resourcefully

together when undirected, worked more willingly, attempted
to escape from the institution less frequently, and were less
destructive of the clothes and equipment.[55]

There was a growing belief by some workers in 1936 that
group work by its very nature had an inherent therapeutic
element and should be used to assist individuals suffering from
emotional problems. In 1936, Emory Bogardus, a sociologist
at the University of Southern California, wrote in *Sociology
and Social Research* that group workers were engaged in activities
that were more strategic than they had ever dreamed. He viewed
group work as augmenting casework and contributing to its
success with disturbed clients. He also felt that the early identification of personality problems could prevent these disturbances
from becoming chronic and unmanageable.[56] Three years later,
he carried this idea a step further when he observed that group
work philosophy included a therapeutic reorganization of un-
adjusted club members. Referring to the writing of S. R. Slavson,
he noted that group opportunities could lead to a better balanced
personality.[57] The therapeutic purpose of group work was
deeply imbedded in everyday activities such as creative handicrafts and art craftwork, club participation and discussion, and
being a functioning member of a democratically operating
association.[58]

NOTES

1. Marcus L. Hansen, *The Immigrant in American History* (New York:
Harper Torchbook, 1964), pp. 1-29.

2. Mary E. Richmond, *Social Diagnosis* (New York: Russell Sage
Foundation, 1917).

3. Milford Conference Report, *Social Case Work: Generic and Specific*
(New York: AASW, 1929), p. 3.

4. Judith Trolander, *Settlement Houses and the Great Depression*
(Detroit, Mich.: Wayne State University, 1975), p. 149.

5. Allen F. Davis, *Spearheads for Reform: The Social Settlements
and the Progressive Movement, 1880-1914* (New York: Oxford University
Press, 1967), pp. 231-32.

6. Lea Taylor to Board of Directors, National Federation of Settlements (December 10, 1932), Social Welfare Historical Archives, University
of Minnesota, Minneapolis, Minnesota.

7. Arthur M. Schlesinger, Jr., *The Age of Roosevelt: The Crisis of the Old Order, 1919-1933* (Boston: Houghton Mifflin, 1957), p. 25.

8. Jane Addams, *Democracy and Social Ethics* (New York: Macmillan Co., 1902).

9. Grace L. Coyle, *Social Process in Organized Groups* (New York: Richard R. Smith, 1930), p. 79.

10. John Dewey, *Experience and Nature* (Chicago: Open Court Publishing Co., 1925).

11. Coyle, *Social Process*, p. 105.

12. Ibid., p. 126.

13. LeRoy L. Bowman, "Application of Progressive Education to Group Work," in Joshua Lieberman (ed.), *New Trends in Group Work* (New York: Association Press, 1939), p. 123.

14. Joshua Lieberman (ed.), *New Trends in Group Work* (New York: Association Press, 1938).

15. Kurt Lewin, Ronald Lippitt, and R. White, "Patterns of Aggressive Behavior in Experimentally Created 'Social Climates,' " *Journal of Social Psychology* 10 (1939): 271-99.

16. Margaret E. Hartford, *Groups in Social Work* (New York: Columbia University Press, 1971), p. 14.

17. J. L. Moreno, *Who Shall Survive* (Washington, D.C.: Nervous and Mental Disease Publishing Co., 1934).

18. Clifford Shaw, *The Jack Rollers* (Chicago: University of Chicago Press, 1930).

19. Frederic Thrasher, *The Gang* (Chicago: University of Chicago Press, 1927).

20. William Foote Whyte, *Street Corner Society* (Chicago: University of Chicago Press, 1943).

21. Muzafer Sherif, *The Psychology of Social Norms* (New York: Harper and Row, 1936).

22. Education for Social Work, reprinted from the *Report of the Commissioner of Education for the Year Ended June 30, 1915* (Washington, D.C.: U.S. Government Printing Office, 1915), pp. 345-48.

23. Elizabeth G. Meier, *History of the New York School of Social Work* (New York: Columbia University Press, 1954), p. 23.

24. Ralph Popple, "The Effects of Professionalization on the Early Development of Social Work Education in St. Louis, Missouri, 1901-1930" (Ph.D. dissertation, Washington University, 1977), p. 137.

25. Paul Simon (ed.), *Play and Game Theory in Group Work: A Collection of Papers by Neva Leona Boyd* (Chicago: University of Illinois, 1971), pp. 1-19.

26. *Social Work: An Outline of Its Professional Aspects* (New York: American Association of Social Workers, 1922), pp. 13-15.

27. *School of Applied Social Sciences: A Graduate Professional School of Western Reserve University in the City of Cleveland, 1916-1917*, (Ohio: Western Reserve University Annual, Catalogue, 1916), p. 3.

28. Sara Maloney, "Development of Group Work Education in Social Work Schools in U.S." (Ph.D. dissertation, School of Applied Social Science, Western Reserve University, 1963), p. 114.

29. Clara A. Kaiser, *The Group Records of Four Clubs at University Neighborhood Centers* (School of Applied Social Sciences, Western Reserve University, Cleveland, Ohio, 1930).

30. Wilbur I. Newstetter, Marc J. Feldstein, and Theodore M. Newcomb, *Group Adjustment: A Study in Experimental Sociology* (Cleveland: School of Applied Sciences, Western Reserve University, 1938).

31. Philip Klein, "Social Work," in Edwin R. A. Seligman (ed.), *The Encyclopedia of the Social Sciences* (New York: Macmillan Co., 1934), Vol. 14, p. 169.

32. Ann Elizabeth Neely, "Current Practices and Problems in Professional Education for Group Work," in Harry K. Eby (ed.), *Main Currents in Group Work Thought: Proceedings of the A.A.S.G.W. 1940* (New York: Association Press, 1941), p. 58.

33. Grace Coyle, *Group Experience and Democratic Values* (New York: Woman's Press, 1947), p. 62.

34. Ibid., p. 65.

35. Margaretta Williamson, *Social Worker in Group Work* (New York: Harper and Brothers, 1929).

36. Ibid., p. 7.

37. Mary Richmond, "Some Next Steps in Social Treatment," reprinted in *The Long View* (New York: Russell Sage Foundation, 1930), pp. 487-88.

38. Mary E. Hurlbutt, Chairman, "The Pugsley Award," *Proceedings of the National Conference of Social Work, 1935* (Chicago: University of Chicago Press, 1935), p. vii. "The Editorial Committee was unanimous in judging Dr. Coyle's paper on 'Group Work and Social Change' to have made the most important contribution to the subject of social work at the conference of 1935. Dr. Coyle discusses the group process as a "significant mode of social action in the contemporary world. Social participation today requires not simply relation to the state but an assumption of responsibility to various group relations. Hence, the opportunity of group work as an educational force for social change. The theme is handled creatively, so that it becomes directly applicable to practice, and is at the same time, serenely rooted in a wider cultural perspective."

39. W. I. Newstetter, "What Is Social Group Work," in *Proceedings of the National Conference of Social Work, 1935* (Chicago: University of Chicago Press, 1935), p. 291.

40. Ibid., p. 299.

41. Roy Sorenson, "Case-Work and Group-Work Integration: Its Implication for Community Planning," in *Proceedings of the National Conference of Social Work, 1935* (Chicago: University of Chicago Press, 1935), p. 311.

42. Ibid., p. 313.

43. Anne Smith, "Group Play in a Hospital Environment," in *Proceedings of the National Conference of Social Work, 1935* (Chicago: University of Chicago Press, 1935), pp. 372-3.

44. Neva Boyd, "Group Work Experiments in State Institutions in Illinois," in *Proceedings of the National Conference of Social Work, 1935* (Chicago: University of Chicago Press, 1935), p. 344.

45. LeRoy E. Bowman, "Dictatorship, Democracy, and Group Work in America," in *Proceedings of the National Conference of Social Work, 1935* (Chicago: University of Chicago Press, 1935), p. 382.

46. Ibid., p. 386.

47. Arthur Swift, "The Essential of Training for Group Leadership," in *Proceedings of the National Conference of Social Work, 1935* (Chicago: University of Chicago Press, 1935), pp. 372-3.

48. Grace Coyle, "Group Work and Social Change," in *Proceedings of the National Conference of Social Work, 1935* (Chicago: University of Chicago Press, 1935), p. 393.

49. Ibid., p. 404.

50. Boyd, "Group Work Experiments," p. 339.

51. Ibid., p. 341.

52. Ibid., p. 343.

53. Ibid., p. 341.

54. Ibid., p. 342.

55. Ibid., p. 343.

56. Emory S. Bogardus, "Ten Standards for Group Work," *Sociology and Social Research* 21 (1936-1937):176.

57. S. R. Slavson, *Creative Group Education* (New York: Association Press, 1937).

58. Emory S. Bogardus, "The Philosophy of Group Work," *Sociology and Social Research* 23 (July-August 1939):567.

Chapter 5

EXPANSION AND PROFESSIONALISM, 1937--1955

By 1937, the United States was slowly emerging from the depths of the depression. Forces leading to another European war were gathering almost unnoticed while Americans were preoccupied with their own economic problems. They placed trust in the protection of their nation's geographic location and were psychologically committed to staying out of future European involvements. There was a growing sense of security. As the foreign situation worsened, America's domestic economy began to improve, stimulated in part by the war and the defense demands on the nation's industrial capacity. The isolationist philosophy came to an abrupt end with the bombing of Pearl Harbor in 1941 by the Japanese.

Unemployment, the key problem of the 1930s, faded into the background, and labor scarcity now became the problem. Industrial and agricultural production demanded all the manpower that could be spared from the armed services, and war prosperity replaced the earlier depressed economy. The additional manpower came from the normal growth of the population, and from the employment of older men, women who were previously housewives, and young people of school age who were not formerly seeking employment. Increased shifts of the population to industrial centers resulted in crowded housing conditions and disruption of previous living patterns. Together, these accumulated tensions contributed to individual, family, and community changes as well as broader societal changes.

The war also brought the importance of mental health into focus, for many men were rejected or discharged from the armed forces because of emotional problems. If more than

1.5 million men were rejected because of neuropsychiatric difficulty, many asked, what similar problems existed in civilian life? It was evident that more services would have to be developed that allowed for working with larger numbers of people than was possible through individual psychotherapy.

When the war came to an end in 1945, the nation was faced with making the change from a war-based to a peace-based economy. The country now had to deal with the return of millions of servicemen, the need for more domestic goods, and America's new dominant position in foreign affairs. In addition, it had to handle the guilt and fear engendered by the use of atomic weapons, and soon it would have to live with the tensions of a cold war. That changes in the social and economic patterns were taking place could be seen in the increased mobility of the population and the growing number of women in the labor force. The impact of these changes was apparent in the lack of adequate housing, the high divorce rate, and increased rates of juvenile and adult crimes.

Another significant change occurred in the 1950s when primarily middle-class groups began moving from large metropolitan areas to the suburbs. They were often replaced in the metropolitan areas by lower economic groups, most of them blacks, who were compelled to live in blighted slum areas and were left with a need for increased social services. One result was an increase in racial tensions, with a greater demand for better schools and services by the nonwhite population.

DEVELOPMENTS IN SOCIAL WORK

The development of the public assistance provisions of the 1935 Social Security Act, created a great demand for personnel to administer the programs. Professionally prepared social workers were usually placed in supervisory or training positions; however, there were not enough workers to fill the thousands of vacant positions. Social workers who functioned in clinical settings as psychiatric social workers found their jobs in jeopardy because funds were reallocated to positions in public assistance agencies. The private agencies with their meager budgets had little to offer in the way of environmental help and found it necessary to become skilled in the art of listening.

The demands for social workers for war services followed this move to public welfare agencies, and again professionally trained caseworkers tended to be placed in leadership positions to guide untrained workers in the administration of services. These workers and those they had supervised provided services in several areas: services centering around the soldier and his family, such as counseling and determining facts about dependency; services involving the broad field of postwar construction; and the continuation of day-to-day services which had become an integral part of most communities. In the last-named, the disruption of family life, increase in divorces, and increase in the number of unwed mothers provided for a more than average load for casework services.

Two major trends in the content of social casework became visible during the 1937-1955 period. The first derived its philosophy and method from the theory of personality, which was developed by Sigmund Freud and his followers, and applied the principles of "dynamic psychiatry" to the casework approach. Conscious as well as unconscious influences were regarded as determining human values and self-control. Diagnostic casework accepted personality organization as a composite of differentiated and interacting elements that reacted on each other but that were also influenced by the people in one's environment and by the social and economic conditions in which one lived.

The second major trend was toward the "functional" approach, based on the writings of Otto Rank and centered around the assumption of an organizing force, the "will," in human personality. Functional casework referred to its function as the "helping process" and did not use the diagnostic term *treatment*. In this process, the client directed himself toward a change of attitude, while the functional caseworker helped him release and redirect his energies toward self-responsibility and self-acceptance.

In 1947, a committee of the Family Service Association, the chief standard-setting body for the field of family social work, was formed to clarify the similarities and differences between these two schools of thought. In 1950, the committee reported that "because of the nature and profundity of the differences in philosophy, purpose and method, the committee is in agreement that the two orientations could not be reconciled." The members of the committee expressed the opinion that the experience in working together had been productive because of the greater knowledge gained about each approach.[1]

BEGINNING OF A PROFESSIONAL ORGANIZATION

The Ligonier Conference held in Ligonier, Pennsylvania, in 1934 and organized by the New York Conference on Group Work drew together people of diverse backgrounds whose common interest in work with small groups provided the basis for continued association. Participants expressed the desire to form an organization made up of individuals interested in groups and committed to the enhancement of group work skills and knowledge. The Ligonier Conference appointed a committee to begin the process of planning an organization that would meet these goals. Prior to the meeting in Atlantic City one hundred letters signed by Arthur L. Swift and Joshua Lieberman and Abel J. Gregg, were sent out for the purpose of convening a meeting during the National Conference of Social Work, to plan in more detail a national organization. According to Charles Hendry, one of the early leaders, fifty persons turned up for the meeting. One point of disagreement was whether the organization should be a professional association or an association for the study of group work. Finally it was unanimously voted to create a National Association for the Study of Group Work. Later, in recognition of Canadian members, the term "American" was substituted for "National."[2]

As the association took shape, a deliberate effort was made to enlist and involve national agency personnel in the NASGW. This was done because these individuals traveled widely and had potential influence among the professionals in their own organizations. There was also a studied cultivation of group workers at local, state, and national conferences of social work. Members of the Central Committee of the Association accepted heavy responsibilities in speaking, leading group work institutes, and participating in or directing numerous community surveys.

The NASGW, in keeping with its purpose, published reports of local study groups and the proceedings of annual meetings. In 1938, a collection of papers written by educators and practitioners for professional meetings was drawn together into a single volume entitled *New Trends in Group Work.*[3] A year later, a bimonthly pamphlet called *The Group in Education-Recreation-Social Work* began to be published. These publications reflected the wide diversity of individuals interested in group work: articles were written by educators, theologians, and recreation workers, as well as social workers.

This wide diversity brought continued confusion as to exactly what profession group work belonged. In its various aspects, group work was a therapeutic tool, a reform movement, an educational method, a small part of the recreation movement, and closely akin to the methods and values of social welfare agencies. To some people, however, it was none of these, but instead something quite new with an identity of its own. These people viewed it as a unique and highly refined skill limited to the worker functioning in small groups of people in intimate psychological interaction, with the goal of helping the group members solve common problems. Many of the early theory-builders in group work felt that it had an identity all its own and that a distinct profession could be established. Others felt it would be more advantageous to wait before making a premature or exclusive identification with one or another field of service. In 1938, Charles Hedley wrote:

It seems quite clear that we are not yet in the position to decide definitely on this question of the professional classification of informal ingroup educational recreation work. Whether we have an independent profession or a substantial segment of an existing profession remains to be determined. Just as a scientist would not want to restrict his participation to a single scientific society, so group work educators presumably would not want to identify themselves solely with one professional organization or to isolate themselves from any professional organization which operates within the area of their social knowledge.[4]

One year later, Hugh Hartshorne, reporting as chairman of the Commission on the Objectives of Group Work of the American Association for the Study of Group Work, said, "It is probably fortunate that the notion of group work has not settled back into a new educational stereotype." He maintained that group work had no objectives of its own but represented the increasing sensitivity of agencies to the conditions under which social skills and attitudes needed in a democracy might be expected to develop.[5]

In 1940, William Kilpatrick, in his book *Group Education for a Democracy*, stressed the generic aspects of group work for education:

The author takes responsibility here for stating his personal opinion assisted at points by publications of the Association, that group work is a highly new interest, whether this goes on in school classes or in recreation and other informal education. This group work is, however, not to be thought of as a separate field of work but rather as a method to be used in all kinds of educational endeavor. "Group work" in this sense is just now more or less of a movement, and as such deserves support and success. But its success will be achieved when and to the degree that effective working in groups has established itself as an essential part of any education of youth, however and wherever conducted.[6]

Kilpatrick believed that group work should be identified with the profession of education. He felt, that although it had many linkages with social work, a formalization of the relationship would stunt the growth and usage of group work.

SEARCH FOR A DEFINITION

During the war years, the controversy over the nature and definition of group work continued. While some agreed with Hedley that it was too early to decide definitely where group work belonged, others saw group work as a social movement that would strengthen democracy through citizen participation in community affairs. Still others were of the opinion that the AASGW was still "too immature as an organization and too underdeveloped in its body of knowledge to have much to offer to society."[7]

Sidney Lindenberg, in the book *Supervision in Social Group Work* (1939) stated, "The concept upon which . . . group workers are now trying to build themselves to a professional status in the eyes of the public . . . is . . . to help people use a group experience positively in terms of their own development, rather than to just help them use their leisure time." He went on to say that the main purpose is to help an individual, through a group to which he voluntarily allies himself, to strengthen worthwhile personality characteristics, to eliminate faulty ones, and broaden his horizon through new interests, better thinking and sounder action.[8]

In 1940, in a pamphlet entitled *Group Work: Roots and Branches*, Charles Hendry defined group work as a method and process in informal education and recreation, which made use of voluntary association in small groups; individualization related to identification with the group. interaction among members and the leader; expression and stimulation of interests, and leadership sensitive to personal and social values.[9] In the same pamphlet, Clara Kaiser referred to the immediate need to clarify the professional content of the job in order to provide a means of transfer of professional experience from one type of organization to another.[10] In another article in the same pamphlet, Coyle stressed the importance of making social action an integral part of the function of group work.

At the National Conference of Social Work in 1942, Gertrude Wilson emphasized the use of group work in effecting changes in the values of individuals and society as a whole. She believed that group work was a process through which group life was influenced by a worker who directed the process toward the accomplishment of a social goal conceived in a democratic philosophy. She defined group work as (1) developmental, as it provided for normal social growth; (2) protective or corrective, in that it could be offered to people without groups; and (3) instrumental in achieving of socially desirable ends. By understanding the personality of each member, the worker influenced the process within the group, and participation in the process helped members use the group for their own growth and development.[11]

SEPARATION OF GROUP WORK AND RECREATION

As group work in the mid-1940s moved closer to social work, many began to raise questions as to the relationship of group work to recreation. In the group work section meeting of the 1946 National Conference of Social Work, G. Ott Romney delivered a paper called "The Field of Recreation," which was followed by a companion paper by Grace Coyle, "Group Work in Recreation." Romney spoke of recreation as an end in its own right, and

as a definable, distinguishable, identifiable something [that] suffers from inaccurate and fragmentary interpretation. It is frequently confused with its dividends (as in health, education therapy, democracy, character building and physical conditioning) and with its methods (as in social group work). . . . Recreation includes everything the individual chooses to do in his own time for the gratification of the doing. . . .[12]

Coyle took this distinction a step further with the following statement on social group work as a method:

Group work arose out of an increasing awareness that in the recreation-education activities which went on in groups there were obviously two dimensions—*the stream of activity*—game discussion or artistic enterprise on one hand; and, on the other, *the interplay of personalities* that creates the group process. To concentrate on one without recognizing and dealing with the other is like playing the piano with one hand only. Program and relationships are inextricably intertwined. The group method developed as we began to see that the understanding and the use of the human relations involved were as important as the understanding and use of various types of program.[13]

A year later, Coyle wrote that group work could make a significant contribution to recreation's function of providing enjoyable experiences. It could contribute by assisting individuals to develop more enjoyable human relations; it could help individuals who were unable to help themselves because of some kind of personal difficulties; and it could contribute to the significant byproducts of recreation by assisting individuals to vitalize interest and improve skills.[14]

GROUP WORK AS PART OF SOCIAL WORK

In 1946, the alignment with social work was becoming more pronounced when the American Association for the Study of Group Work changed its name to American Association of Group Workers (AAGW). The reconstructed association, described as "an organization of professional workers," joined with the group work section of the National Conference of Social Work to develop professional standards in group work.[15] During the 1946 meeting of the AAGW, social workers presented a significant number of papers. Three papers stated unequivocally that group work was a social work method. Nathan Cohen asserted that he had to discuss his topic "Body of Knowledge and Skills Basic to Group Work" from the premise that group work was "an integral part of the social work family."[16]

Grace Coyle, drawing attention to the question of professional "belonging," said that group workers

must . . . it seems, be either educators or social workers. When a problem persists for so long among intelligent people, as of course we are, it is usually a proof that we are trying to solve it by a wrong set of assumptions. It is not an either-or proposition, and we shall never solve it by organizing teams and instituting a tug of war. Like all persistent problems, it has its accretions of the irrational—old loyalties and prejudices, an occasional vested interest and a considerable admixture of misinformation or once good information now out of date.[17]

According to Coyle, although the group work methodology was developed by the recreation and informal education agencies, it was increasingly being used in social work-oriented agencies with other functions such as children's institutions, hospitals, and churches. Arguing that group work did come within the scope of the social work profession, Coyle expressed the hope that

the emerging definition of social work may define it as involving the conscious use of social relations in performing certain community functions, such as child welfare, family welfare, or health services, recreation and informal education. Case work, group, and community organization have this common factor, that they are all based on understanding human relations. While the specific relations used in each are different, the underlying philosophy and approach are the same; a respect for personality and a belief in democracy. This we share with case workers and expert community organization people. It is for this reason that I believe group work as a method falls within the larger scope of social work *as a method* [*sic*] and as defined above.[18]

Gertrude Wilson viewed group work as a basic method of the profession of social work and not as a field, movement, or agency. Calling attention to the difficulty in delineating content for professional education when the professional identification was so uncertain, she felt a great deal had been accomplished in the past decade. She expressed hope that

by the end of another decade, group workers will have settled these basic problems, and that they will be absorbed in advanced research in knowledge and skill in practice that will make the group-work method more effective in helping individuals and groups to create a better world for all mankind.[19]

In 1949, after several years of study, an AAGW committee under the chairmanship of Grace Coyle produced a report entitled "Definition of the Function of the Group Worker." The AAGW adopted this statement, which became the official description of the function of the professional group worker:

The group worker enables various types of groups to function in such a way that both group interaction and program activities contribute to the growth of the individual and the achievement of desirable social goals.

The objectives of the group worker include provision for personal growth according to individual capacity and need, the adjustment of the individual to other persons, to groups and to society, and the motivation of the individual toward the improvement of society; the recognition by the individual of his own rights, limitations and abilities, as well as his acceptance of the rights, abilities and differences of others.

Through his participation the group worker aims to effect the group process so that decisions come about as a result of knowledge and a sharing and integration of ideas, experiences and knowledge, rather than as a result of domination from within or without the group.

Through experience he aims to produce those relations with other groups and the wider community which contribute to responsible citizenship, mutual understanding between cultural, religious, economic or social groupings in the community, and a participation in the constant improvement of our society toward democratic goals.

The guiding purpose behind such leadership rests upon the common assumptions of a democratic society; namely, the opportunity for each individual to fulfill his capacities in freedom, to respect and appreciate others and to assume his social responsibility in maintaining and constantly improving our democratic society.

Underlying the practice of group work is a knowledge of individual and group behavior and of social conditions and community relations which is based on modern social sciences.

On the basis of this knowledge the group worker contributes to the group in which he works a skilled leadership which enables the members to use their capacities to the full and to create socially constructive group activities.

He is aware of both program activities and of the interplay of personalities within the group and between the group and its surrounding community.

According to the interests and needs of each, he assists them to get from the group experience the satisfactions provided by the program activities, the enjoyment and personal growth available through the social relations and the opportunity to participate as a responsible citizen.

The group worker makes conscious use of his relation to the group, his knowledge of program as a tool and his understanding of the individual and of the group process and recognizes his responsibility both to individuals and groups with whom he works and the larger social values he represents.[20]

Although the statement was more specific about goals and purposes desired than about systematic ways by which they could
be accomplished, it identified three components of method
more clearly than had previous statements, specifically, (1) the
interaction between group members and between workers and
members; (2) the use of program as a tool; and (3) the interrelatedness of individuals and the community or larger social
body in which humans and the group operate.

Caseworkers were slow to accept group work. Group workers
were identified with recreation, and it was hard for many caseworkers to think of activities such as "play," "arts and crafts,"
and "dances" as serious means of assisting people develop their
personality or work on their problems. An early attempt to
articulate the interrelatedness of these two methods of helping
was Gertrude Wilson's book *Group Work and Case Work:
Their Relationship and Practice.*[21] Read by hundreds of caseworkers, it underscored the generic skills common to group
work and casework. It led caseworkers to experiment with
groups, and it resulted in the introduction of group services
into agencies that had formerly provided help on a one-to-one
basis. It also served as a reminder to group workers that a
significant amount of time was spent working with individuals
and that similarities far outweighed differences.[22]

INDUSTRIALIZATION AND HUMAN RELATIONS

As in previous periods, many people were concerned with
the problems created by an industrial society. One of these
concerned individuals, Elton Mayo (1880-1949), a Harvard
professor, had an important effect on social work and group
work practitioners. Influenced by Robert Parker, Clifford
Shaw, and the writings of Emil Durkheim, Mayo viewed the
large industrial community as the major factor in the increased
rate of suicides, the high number of divorces, and the growing
problem of juvenile delinquency. As countries became industrialized, he stated, the people became susceptible to unhappy and
"obsessive personal preoccupation" because they lacked social
function and had lost their desire to cooperate with other groups.

Mayo's writings on small work groups were based on his research on the Hawthorne Plant of the Western Electric Company. In this study, he concluded that work output was a function of the degree of work satisfaction, which in turn depended on the informal social pattern of the work group. By belonging to small groups and influencing the outcome of the group's behavior, individuals functioned at a higher level. Restoration was to be the task of the industrial managers who until that time had done little more than create a sense of futility. Mayo's confidence in the ability of this group was based on the Hawthorne studies and the positive effects of a human relations approach to workers. He assumed that managers could organize production with minimum exercise of authority and maximum attention to the individual's work satisfaction.

Mayo maintained that the social dislocations of the time were producing a lack of opportunities for many individuals to acquire the social skills in the ordinary course of the maturing process or to find satisfactory personal relations. Unless this lack of "social skills" could be compensated for, the very survival of industrial civilization was threatened.[23]

THE INFLUENCE OF THE WAR ON GROUP WORK

The war years had a strong impact on the development of group work in the United States. The Nazis' assumption of power in Germany highlighted the importance of citizen participation in a democratic society. Eduard C. Lindeman, in 1939, wrote:

. . . the roots of a democratic culture do not lie in theories and conceptions, but rather in conduct, in experience and its satisfactions. If these roots do not strike deep into the "soil" of human personality, they will be easily destroyed by their external enemies, or they will wither away and die for want of nutrients and exercise. Whenever in history the people have thought and felt and lived democracy, there has been cast upon human experience a sharp luminosity. Fears were dispelled and hopes renewed and whenever, in history, tyranny and despotism have succeeded to power, human experience has been shadowed by suspicion, anger, and bitterness.[24]

The lessons of Nazi Germany underscored the need for increased participation in community life, for strength that grows in the individual and in the group from working together, and for intelligent leadership in all population sectors and all groups. At the same time, it was recognized that group association could be extremely powerful and dangerous and should be used with caution. The Nazi experience taught group workers, who at times had thought of group activities as having a value in themselves, that these activities could be used to enslave youth as well as to help them freely participate in society. It forced them to look deeper into human movements to learn about the unique forces within each individual and not to rely solely on programs and group process.[25]

Group work was also influenced by refugees from Central European countries, such as Fritz Redl, Bruno Bettelehim, and Gisela Konopka, who brought over a tradition of psychoanalytic thinking combined with group experience. Having grown up in an authoritarian family culture, they realized the significance of voluntary group participation to individual development. Psychoanalysis had neither the dramatic nor the exclusive impact on them that it frequently had on those reared in a highly individualistic and puritan culture such as America during the 1940s. Unlike their American counterparts, who viewed analytic therapy as a panacea for solving an individual's problems, most of the middle Europeans saw it as only one of many treatments available. In addition, their painful experiences in Nazi Germany and Austria increased their interest in human relations.[26]

In October 1940, the Committee on an Emergency Program of the AASGW prepared a report entitled *Group Workers in the Present Emergency*. The report grew out of a concern that democracy was under attack and was endangered by the onrushing conquest by the major totalitarian powers. It was also felt that if England were defeated, the danger of aggression against the United States would become imminent. If group workers were to have a significant function in the emergency and in building up a defense against an aggresive war, it would probably be in the area of morale, particularly civilian morale.[27]

To many, the war forced group work to look at its methods, assumptions, and practices. Ray Johns, in a paper entitled "Practices and Applications During Wartime," wrote that the major changes in group work were: the reemphasis on the importance of group relationships; the broadening of constituencies; the influence of group practices; the greater fusion of individual services and large-scale activity in group work; the importance of social settings; the lessened emphasis on current issues in program content; and adaptations in leadership practices.

According to Johns, the traditional group work agencies had to learn how to deal with transitory groups, a type of group unfamiliar to most group workers.

Soldiers and sailors who joined a dramatic or music group might after a few rehearsals, be transferred to another camp, or shipped overseas. Replacements oftimes replaced replacements. The proportion of club groups declined sharply. Short-time special interest groups and individual activities which could be completed in a brief time or finished elsewhere predominated in many programs.[28]

As the war progressed, large scale activities seemed to predominate in group serving agencies. Congeniality, which had long been considered essential to sound grouping, took a back seat to diversity, and short acquaintances and constant shifts of people gave many groups a diversity of membership unknown in prewar years. The war required a more extensive use of volunteers, and creative means of training needed to be developed to assist these individuals lead groups.[29]

Special services of a recreational and counseling nature for men in the armed forces were carried out through the Red Cross, through its military and naval posts, stations, camps, and hospitals. Another major project was the work in the hospitals, where recreation programs had to be adapted to the physical and emotional conditions of the patients. While this adaptation was not difficult, it underscored to Red Cross leaders that their teachers and recreation and physical education personnel did not have the essential knowledge to assist returning injured servicemen in dealing with social problems that interfered with their rehabilitation. These injured servicemen were initially considered "normal" people who were rendered help-less, and sometimes hopeless, because of the war. The adaptation also brought into focus the use of groups as a means of helping. Many of those working with servicemen came to realize that it was helpful for the men to be able to discuss their difficulties with the social worker on the ward, where they were receiving treatment and could turn to their "buddies" for support and mutual interchange in surroundings familiar to them.

The American Red Cross employed 800 persons in 1939 and by June 1942 had increased its total staff to nearly 6,000. Of these, half were in the armed forces and 1,400 were in social work and recreation. By 1945, the number of social work positions had increased to 2,500 distributed among hospital services (medical and psychiatric social work and education), army and navy posts in the United States, and overseas club programs.

GROUP DYNAMICS AND SOCIAL GROUP WORK

Group workers were significantly influenced by Kurt Lewin (1890-1947) and his research into group dynamics and human relations. Lewin, a German psychologist known for his work in field theory, visited America on a lecture tour shortly before World War II. Once out of Germany, he accepted a visiting professorship at Harvard for a short time and, while there, met Lawrence Hall, who was teaching group work at Springfield College and who provided Lewin with his first introduction to the small group field.

Lewin's interest in group dynamics grew, in part, from his observations in Nazi Germany, which stimulated in him a deep interest in such problems as the eventual reeducation of the Hitler Youth and the changing of anti-Semitic attitudes. His interest in the effects of the social climate on individual attitudes[29] led him to research into various forms of leadership. Lewin also studied patterns of aggressive behavior and the resolution of social conflict. During the war, he studied changing attitudes toward foods, and through trained leaders using group methods, he attempted to persuade people to increase their intake of such available but, to some, unappealing foods as brains

and kidney. While the results of these studies influenced the
leadership styles and the group structure utilized in club leadership, many social work leaders objected that human emotions
should not be the subject of experimentation. The very valuable
results of these and later studies had less effect on the use of
groups in social work than they might have had if at the time
there had been more receptivity to experimental methods of
inquiry.[30]

Along with several associates, Lewin established the Research
Center for Group Dynamics at the Massachusetts Institute of
Technology, in 1944. In the summer of 1947, the year of
Lewin's death, the first National Training Laboratory in Group
Development was held at Gould Academy in Bethel, Maine.
A central feature of the laboratory was "basic skills training,"
in which an observer reported on group processes at set intervals.
The skills to be achieved were intended to help an individual
function in the role of "change agent." A change agent was
thought to be instrumental in facilitating communication and
useful feedback among participants. He was also to be a
paragon who was aware of the need for change, could diagnose
the problems involved, and could plan for change, implement
the plans, and evaluate the results. To become an effective
change agent, an understanding of the dynamics of groups was
believed necessary.[31]

While Lewin was not directly involved in the National Training Laboratory, his philosophy and the results of his research
were a part of the organization. For example, the laboratory
adopted the attitude that behavior and long-term beliefs could
be changed when individuals could examine them closely and
conclude they were unsatisfactory. Methods of changing attitudes or retaining them, based on Lewin's theories, proved
effective. The participants were provided with opportunities
for discovering the negative effects of these behaviors on themselves and others. Only when the person could see himself as
others perceived him would his attitudes and subsequent behavior change.

Lewin and his associates made a great contribution to the
development of group theory, as it relates both to experimental
groups and to real life groups pursuing long-term tasks. At the

same time, there was resistance to their contributions, partly because of the Gestalt base.[32] Another objection was that human relations training was a fad, poorly conceived and lacking in any real substance. Grace Coyle, who had spent time at Bethel, felt that in many instances training groups handled group situations very badly. She also criticized the laboratory on the basis that the leaders were beginning to believe they had discovered everything there was to know about group relations and were unaware of the inquiry and work of others.[33]

A CHANGE OF FOCUS

By World War II, group work was beginning to change its emphasis from social action and preparation of group members for social responsibility to problems of individual adjustment. In 1940, Ray Johns made the following observations:

Relating young people to social change is apparently difficult to accomplish. The close identification of agency financing with conservative community interests, combined with the problems of discovering specific enterprises in which young people can participate and which contribute toward needed social change, makes participation far less effective than Grace Coyle's challenging Pugsley Award paper suggests may someday be possible.[34]

In one Eastern city, 538 persons, many of them active in group work programs have already been identified as revealing personality difficulties. Two functions for agencies doing group work are suggested: (1) early recognition by staff and volunteer workers of incipient personality problems and quick referral for proper social treatment through well-established social work channels; and (2) treatment as an important part of the social work program of service for some problem cases.[35]

In schools of social work, group work students were being prepared for professional practice rather than for professional responsibilities. Like casework students, they were becoming skillful in the diagnosis that the workers met in day-to-day practice, but they were not being prepared to speak with knowledge and understanding of the wider social issues involved or with authority on possible courses of action and development for society as a whole.[36] By the 1950s, many questioned whether the "social" was being lost in social group work. At the 1952 Conference of Social Work, two speakers urged workers not to limit the practice of group work to the narrow confines of individual adjustment and interaction within the group. William Brueckner said not enough work was being done in the social change aspect of social group work.[37] Clara Kaiser stated that social purposes needed further emphasis, and she urged workers to work within the limits of the 1949 definition.[38] This same note was sounded in 1955, when Nathan Cohen said that group work practice might become too technical and lose its historical roots and its ethical commitment. He maintained that "Group work as a method or process cannot operate in a vacuum, but must be within the present social scene."[39] Cohen stated that group work must develop ethics and keep its democratic goals.

GROUPS IN THERAPEUTIC SETTINGS

The military provided psychiatrists, psychologists, and social workers opportunities to communicate with each other and to work together. It also forced the various professionals to devise new ways of cutting down on traditional detailed case histories, paperwork, and waiting lists. One of these ways was through group psychotherapy, which had been used before the war to treat emotionally disturbed children. William Menninger, reflecting on the social workers' use of group psychotherapy in the armed services, said that it had good potential for the civilian scene, and he saw a role for the social worker in using it. He asserted that social workers in the army had the opportunity to participate in a program of prevention and in active treatment programs (in both, they were concerned with groups of individuals) and that the practice of group psychotherapy was far more extensive than individual psychotherapy. In many instances, the social worker had the major responsibility for conducting the group.[40]

Although many social workers expressed interest in this use, group workers in the more traditional fields of informal education and recreation felt it would only detract from group work's tasks of citizen action and service to normal youth. Also brought into focus was the question of whether group work with emotionally ill individuals was group therapy. Fritz Redl, calling attention to the problem of terminology between groups for educational and clinical purposes, wrote:

I find many people calling "educational value" what others would claim as "group therapy," and the other way around. . . . By "educational," I mean all those cases where an existing growth trend is helped to develop without anything being "wrong" to begin with. The term "clinical" refers to all attempts at doing some sort of a "repair job." Among these are cases where rather far-gone disturbances are attacked and elaborate processes are installed to bring about the repair. These more elaborate and noticeably complex forms of clinical work, I refer to as "therapy."[41]

By 1949, a committee of the American Association of Group Work had begun working on the relationship of group work to treatment. The committee defined therapeutic group work as "the use of the group work method in working with groups of patients in a psychiatric setting." Like general group work, therapeutic group work focused on helping the individual move toward health and emotional adjustment. The role of the worker and the type of group, however, were different. According to the committee, the general group worker, moved from the central role as soon as possible, enabling the group to determine its own goals and leadership. The psychiatric group worker was the central figure in the group, often assuming the role of mother or father figure. The group worker in the general setting worked with formed or natural groups, while the psychiatric group worker worked with specifically formed groups.

In general group work the agency determines groupings in relation to social goals and the individual preferences. In psychiatric group work, grouping is an important factor in helping the individual. The agency [hospital or child guidance clinic] determines and controls groupings on the basis of individual therapy needs only.[42]

Both types of group work had "knowledge needed" in common. In each, it was considered important to have understanding and skill in working with individuals in groups. In addition, both

were concerned with the recognition of sickness and strength
in the individual. S. R. Slavson, a group therapist in 1934 with
the Jewish Board of Guardians of New York, also contributed
to group work's move toward the treatment of emotionally ill
individuals. Slavson classified his work as "activity group therapy,"
which he differentiated from "interview group therapy" because
of its almost total absence of discussion and its emphasis on the
group members' physical and manual activity and interplay.
Activity group therapy also differed from social group work
in its stress on the involvement of the individual as opposed to
concern with the totality of the group process. The therapist's
role was that of a neutral person who stayed in the background,
allowing the acting out of hostilities in a permissive environment.[43]

Child Guidance

In 1942, when Fritz Redl was a faculty member at the
School of Social Work at Wayne University in Detroit, he initiated a project in various community agencies for small groups
of emotionally disturbed children who needed more specialized
services than the more traditional agencies could provide.[44]
Called the Detroit Project, it provided diagnostic services through
the use of groups led by trained group workers. The purpose of
the project was based in part on the limitations that had been
revealed in gathering diagnostic data through the use of interviews. Diagnostic study in the group avoided the artificiality
and treatment consciousness usually associated with therapy.
It also provided first-hand knowledge as to symptoms and
the child's behavior under stress. It was also felt that using
the group for treatment and diagnostic purposes had certain limitations. According to Redl, little was actually known
as to what groups were best for what children, and this lack of
knowledge often resulted in negative results for both the child
and the group. Some children opened up and expressed themselves more freely, while others "snapped shut like clams."[45]

In 1938, the faculty of the University of Pittsburgh together
with the Pittsburgh Child Guidance Center, began to explore
the possibility of setting up a demonstration project using the
group work method. After two years of discussion, a plan for

using the center for graduate field placement was finalized. By
the mid-1940s, group work services were an integral part of the
Child Guidance Center's program. Gisela Konopka, using the
terms *group therapy* and *psychiatric group work* interchange-
ably, wrote that the use of group work in a child guidance
setting such as at the center would provide an opportunity for
a child to test out reality in a safe environment. Hostility, for
example, usually played out through symbolism in individual
interviews either by talking or with play materials, was acted
out in the group by real fights. In addition, children with strong
sibling rivalry, having to share the worker with other members
of the group, were able to work out some of their feelings in
the group.[46]

With increased acceptance of the group work method as a
means of working with disturbed children, other facilities and
settings began to seriously consider the use of groups as a means
of treatment. In 1947, the Toronto Big Brother Movement conducted a three-week camp for children whom the agency's
psychiatrist and other staff considered to be too disturbed to
cope with regular camp programs. Once it was recognized that
the camp experience could have therapeutic benefits, less
emphasis was placed on activities and greater emphasis was
placed on individual needs and attitudes. It was the thinking of
the staff, in their assessment of the camp program, that a relatively permissive setting such as a camp allowed for certain
behaviors to come to the surface that might be concealed in a
more controlled setting.[47]

Psychiatric and General Hospitals

In 1945, the state hospital for the mentally ill in Cleveland
began using a part-time group worker who was employed at a
nearby settlement house. Initially, there were many questions
as to why he was there and what he was to do. Typical of many
group workers in the 1940s, he knew little about mental illness
and hospital settings. Time had to be spent becoming acclimated
to the setting and learning about hospital procedures and
methods of working as a member of a team that included other

professional disciplines. Raymond Fisher, reflecting on his experience, notes:

We had to have enough experience with patients so that we ourselves could be comfortable in our relationships with them before we could proceed further. We counted on the fact that our basic concepts in working with people would be sound and applicable in this setting too, and indeed before too long, found they were. We, of course, recognized that there would have to be adaptations in how to apply these concepts to these specialized settings to meet the particular needs of the emotionally disturbed individuals, but we were encouraged by the psychiatrists in our work and we learned as we went along.[48]

The Menninger Clinic at Topeka, Kansas, a private psychiatric hospital, began operating an outpatient club in 1948 after a group of patients requested that a club of this nature be formed. At first, a caseworker served as staff person with the group; however, in 1949, a trained social group worker was employed to assume responsibility for the outpatient club. The club was successful and in a short time became accepted by the clinic staff as an important vehicle in assisting patients to return to the community. Three years later, another social group worker was hired to develop groups inside the hospital so as to enhance the patient's functioning in the treatment program. Eventually, a patient government was formed along with small interest groups.[49]

Field placements for graduate students interested in mental health began to be developed. One of the first was the Aspinwall Veterans Administration Hospital which served as a placement for University of Pittsburgh students in 1948. By 1949, the program had expanded, and students were working with both physically and mentally ill patients in the hospital. Groups were formed around specific problems such as epilepsy, sclerosis, heart disease, and diabetes. In addition, groups were established for geriatric patients and for those who planned to leave the hospital. The groups were engaged in a variety of activities ranging from discussions and outside speakers to games, music, crafts, and recreational trips. A concerted effort was made to integrate the program with total hospital treatment. For instance, physicians made all the referrals, groups were organized along diagnostic lines to correspond with the administrative line structure of the hospital, and there was a high ration of concurrent casework services.[50]

The growing interest in the use of the group and group workers for treatment is evident in the articles published in professional journals and the papers presented at national and regional conferences in the 1950s. It is also indicated by the statistics of several studies on group work graduates during this period. "The figures serve to confirm the fact," wrote Grace Coyle, "that there is a trend for group work to spread especially into group living situations where treatment is recognized as a social work function."[51] The study by W. L. Kindelsperger and others of the employment characteristics of the group work graduates for the years 1950, 1951, and 1952 shows that 14.9 percent of the graduates were employed in what are termed "nontraditional settings."[52]

Charles Levy's study of the graduates of group work programs during the years 1953 and 1954 reveals that out of a sample of seventy-nine graduates employed in group work settings, sixty-two were employed in the so-called traditional settings and seventeen in "specialized settings"—that is, psychiatric hospitals and clinics, residential treatment institutions, and other agencies not primarily identified with the use of the group work method, or only recently established to render group work service to special groups such as street gangs, physically or emotionally handicapped children, and similar agencies.[53]

Another study, conducted for the Council on Social Work Education, also dealt with the characteristics and employment responsibility of graduates for the 1953-1954 period. The study discloses that thirty-one out of ninety group work graduates, or 25.6 percent, accepted positions in special settings. A further analysis of the titles and responsibilities of these thirty-one graduates divided them into two groups. One group of twenty-one was deemed as practicing social group work, and the other ten had responsibilities or titles indicating functions other than social group work.[54]

ARTICULATION OF SKILL AND THEORY

The mid-1940s were marked by a relative proliferation of written work on the use of groups as a way of enhancing growth and socialization and strengthening the democratic process. Until then, the professional literature had consisted of a few books, articles in *The Group*, small pamphlets, agency magazines, and house organs. Unfortunately, this material was unevenly spread about and not always easily obtainable. Another problem that haunted both the writer and the reader was that of having to deal with the variety of meanings given to group work. Some writers used the term to designate a field, others a movement, and still others a method.

In 1947, Grace L. Coyle published a collection of papers that dealt with the importance of groups in a democracy.[55] The following year she published a second book, *Group Work with American Youth: A Guide to the Practice of Leadership*, in which she presented practical information for youth leaders, recreation workers, social workers, and others working with groups.[56] The worker, she reported, was a problem-solver who, through his understanding of psychology, sociology, and social psychology, was able to assist the members deal with their personal and group problems. Coyle also applied the findings of small group research to processes within the group such as structure, leadership, roles, and decision-making.

One of the earliest books on the "how" of working with groups was *Social Group Work: Principles and Practices*, written in 1948 by Harleigh B. Trecker who was a faculty member in the Graduate School of Social Work at the University of California.[57] Trecker clearly identified group work as a method of social work along with social casework and community organization. He gave attention to such issues as the agency and community, the group, the individual and the group, the role of the worker, individual guidance, recording, and evaluation.

In the same year, Charles E. Hendry edited a collection of papers to mark a decade since the formation of the American

Association for the Study of Group Workers.[58] The papers
covered a wide range of issues, including the philosophical and
scientific frontiers of group work, major trends, formulation
of priorities, and directions for the future. A common thread
that ran through most of the articles was the sense of excitement and mission felt by the contributing writers. While they
varied on how they worked with groups and even on how they
defined group work, they shared the belief that group work
was a special tool with which to make the world a better place
to live. Only four of the twenty-five authors of the chapters
had graduate degrees in social work, and their affiliations
included posts with such federal departments as the Veterans
Administration, the Social Security Administration, and the
Extension Service of the U.S. Department of Agriculture, the
Adult Education Service, and some youth service agencies.[59]

Perhaps the book that had the greatest influence on the use
of groups in social work was *Social Group Work Practice* by
Gertrude Wilson and Gladys Ryland.[60] Known affectionately
as the "green Bible," it provided practitioners and group work
faculty alike with a practical guide to working with groups.
Wilson and Ryland, who had been on the faculty of the School
of Social Work at the University of Pittsburgh, drew liberally
from the records of students and workers carrying groups.
The authors brought together knowledge from the social
sciences, social work, and psychiatry. They also presented an
in-depth examination of program media and their purposeful
use by group workers in the service of objectives related to
individual and group development and problem-solving.

In 1949, Gisela Konopka, who had been a student of Wilson
and Ryland at the University of Pittsburgh, was instrumental
in drawing attention to the use of the group work method in
working with disturbed children. In her book *Therapeutic
Group Work with Children*, which consisted mainly of records
of group meetings, she showed how the group work method
could be useful.[61] In 1954, she published a second book on
the role of the group worker in institutions.[62] In this book
she dealt with such settings as institutions for disturbed
children, unmarried mothers, handicapped children, delinquents,

the aged, and criminals. Referring to it as a sober and practical book, she noted that people in institutions had some of the greatest unmet needs and that social group workers could make a unique contribution to their treatment and to the therapeutic process of the total institution.[63]

The connection between group work and democracy was underscored in 1953 with the publication of Alan Klein's book *Society, Democracy, and the Group.*[64] Klein explored in depth the importance of building the democratic process into groups, agencies, neighborhoods, and communities, and of developing citizens who know how to live and function in a democracy. Group work, Klein said, was a vehicle for teaching democratic concepts inasmuch as it provided a laboratory for individuals to learn constructive values and become educated to their roles as citizens.

Helen U. Phillips developed a functional approach to the use of groups in 1957 based on her doctoral dissertation.[65] She emphasized the need for cooperation, mutuality, and inter-dependency within a society. Phillips viewed social group work as a means of preparing individuals for cooperative living within a democracy. An especially valuable contribution at the time and in ensuing years was her discussion of the worker's aware-ness as to his own feelings both within the group and in inter-action with members outside the group. She noted that the worker had to be aware of his feelings and previous experiences so that they did not prevent him from being genuine within the group. The worker, Phillips said, had to find in himself a balance between spontaneity and discipline, and freedom and control.

FORMATION OF THE NATIONAL ASSOCIATION OF SOCIAL WORKERS

The first regular association of individuals in a national organ-ization concerned with welfare institutions and social problems was the National Conference on Social Welfare (NCSW) founded in 1874. The primary purpose of the conference was communica-tion among people committed to a more humanitarian and effective administration of social programs concerned with poverty, social degradation, and crime. After World War I, as paid professionals began to outnumber volunteers in agencies, a number of special interest groups formed. The first was the National Social Workers Exchange founded in 1917, which served as the nucleus around which the American Association of Social Workers was formed in 1921. In 1918 the American Association of Hospital Social Workers (later to become the American Association of Medical Social Workers in 1934) came into existence. The American Association of Visiting Teachers, which formed in 1919, became the National Association of School Social Workers in 1945. These groups were followed by the American Association of Psychiatric Social Workers in 1926, the American Association for the Study of Group Work in 1936 (in 1946 called the American Association of Group Workers), the Association for the Study of Community Organization in 1946, and the Social Work Research Group in 1949.

After World War II there was a growing effort to shift attention from the specializations that had divided the social work field to the identification of a common core that would bring unity. To this end, a committee on interassociation structure called the Temporary Inter-Association Council of Social Work (TIAC), was organized in 1949 to develop a plan for promoting closer cooperative relationships among the social work professional membership associations. The council studied the various objectives, programs, and procedures of the different associations in addition to areas of cooperation. Their deliberations caused them to realize that they had a great deal in common and that there was a base for a single professional association.

In spite of the apparent advantages of being directly related to the profession of social work, not all group workers favored the merger. To some, it meant selling out on group work's original task of working with normal individuals so as to help them develop to the fullest extent possible. To others, it meant joining a profession that had little interest in social reform or in helping communities take responsibility for their own development through community action.[66] In 1952, however, the American Association of Group Workers voted overwhelmingly to participate in the program to combine the social work professional organizations into one social work organization. The move was a final step in social work identification, which resulted in the formation of the National Association of Social Workers in 1955.

NOTES

1. *A Comparison of Diagnosis and Functional Casework Concepts* (New York: Family Service Association of America, 1950), p. 3.

2. Charles E. Hendry, "All Past Is Prologue," *Toward Professional Standards*, American Association of Group Workers. 1945-46 (New York: Association Press, 1947), p. 160.

3. Joshua Lieberman (ed.), *New Trends in Group Work* (New York: Association Press, 1938).

4. Charles Hedley et al., *A Professional Outlook on Group Education* (New York: Association Press, 1938), p. 47.

5. Hugh Hartshorne, "Objectives of Group Work," in *Group Work, 1939* (New York: Association Press, 1939), p. 39.

6. W. H. Kilpatrick, *Group Education for a Democracy* (New York: Association Press, 1940).

7. Grace Coyle, *Group Experience and Democratic Values* (New York: Woman's Press, 1947), p. 95.

8. Sidney Lindenberg, *Supervision in Social Group Work,* (New York: Association Press, 1939).

9. *Group Work: Roots and Branches* (1940), "Social Work Today."

10. Ibid.

11. Gertrude Wilson, "Human Needs Pertinent to Group Work Services," *Proceedings of the National Conference of Social Work, 1942* (New York: Columbia University Press, 1942).

12. G. Ott Romney, "The Field of Recreation," *Proceedings of the National Conference of Social Work, 1947* (New York: Columbia University Press, 1947), pp. 195-96.

13. Grace Coyle, "Group Work in Recreation," *Proceedings of the National Conference of Social Work, 1947* (New York: Columbia University Press, 1947).

14. Grace Coyle, "Group Work: A Method in Recreation," *The Group* 9 (April 1947): 8-11.

15. Helen Rowe, "Report of the Central Committee," in AAGW (comp.), *Toward Professional Standards,* (New York: Association Press, 1947), p. 169.

16. Nathan E. Cohen, "Body of Knowledge and Skills Basic to Group Work," in AAGW (comp.), *Toward Professional Standards* (New York: Association Press, 1947), p. 8.

17. Grace Coyle, "On Becoming Professional," in AAGW (comp.), *Toward Professional Standards* (New York: Association Press, 1947), p. 18.

18. Ibid., p. 19.

19. Gertrude Wilson, "Trends in Professional Education in Group Work," in AAGW (comp.), *Toward Professional Standards* (New York: Association Press, 1947), p. 33.

20. American Association of Group Workers, "Definition of the Function of the Group Worker," Mimeographed.

21. Gertrude Wilson, *Group Work and Case Work: Their Relationship and Practice* (New York: Family Welfare Association, 1941).

22. Gertrude Wilson, "From Practice to Theory," in Robert Roberts and Helen Northen (eds.), *Theories of Social Work with Groups* (New York: Columbia University Press, 1976), p. 27.

23. Elton Mayo, *The Social Problems of an Industrial Civilization* (Andover, Mass.: Andover Press, 1945).

24. Eduard C. Lindeman, "The Roots of Democratic Culture," *The Group* (New York: NASGW, 1939).

25. Gisela Konopka, *Social Group Work: A Helping Process* (Englewood Cliffs, N.J.: Prentice-Hall, 1963), p. 8.

26. Gisela Konopka, an outstanding leader in the field of group work, notes:

For myself, if I represent at all—at least in some ways—this group of immigrants, I must say that my first encounter with social group work in 1941 was a revelation. Having just come from a society that seemed to present an inescapable gulf between the individual and the group—which insisted that the individual be sacrificed to the interests of the group—I found the concept of individualization in and through the group exhilarating. (Ibid., p. 9.)

27. "Group Work in the Present Emergency," Committee on an Emergency Program, AASGW, October 1940.

28. Ray Johns, "Practices and Applications During Wartime," in Charles E. Hendry (ed.) *A Decade of Group Work* (New York: Association Press, 1948), p. 116.

29. Ibid., p. 119.

30. Margaret Hartford, *Groups in Social Work* (New York: Columbia University Press, 1972), p. 15.

31. Miriam R. Ephraim, "Introduction," *The Group* 10, No. 2 (January 1948): 3. See also Leland P. Bradford, "Human Relations Training at the First National Training Laboratory in Group Development," *The Group* 10, No. 2 (January 1948): 4.

32. Hartford, *Groups in Social Work*, p. 14.

33. Based on correspondence between Grace L. Coyle and Alfred Sheffield, September 11, 1952.

34. Ray Johns, "An Examination of Group Work's Practices," *Proceedings of the National Conference of Social Work, 1940* (New York: Columbia University Press), p. 560.

35. Ibid., p. 557.

36. Nathan E. Cohen, *Social Work in the American Tradition* (New York: Dryden Press, 1958), p. 192.

37. William Brueckner, "Group Work Commitment to Social Responsibility," paper presented at the National Conference of Social Work, 1952 in Chicago, Illinois.

38. Clara Kaiser, "Social Group Work Practice and Social Responsibility," *Proceedings of the National Conference of Social Work, 1952* (New York: Columbia University Press, 1952), p. 161.

39. Nathan E. Cohen, "Implications of the Present Scene for Social Group Work Practice," *Proceedings of the National Conference of Social Work, 1955* (New York: Columbia University Press, 1955), p. 103.

40. William C. Menninger, "Psychiatric Social Work in the Army and Its Implications for Civilian Social Work," *Proceedings of the National Conference of Social Work, 1945* (New York: Columbia University Press, 1945), p. 13.

41. Fritz Redl, "Diagnostic Group Work," *American Journal of Orthopsychiatry* 14 (January 1944): 53-67.

42. Gisela Konopka, "Similarities and Differences Between Group Work and Group Therapy," Report of the Group Therapy Committee, AAGW (Mimeographed) ST-451-8.

43. S. R. Slavson, *Introduction to Group Therapy* (New York: Commonwealth Fund, 1943).

44. The Detroit Project was a joint enterprise of the Wayne University School of Social Work, the Consultation Bureau, and the Jewish Social Service Bureau. See Fritz Redl and David Wineman, *The Aggressive Child*, (Glencoe, Ill.: Free Press, 1957), p. 29.

45. Ibid., p. 66.

46. Gisela Konopka, "Therapy Through Group Work," in AAGW (comp.), *Toward Professional Standards* (New York: Association Press, 1947), p. 140.

47. Gordon J. Aldridge, "Program in a Camp for Emotionally Disturbed Boys," *The Group* 16, No. 2 (December 1953): 13.

48. Raymond Fisher, "Contributions of Group Work in Psychiatric Hospitals," *The Group* 12, No. 1 (November 1949): 3.

49. Based on personal correspondence between Minnie M. Harlow (Chief Group Worker, the Menninger Foundation, Topeka, Kansas) and the author, January 30, 1974. According to Harlow, Drs. Karl and William Menninger became interested in the use of groups in psychiatric settings through their acquaintance with Gertrude Wilson and Gladys Ryland, who had a group of students at the Winter VA Hospital in Topeka during the summers of 1947 and 1948.

50. Claire R. Lustman, "Group Work Within a Medical Setting." Paper presented at the National Conference of Social Work, Atlantic City, N.J., May 1950.

51. Grace Coyle, "Social Group Work," *Social Work Yearbook, 1954*, (New York: Russell Sage Foundation, 1954), Vol. 12, p. 483.

52. Ibid., p. 484.

53. Charles S. Levy, "From Education to Practice in Social Group Work," *Journal of Jewish Communal Service* (Winter 1958): 175.

54. Gladys Ryland, *Employment Responsibilities of Social Group Work Graduates* (New York: Council on Social Work Education, 1958), p. 4.

55. Grace L. Coyle, *Group Experience and Democratic Values* (New York: Woman's Press, 1947).

56. Grace L. Coyle, *Group Work with American Youth: A Guide to the Practice of Leadership* (New York: Harper Brothers, 1948).

57. Harleigh B. Trecker, *Social Group Work: Principles and Practices* (New York: Woman's Press, 1948).

58. Charles E. Hendry (ed.), *A Decade of Group Work* (New York: Association Press, 1948).

59. Gertrude Wilson, "From Practice to Theory: A Personalized History," *Theories of Social Work with Groups*, Robert W. Roberts and Helen Northen (eds.), (New York: Columbia University Press, 1975), p. 36.

60. Gertrude Wilson and Gladys Ryland, *Social Group Work Practice* (New York: Houghton Mifflin Co., 1949).

61. Gisela Konopka, *Therapeutic Group Work with Children* (Minneapolis, Minn.: University of Minnesota Press, 1949).

62. Gisela Konopka, *Group Work in the Institution: A Modern Challenge* (New York: Association Press, 1954).

63. Ibid., p. 286.

64. Alan Klein, *Society, Democracy and the Group* (New York: Woman's Press, 1953).

65. Helen U. Phillips, *Essentials of Social Group Work Skill* (New York: Association Press, 1957).

66. For a summary of the struggle of social group work to find a definition, see Margaret Hartford, "Social Group Work 1930 to 1960: The Search for a Definition," in Margaret E. Hartford (ed.), *Working Papers Toward a Frame of Reference for Social Group Work—1959-1963* (New York: NASW, 1964).

Chapter 6

WINDS OF CHANGE, 1956-1970s

After World War II, a majority of Americans were lulled into a false sense of security as to their country's ability to solve both national and international problems. From kindergarten to graduate school, the nation's educational facilities were pressed to the breaking point by the increase in population and the acceptance of a college education as a norm for every middle-class American boy and girl. There was the belief that poverty would disappear, and there would be an equitable distribution of the nation's wealth. There was the feeling that, while many schools were segregated, children, both black and white, would receive equal education. There was the attitude that a half century of reform had established social justice; and most Americans were content to keep the status quo.

In many ways, the experiences of the last half of the 1950s and the following two decades brought an end to these illusions under which America had been living. It was becoming increasingly apparent that poverty was not disappearing, the nation's wealth was not equally distributed, children were not receiving equal education, and social justice for all citizens had not been achieved. This was also a period of tremendous change and violence in America. A president, a U.S. senator and presidential candidate, and two leaders of major black organizations were assassinated, there were riots in many of the nation's cities, a man walked on the moon, America lost a war, and in 1974 a president was forced to resign from office. A whole new set of words was added to the American lexicon, including cold war, Vietnam, busing, Watergate, impeachment, and cloning.

A major element in the changes that took place during this period was the rising dissatisfaction of blacks in America with

their unequal status and lack of social justice. Beginning with
the 1954 Supreme Court decision which ended legal school
segregation, blacks began to seriously question their powerless-
ness and the systematic attack on their human dignity. Their
new militancy gave birth to or renewed vitality in a number of
organizations such as the National Association for the Advancement of Colored People, the Student Non-violent Coordinating
Committee, the Black Panther party, and the Black Muslims.
With these groups came the quest for black power and the goal
of social justice. Classic forms of violence erupted; terrorism
by whites against blacks and terrorism against whites who sided
with blacks. There were riots by blacks, causing death and
property loss.

Stimulated by the civil rights movement, both white and
black students entered a phase of political activism. By the late
1960s, the focus of the student movement became the Vietnam
War, the "military industrial complex," and the government's
allocation of resources for war efforts rather than the problems
of the cities. Finding the field of social work compatible with
their personal commitment, many student activists entered
schools of social work, while others became involved in programs such as the Peace Corps and VISTA.

During the Kennedy and Johnson administrations, there was
a rediscovery of poverty in the United States, based partly on
the recognition that the number of individuals receiving welfare
was increasing at an incredible rate. Perhaps more important
was the growing indignation against the persistence of poverty
in a land of plenty. President Johnson in a message to Congress
on March 16, 1964 urged that war be declared on a "domestic
enemy which threatens the strength of our nation and the welfare of the people."[1] Under the Economic Act of 1964, programs
were established to combat poverty in rural and urban areas:
youth programs such as the Job Corps and College Work-Study
programs, community action programs, employment and investment incentive programs, and work experience programs. By
design, there was to be "maximum feasible participation" of
the recipients of the various programs.

To many, the patterns of American life during the 1960s seemed strangely awry. The annual gross national product had reached $800 billion, but at the same time employment in the black ghettos remained low and inflation was reducing the purchasing power of individuals and families. Men and equipment poured into Vietnam, but the war seemed never-ending: only the number of casualties increased.

The interface of wealth and success, poverty and failure was very much a part of American life. John Kenneth Galbraith, observing this paradox, wrote:

The family which takes its mauve and cerise, air-conditioned, power-steered, and power-braked automobile out for a tour passes through cities that are badly paved, made hideous by litter, blighted buildings, billboards, and posts for wires that should long since have been put underground. They pass on into a countryside that has been rendered largely invisible by commercial art. . . . They picnic on exquisitely packaged food from a portable icebox by a polluted stream and go on to spend the night at a park which is a menace to public health and morals. Just before dozing off on an air mattress, beneath a nylon tent, amid the stench of decaying refuse, they may reflect vaguely on the curious unevenness of their blessings. Is this, indeed, the American genius?[2]

The year 1968 brought a new president to the White House along with a change in philosophy toward social welfare services. Richard Nixon dismantled many of the agencies that had been established as part of Johnson's War on Poverty. Programs in mental health, public welfare, education, and public health that had grown at an unprecedented rate during the Kennedy and Johnson administrations began to feel a serious reduction in funding for research, scholarships, and hiring of professional staff. While money to support social welfare programs declined, social problems continued. Urban communities such as New York and Detroit bordered on bankruptcy and decayed faster than they were renewed. Even with the rise in illegitimacy rates, birth rates approached zero population growth. The popularity of marriage was balanced by rising divorce rates, and an increase in the number of single-parent families. More and more, the viability of the nuclear family was under attack, and alternative life-styles were tested.

Problems such as poverty and racism were not conquered, and the discrepancies between reality, possibility, and hope seemed to widen. In 1959, the number of persons earning below the poverty level income ($4,540 for an urban family of four) was about 39.5 million; in 1973 (with poverty level set at $6,355) the number had been reduced to about 23.0 million, 11.1 percent of the population. This was certainly progress, but not the victory that had been anticipated. In general, white families fared better than black families. In 1959, 18 percent of all white families and 57 percent of all black families were defined as poor. By 1973, the poverty rate for whites had been reduced to 8 percent, but remained almost 33 percent for blacks.[3]

Although concern for the rights of oppressed groups continued into the seventies, there was retrogression in some areas. The rights to privacy, to equal protection, and to due process were aggressively diminished. One example of this was Health, Education, and Welfare's failure to include in its requirements that welfare agencies refrain from searching homes under false pretenses or during sleeping hours and respect the dignity and right to privacy of clients. Another, was New York State's subversion of the Supreme Court's ruling against residency requirements, thus refusing welfare to newcomers who had not managed to find standard housing.[4]

The status of women in America was also challenged during the 1960 and 1970s. Like other minorities, women developed a new consciousness in the militant-reform oriented 1960s and rebelled against the social, educational and economic discrimination they experienced. Several diverse factors fed female activism, including more women with college degrees entering the work force and efforts by some politicians to interest women in government as an occupation. Another factor was the publication of books such as the *Feminine Mystique* (1963) by Betty Friedan, which called on women to recognize what society was doing to them and urged them to reclaim their identities. In 1966, the National Organization for Women (NOW) was established. It concentrated on economic and social issues; an equal rights amendment; equal pay for equal work; the abolition of sexual discrimination in employment; child care centers; equal access to education and the professions; and birth control and abortion. By the late 1970s there was evidence that the women's movement was having impact. Barriers to female participation were falling throughout American society. Forty-three percent of all adult women, including a third of all married women, were in the labor force. The proportion of women in higher education, the professions, and managerial positions was growing. Another important achievement was the Senate's approval of the Equal Rights Amendment, which, when ratified, would guarantee that the equality of rights under the law would not be denied or abridged by the United States or by any state on account of sex.

An important phenomenon of the 1960s and the 1970s was the interest in self-actualization and psychology by the public at large. Hundreds of self-help books written by psychologists and psychiatrists flooded the market. New growth centers were established throughout America, offering encounter groups and sensitivity training. By the mid-1970s, the movement had become a cultural force, in that it was a part of education, business, and the arts. Schools were using growth exercises as a part of their curriculum. Theaters were consciously using group techniques for training and for audience involvement. Businesses were using sensitivity training to improve communication and establish better relations between employees and management.

DEVELOPMENTS IN SOCIAL WORK

The decades following the formation of the National Association of Social Workers and group work's formal integration into the profession of social work were years of ferment. The changes in this period were so great that practically a new history for social work was begun. Influences from both within and outside the profession brought about changes in the composition of social work, educational goals and structure, and the focus of practice. One of the most apparent changes was in the number of individuals entering the field of social work. Between 1953 and 1954, 566 men and 1,085 women graduated with Master's degrees from schools of social work; by 1974-1975, these numbers had increased to 3,037 men and 5,730 women. In 1975, it was estimated that 16,675 students were enrolled in Master's degree programs in eighty-one schools of social work.[5]

Another change had to do with the expansion of those who were to be called professional social workers. Over the years, the term was used to designate those holding a Master's of Social Work (MSW). In 1963, the National Association of Social Workers proposed a six-level classification plan for social work manpower: two preprofessional levels—social work aide and social work technician; social worker—Bachelor's of Social Work (BSW); graduate social worker—the MSW; certified social worker—one who has met the qualifications for the Academy of Certified Social Workers; and social work fellow—Doctorate of Social Work (DSW), or its equivalent. More and more of the direct service work that had been done by MSWs in the 1950s and 1960s became the province of the BSW in the 1970s. In like manner, the MSW found himself moving into such roles as consultant, teacher, planner, supervisor, evaluator, and clinical social worker.

The Kennedy and Johnson administrations furthered the development of social welfare services. Programs such as the Community Mental Health Act and the War on Poverty stimulated new forms of services, creative methodologies, and a renewed enthusiasm for some of the problems social workers had been struggling with for years. They also led social work to reexamine its function as well as its definitions. The antipoverty efforts, for example, with the basic thrust of attacking racism and facilitating racial integration brought education to the forefront as a pivotal social welfare measure, and social workers became part of the planning of new basic educational approaches. Of special interest were the measures that helped disadvantaged children overcome environmental and interpersonal deprivation so that they could compete successfully in school and work.

As attention shifted to the urban community, poverty, and discrimination in the 1960s, social casework's emphasis on psychotherapeutic functions, other than social change at a broader level, came under fire. At this time, the poor and other recipients of social welfare services were making demands for local community-controlled schools, higher public assistance allowances, and improved services in general. New roles based on old functions were suggested for caseworkers, such as "advocate" and "social broker."[6] Both roles, it was felt, had been part of social work's heritage but had been given up for the more attractive role of "therapist." As an advocate, the worker would serve as a spokesman for the client by presenting and arguing his cause when necessary. As a social broker, the worker would steer people toward the existing services that could benefit them. He would then help the client use the system and negotiate its pathways.

Since the late 1950s, social work had been simultaneously moving away from its preoccupation with psychoanalytic theory to that of ego psychology and other theories that dealt with conscious and preconscious motivation. In contrast to the intrapsychic view of behavior, the individual began to be seen in the context of a family or group structure and to be understood in relation to such facts as culture, class, and socioeconomic conditions. By the end of the 1960s, a whole array of approaches was available to practitioners, including client-centered therapy, crisis intervention, transactional analysis, behavior modification, and family therapy.

As new information began to flood social work from both within and outside the profession, some of the artificial barriers that existed within social work were weakened. One such barrier was the reluctance of caseworkers to work with groups, as well as the group workers' discomfort in singling out individual members for interviews. Helen Harris Perlman, describing the discovery of groups by caseworkers, wrote in 1965:

The use of group sessions by case workers has had many spokesmen in casework's literature and many values attributed to it as a substitute for or as a supplementary method to, the one-to-one interview. These attributed values range from experience and economy of time and effort to the connections assumed to exist between the group process and ego support, between group participation and facilitated social functioning, between enhanced communication and enhanced happiness.[7]

Perlman observed that caseworkers' writings on the use of groups did not seem too troubled about group dynamics or group process and their differences from the one-to-one interview. Similarly, questions such as what principles governed the worker's relative activity or passivity in the groups did not seem to prevent caseworkers from beginning to use groups.

As noted earlier, what was gained in the area of social welfare in the 1960s was diminished by the Nixon administration. The threat by John Erlichman, an assistant to the president, that "now social workers would be looking for honest work" accurately reflected the administration's attitude toward services. Hence, there was a definite decrease in expenditures for social welfare services along with a reduction in imaginative planning. For the first time since the depression of 1929, social workers found it difficult to obtain jobs.

The reduction in federal support also caused government, business, and management leaders to urge social work to become more accountable both for what it was doing and for what it was not doing. Some even suggested that all social services be reduced to a systems analysis process to measure the impact of the delivery of human services. Those programs that did institute such a system faced the herculean task of reducing the dynamics that went on in the helping relationship to measurable units. Workers objected to measuring outcome and argued that clients would be hurt if efficiency and effectiveness were to be measured purely in terms of cost. It was found that it was nearly impossible to measure factors such as affect and impact with any accuracy.

As pressure was put on social workers to be more accountable, there was a move by a number of states to license social workers. For the most part this was encouraged by social workers, who

were alarmed by the increasing number of individuals taking
social work jobs but not professionally trained. In 1974, the
NASW reported that fourteen states had some form of regulating social work, nine of which had acts providing title protection
only and six that licensed social work practice or some part of
it. In some states, such as Michigan, there was a deliberate move
by the Civil Service Commission to declassify jobs in mental
health and public welfare that traditionally required a masters
degree in social work. The declassification made the jobs open
to anyone with a Master's degree in any field and adequate
experience.

In addition to such issues as the limited number of jobs,
accountability, and licensing, social work came under devastat-
ing criticism during the 1960s and 1970s, primarily from within
the profession. Some critics declared that casework was not
effective and had little impact on those it claimed to help. As
proof, they cited the findings of research studies such as *Girls
at Vocational High*[8] and suggested there was no solid research
evidence that any of the traditional casework approaches provided significant change in clients attributable to the intervention. Others criticized social work's inability to relate to the
poor. Many viewed it as a strictly middle-class form of service,
performed by middle-class workers and effective only with
middle-class clients. Richan and Mendelsohn, in the book
Social Work: The Unloved Profession, wrote:

Once upon a time, social workers mainly served the poor and the more
"professional" the field has become, the more its members have dis-
engaged themselves from the grimy problems of poverty, discrimination
and urban decay.

It is ironic for the existence of the social work profession can be best
justified by the continuing presence of the poor in a society, and the
poor are what social work purports to be all about. It may come as a
considerable surprise to some that social work—with its emphasis on the
development of knowledge and skills in dealing with social problems,
with its highly organized agencies for the delivery of needed services, has
so very little to do with the poor today.[9]

It was also observed that, over time, agencies tended to become bureaucratically oriented rather than client oriented. As rules and regulations increased, emphasis on professionalism and innovation often decreased.

Social work, like other professions, had various specializations both in method and fields of service. In the 1950s and 1960s, students enrolling in schools of social work were required to select a method, for example, casework, group work, or community organization, and focus on a specific field of social work such as child welfare, school social work, or psychiatric social work. This quasi-form of apprenticeship was derived from the settings in which social work had historically developed. It was presumed that while a practitioner might move from one agency to another within the field, there would be relatively little shifting from one field to another. After two years, graduates of a school of social work generally had solid knowledge of one method and one or two fields of practice. At the same time, they often carried with them a somewhat insular view of clients and their situation which caused them to fit the client to the worker's problem-solving framework. This form of departmentalization did not follow the natural life-style of people in trouble but rather forced the client into a mold that fit the worker's needs and knowledge framework.

Increasingly, as this single method-single field concept came to be questioned, new interest began to be generated around the common and specific knowledge bases of casework, group work, and community organization. Some schools retained this three-methods approach to teaching but required that students in one specialty take courses in another to achieve some acquaintance with the various aspects of the methods. Other schools attempted to integrate the three methods into one or two courses that identified both the common and the unique characteristics of each. By the mid-1970s, a significant number of schools were committed to preparing practitioners who could direct their attention to the totality of the person-situation interaction, and were not limited by any preferred relational system or prior methodological bias.

EXPANSION OF COMMUNITY ORGANIZATION

The roots of social group work are intertwined with those of community organization. The first community organization efforts were those of the Charity Organization Society (COS), which sought to organize and coordinate the work of the numerous agencies that provided for the poor. The COS maintained a central registration bureau to avoid duplication of services and sought services from private sources in the community. Because of the COS's basic distrust of governmental involvement in social services, it excluded public welfare departments from its efforts.

Members of the settlement movement, besides being concerned with assisting their immediate neighbors, attempted to alleviate social problems at the local, state, national, and international levels. The early settlement leaders believed it was important to change the system through some form of social action. Hull House, for example, became a center for research and action in the interest of better labor conditions, improvements to slum housing, industrial hygiene, more humane courts and prisons, adjustments of immigrants, and improved educational facilities.

During the 1920s, the coordination activities of the COS were dominant in the welfare field. The Community Chest movement, with the companion councils of social agencies, began just before World War I, when the advantage of unified fundraising drives led to joint financial efforts in such cities as Denver, Cleveland, and Cincinnati. By the time of the Great Depression, most large cities had some form of community welfare council that could provide resources for community-wide planning. Increasingly, however, it was becoming apparent that an effective resolution of social disorganization problems required going beyond the bounds of the social agencies. Steiner notes that community disorganization

includes far more than the problem of ill-coordinated social agencies. In fact, the more serious aspects of disorganization are frequently found in connection with economic, political, educational, and religious institutions of the community. . . . As long as we give a minimum of attention

to the problem of regulating industry in the interest of community welfare, it is useless to expect a community council to accomplish the far
reaching results that its supporters frequently claim for it. If community
organization is the way out it must be sufficiently inclusive to deal with
the fundamental forces that are making for disorganization.[10]

Councils throughout the country shifted from an immediate
concern with coordination for greater economy toward an expanded concept of social planning around unmet needs. They
gave renewed consideration to the use of the survey as a tool
in community organization and to fact-finding for evaluating
the various programs. In some areas, agency-centeredness gave
way to community-centeredness in studying and dealing with
community problems.

Those working with groups, whether in the settlements,
youth service agencies, charity societies, or community planning
councils, came to be influenced by the writings of such people
as Joseph Hart, Eduard Lindeman, Bessie A. McClenahan,
and Robert Lane. All of these writers had a basic concern for
the disintegration of the democratic process within the United
States and a desire for a more effective means of initiating and
sustaining the democratic process within a community. These
early students of community life looked to the contemporary
theories of society and social psychology for their knowledge
and theory. McClenahan[11] and Steiner envisioned the development of a study-diagnosis treatment approach for community
organization practice that would take into consideration the
uniqueness of each community, even though the problems of
the communities might be similar. These writers were aware
that few communities were cohesive and unified. Lindeman
wrote that, although the community was an association of
groups rather than of individuals, it seldom acted with any real
solidarity.[12] Steiner noted the same situation in city neighborhoods and underlined the need for community organization at
a regional level rather than in a town or city.[13]

In 1939, Robert Lane presented a report entitled "The Field
of Community Organization" at the National Conference of
Social Work. His report was based on the findings of discussion

groups in six cities which sought to define community organization as a method of social work similar to casework and group
work. He outlined agreement on the following propositions:
(1) the term *community organization* refers to both a process
and a field, (2) the process of organizing a community is carried
on inside as well as outside the general area of social work,
(3) within the area of social work, the process of community
organization is carried out as a primary function by some
organizations and as a secondary function by others, (4) the
process exists on local, state, and national levels and also between levels, and (5) organizations whose primary function is
the practice of community organization do not, as a rule, offer
direct help to clients.[14]

After World War II, a new concept, social intergroup work,
was added to community organization. Introduced by W. I.
Newstetter, it was based on a paraphrase of Earle Eubank's
definition of a group: specifically, "A group is two or more
persons in a relationship of psychic interaction whose relationship with one another may be abstracted and distinguished
from their relationship with all others so that they may be
thought of as an entity."[15] Newstetter's definition of community substituted the word "community" for group and
"groups" for persons. This definition was based on the idea that
genuine relationships and psychic interaction between groups
must precede any feeling of community. According to
Newstetter, the community organization worker sought to
achieve mutually satisfactory relationships between the groups
responsibly represented and their representatives. Thus, the
worker had two purposes: to achieve mutually satisfactory
relations between groups and to attain selected social goals.
The role of the worker was that of "enabler" rather than of
"doer." He would enable (1) the intergroup to develop structure
and operating practices suitable to attaining the social goals
selected, and (2) the groups represented to participate appro-
priately in the process.[16]

An examination of one approach to community organization
reveals considerable variation, transition, and confusion. One
leader in the field describes the situation as such:

In the past five years, in large measure, under the influence of the federal comprehensive projects, community organization practice has undergone great change. From a method confined largely to Chest and Council social planning and the staffing of national social welfare agencies, it has moved into extensive grass roots organization and participation in political areas. From a method concerned largely with the orderly dispensing of existing welfare services, it has added an emphasis on social change and serving groups in the community by altering institutions and other aspects of their environment. From a method largely utilizing amelioration and consensus, it has consciously moved to include the use of conflict and power. Community organization has added initiating to enabling. It has added working with the impoverished poor to work with the elite; and social agency criticism to social agency support.[17]

There are at least three important orientations that deliberate change in contemporary American communities: locality development, social planning, and social action.[18] The locality development orientation presupposes that community change can be best pursued through the broad participation of a wide variety of people at the local community level. By citizens working together, there will be a heightened sense of community, and the individuals will take a greater interest in achieving their goals. Some themes emphasized in locality development are democratic procedures, voluntary cooperation, self-help, development of indigenous leadership, and self-determination. According to this approach, the role of the community organizer is that of enabler. The clients or constituents are likely to be viewed as normal citizens who possess considerable strengths that are not fully developed. Because of the benign organization of the community, the worker is concerned primarily with coordinating, consulting, or lending a vision to the community representatives.

The social planning orientation as described in the writings of Roland Warren emphasizes a more technical, problem-solving approach in regard to reducing or eliminating social problems. This approach is based on the premise that change in a complex, industrial environment requires expert planners, technology, and ability to influence large bureaucracies. In this role of expert, the worker must be able to gather facts, assess the data, and intervene. Hired because of his knowledge, he views the community members as consumers of his knowledge and skills.[19]

The social action orientation, exemplified by the work of Saul Alinsky, regards process and planning as a device used by the establishment and the community power structure to forestall needed action. The goal of the social actionist is to redistribute the power relationship in the community. To achieve this end, the organizer attempts to crystallize issues, determine the target population, and take action to resolve the problems the target population faces. The role of the worker is that of activist and advocate as opposed to the therapist, and the method is one of contest and conflict.[20]

A FRAME OF REFERENCE FOR GROUP WORK

A recurring issue that haunted both practitioners and those teaching group work in the 1950s was that of the current state of group work as being practiced. To answer this and basic questions as to the professional background and present position of group workers, a statistical study was initiated in 1956 using as a sample 25 percent of the membership of the group work section of the NASW. A major finding of the study was the uncertainties with regard to the purpose and essential nature of group work as a part of social work. Members were confused as to the generic components and basic concepts underlying the profession of social work in general and social group work as a specialization in particular.[21]

In 1959, the Practice Committee of the NASW gave to the group work section the charge of preparing a statement on the nature of the social group work method. Rather than arriving at a consensus or an official definition, the committee was to clarify and state those concepts, ideas, and principles of the method as they existed. With this in mind, the committee chose not to develop a working definition, but instead, a frame of reference in order to communicate the tentative nature of the statement. A number of individuals engaged in practice and education for practice were asked to define group work. In addition, papers by such leaders as Gertrude Wilson, Grace

Coyle, Gisela Konopka, and Clara Kaiser were used as a framework. Others, including Robert Vinter and William Schwartz,
submitted papers on particular approaches to working with
groups.[22]

Several important issues came up in the committee deliberations regarding the type of individual served and the form and
focus social group work should take. Some contributors wanted
the term *social group work* to be limited to those services for
normal individuals and groups, while the use of group work,
with persons who had needs for corrective services, was to be
given some other label. Likewise, those who saw social group
work as primarily focused on corrective services for social
dysfunction, for example, delinquents, retarded individuals,
and the mentally ill, could not accept a formation that contained only the normal growth function. Subsequently, it was
decided to include both views.

A second significant issue had to do with the group as a means
or an end of service. Some of the contributors argued that the
total focus of practice should be on the individual who is helped
to grow in and through the group. Others felt strongly that
formation and work with the group was an end in itself. Still
others maintained that both the individual and the group were
means and ends depending on the particular situation. In broad
terms, social group work was described as a method of social
work in which the group experience was utilized by the worker
as the primary medium of practice, for the purpose of affecting
the social functioning, growth, or change of the group members.
As a part of social work, social group work incorporates values,
purposes, knowledge, and sanctions common to all of social
work. The social group work *method* could be distinguished
by the specific activities of the worker with or in behalf of the
group in which the group experience is used for the benefit of
the members.

The difference between social group work and other methods
of social work lies in its methodology, differential use of
common bodies of knowledge, and different emphasis on some
of the purposes. In its methodology, the worker functions primarily with the group as his major method of helping. The use
of individual intergroup methods, while vital to his practice,

is secondary. The social group worker draws heavily on individual personality theory and interactional theory, but he may draw on social psychology and group dynamics more heavily than sociocultural theory of society and personality. The purposes of social work include the restoration of personal and social dysfunctioning, the prevention of social and personal breakdown, the promotion of normal social growth, especially in stress periods, and the provision of opportunity for personal enhancement and citizen participation. In the last three purposes, social group work may differ in some degree from other methods of social work practice.

The social group work method is employed in a variety of settings or types of agencies and organizations, including neighborhood and community services, group services, youth services, hospitals and clinics, correctional institutions, schools, residential treatment centers, institutions for the aged, ill, or people with special problems, churches, family and child welfare services, public assistance, and camps. Although the purpose, focus, goals, and sanction of the services are conditioned by the setting and the clientele, the method is practiced in essentially the same form.

Purposes

According to the Practice Committee, social group work maintains or improves the personal and social functioning of group members within a range of purposes. Groups may be used for corrective purposes when the problem involves the behavior of the group member; for prevention when there is the potential danger of dysfunction; for normal growth, particularly at critical growth periods; for enhancement of the person; and for the purpose of education and citizen participation. A group may be used for any one or all of these purposes simultaneously and may change as the particular needs of the client change.

The corrective purpose has to do with those situations where there is or has been some form of personal dysfunctioning or breakdown within the individual members or within their social situation. In these instances, something may have gone wrong or may never have developed within the social situation. The group with the group worker can provide the necessary corrective experiences to promote growth or change.

The preventive purpose is manifest in situations where individual members or the group as a whole may face circumstances where there is danger of deterioration in personal or social functioning. Here the group may help maintain current levels of functioning so as to prevent further deterioration.

Through the group experience, individuals may be guided in the normal social growth process. The worker's interventions help the group prepare for and adapt to new situations such as marriage, parenthood, adulthood, or old age. The guided group experience can provide social associations and peer relations necessary to help the individual through the normal developmental periods and to extend the quality of friendships and other social relationships.

With regard to the personal enhancement purpose, as part of the group, members develop skills, express latent talents, fulfill potential for growth, and find enrichments that could not be achieved through an individual experience. Groups of this nature include some of the creative arts, athletic interests, intellectual and philosophical discussions, or action groups in which the individual members grow and find a fuller life through the group.

Finally, the worker in the group guides the group toward experiences that enable the members to incorporate democratic values for themselves, the group as a whole, and for the wider society. Inherent in this purpose is the value of the rights and dignity of all human beings. Through active involvement in the group, individuals may learn to lead, follow, take part in decision-making, assume responsibility for themselves, delegate responsibility, think independently and collectively, abide by decisions to which one has agreed in the group, and assume some responsibility for society as a whole.

Knowledge

The social group worker draws upon, integrates, and applies knowledge from several areas, including personality theory, group theory, sociocultural theory, social welfare organization, program media and theory of group work method.

(1) Personality Theory: The worker uses dynamic theories of personality by which he can understand the meaning of individual behavior from an intrapsychic and interpersonal or social view. He uses generalized knowledge about expectations of personal and social behavior at various stages of development within the cultural context and group experience on personality development. (2) Group Theory: The social group worker uses theories and concepts about groups by which he can understand and also intervene effectively in the processes of groups. Some of the elements of processes which he needs to understand are the group formation, continuity, and dissolution functioning, patterning of relationships, group influences, group cohesion and morale, and cultural properties of groups. (3) Sociocultural Theory: The worker utilizes knowledge of the nature, function, and structure of society and culture, subcultures, and substructures, including reference groups, ethnic background, social class, family, geographical and occupational organization. (4) Knowledge of Social Welfare Systems: As part of his practice with groups, the worker uses a body of knowledge about the organization of social welfare systems, public and private, the nature and function of resources, and the interrelatedness of the social welfare services. (5) Knowledge of Program Media: The social group worker uses knowledge about the nature and functions of various program media for personality development, for facilitating social, intellectual, and physical growth, for stimulating motivation for change, and for facilitating group development or change. Program media used in social group work may be verbal and nonverbal; they include arts and crafts, drama, music, games, discussion, and camping. (6) Practice Theory: The committee felt that practice theory relative to the use of social group work remained to be fully developed and tested. Some of the elements of practice theory presently in use include the following:

The group is the means for providing social group work service. The worker gives attention to the growth of members in the development of themselves and their group through their interactions and activities with each other and with the worker. As part of the service the worker may find it necessary or deem it important to engage in individual conferences with members or in behalf of members, but this is related to the use of the group as the major medium of service.

Service is provided to groups and individuals by the social group worker on the basis of diagnostic thinking about and feeling for the particular people in the specific group in their circumstances and within the defined service area of or agency framework. . . . diagnostic thinking includes an awareness of the differential social functioning, needs and strengths of the particular individual which may be amenable to growth or change within the group experience. Diagnostic thinking also includes an assessment of the group as an entity in light of a theoretical formulation of the nature of groups.

The social group worker's interventions take the form of interaction or relationships with members and promotion of group action through various group activities or program media toward the end of growth or change of the group and the individual members in accordance with member's and worker's goals determined in the diagnostic process. The social group worker's constant evaluation of the process of growth and change taking place within the group and with the individual effect his intervention and methods of procedure.[23]

Historically, the social group worker's knowledge has come from many sources, including biology, physiology, psychiatry, psychology, social psychology, anthropology, education, sociology, political science, and economics. Increasingly, practice knowledge has been derived from empirical research done by social workers on group process, worker interventions, behavior of members, and the impact of the various approaches to working with groups.

Technical Skills

The worker's technical skills are developed from clinical experience and the application of existing theory. He uses his knowledge, makes an assessment of the needs and strengths of the members of the group, and intervenes with the group using a range of technical skills, including skills in relationship with members and in facilitating the relationships between and among members; in diagnosis or assessment of the social functioning needs of individuals and of the group using an integration of the several bodies of knowledge; in systematic observation and assessment of individuals, groups, social situations, and problems to determine need for service; in forming, continuing, and terminating groups; in intervention in group processes; in leadership in handling structure and authority, facilitating and guiding the group; in involvement of group members in planning and group activities; in the analysis of program media and in the use of program media with groups; in recording; in the use of agency resources; in the use of professional judgment in the choice of actions related to individuals and groups; in the evaluation of professional activity and of individual and group movement; and in communication of attitudes, feelings, and opinions.[24]

PRESENT APPROACHES

One important result of the study completed by the Practice Committee was the visibility given to theoretical differences held by those working with groups. William Schwartz distinguished three different models, each with its own implications for how group work is practiced. The first, the *medical* model, bases the helping process on a sequence of movements through which the worker investigates, diagnoses, and treats the problem under consideration. The second, the *scientific* model, uses steps in the helping process that closely resemble the problem-solving sequence by which the scientific worker moves from the unknown to the known. The third model, that of the *organic system*, views the total helping situation as a network of reciprocal activity.[25]

In 1966, Catherine Papell and Beulah Rothman, expanding on Schwartz's typology, identified three separate models of group work. They noted that the sequence in which the models emerged was exclusive in that the rudiments of these models were to be found scattered historically throughout the development of group work. "Each had periods of ascendent [sic] or waning commitment as practitioners have responded to the social scene and innovative calls for our professional services."

The models identified were the remedial model (similar to Schwartz's medical model); reciprocal model (similar to Schwartz's organic system model); and the social goals model (similar in purpose to community organization).[26]

The 1971 *Encyclopedia of Social Work* underscored the differences in working with groups by presenting three approaches, each described by its major proponent(s). These included the preventative and rehabilitative approach (Charles Garvin and Paul Glasser),[27] the developmental approach (Emanuel Tropp),[28] and the interactionist approach (William Schwartz).[29] The approaches were discussed with attention given to such issues as practice assumptions, methodology, and theoretical base. In attempting to understand and compare the various approaches, one runs into several difficulties. In the first place, even though the major theorists are writing about things in common, that is, the use of groups, similar types of social problems, and workers with values in common, they communicate their ideas at various levels of abstraction and specificity. Second, each proponent tends to highlight a selected dimension of history, giving credit to certain early social workers and scholars while ignoring others. Third, despite a universal commitment to the scientific method and dependence on the findings of empirical research, there is little agreement on definitions of an appropriate philosophy of science and criteria for labeling knowledge as factual or relevant.

Struggling with a similar problem in making comparisons, Roberts and Northen note that a comparative analysis of the approaches presently identifiable in group work is both difficult and unsatisfactory.

The extreme complexity of groups and of practice with them, and the many dimensions from which such complexities are analyzed led to the conclusion that a comparison of the position papers as totalities would do injustice to their component parts. Attempts to use content-analysis procedures were also unsatisfactory because specific statements often assumed meanings that were different from those communicated when the statements were read in the context of the total papers.[30]

On a continuum, there are two polar views with various people taking stands at stages in between. At one extreme is the preventative and rehabilitative approach where the group serves as a means by which the worker can meet individual goals that are carefully studied, diagnosed, and presented for each individual in the group. The proponents of this approach emphasize the importance of restricting the profession's study to behavior that can be operationally defined and of giving priority to research procedures that satisfy the test of documented proof as derived from laboratory and experimental studies. At the other extreme is the interactionist approach in which the group is seen as a system of mutual aid wherein the worker and the members are engaged in the common enterprise of carrying out the group's goals. Proponents of this approach tend to identify themselves as humanist and existentialists.

The preventative and rehabilitative, interactionist, developmental, and social goals approaches embody the present range and diversity of approaches presently used by practitioners. It is important to note that while there are differences between them, they have a great deal more in common. These approaches are summarized in the following section.

The Preventative and Rehabilitative Approach

This approach (often referred to as the remedial model and, more recently, as the organizational model) was first influenced by the writings of Fritz Redl and his work with institutionalized children, and was later elaborated upon by such group workers as Marion Sloan and Gisela Konopka. In recent years, Robert Vinter, Paul Glasser, and Charles Garvin have come to be recognized as the leading proponents of this approach. These and other writers have asserted that group work's historic mission is service to those most in need and that emphasis should be on ameliorating or preventing the adverse conditions that negatively influence individuals and result in deviant behavior.

Function and Focus

According to Garvin and Glasser, organizations that employ several workers can be categorized as those that provide service to people in the midst of *transition* from one status or position to another and those that provide service to people in the midst of *social conflict*. The former emphasizes socialization into new developmental positions, or choice among alternative and sometimes ambiguous norms in an anomic environment. The latter emphasizes social control of those who have violated the legal and normative systems of society or resocialization of those whose adaptation to their present environment is no longer functional.[31]

The most appropriate clientele for groups that are based on the preventative and rehabilitative approach include the physically or mentally handicapped, legal offenders, the emotionally disturbed, and isolated or alienated persons: "Recipients of such group work services are individuals who exhibit or are prone to exhibit problems while performing conventional social roles. The behavioral difficulties and the situations which support them are the specific foci of the helping efforts; improved performance is the desired change.[32] The client's behavioral difficulties may be few and may appear in only one of the individual's numerous social roles. Cultural and social norms provide general criteria of the nature of the problem behavior and the degree of change actually effected.

The treatment group envisioned by this approach is the "formed" group wherein membership is predetermined and the individuals are selected by the worker. In this respect, the group is both a means and a context for treatment. As a means, it serves as a vehicle through which peer interaction and influence can be used to affect the client participation. As a context, it affords opportunities for direct worker-client interaction which can contribute to change. Processes within the group which help members to help each other are given recognition, but the limit of the self-help system is contained within the boundaries of the diagnostic plan.

Under this approach, the individual is the focus of change, whereas under the developmental and interactionist approaches the focus is on the group as the primary client. The worker tries to attain specified group conditions only as they help to achieve relevant goals for the individuals. He may use a highly organized group with an extensive division of labor, or a loosely organized short-term group. In either situation, the goals which the worker identifies for the members determine the format.

Assessment and Group Formation

The treatment process is made up of four sequential tasks that begin at intake and continue to termination. The worker assesses the client situation with reference to problems, causal conditions, and goals; plans his own activities in relation to this assessment; executes his plan; and evaluates the outcome. At any phase of the cycle, he may revise the plan to meet the particular need of the client. From his first contact with the client, the worker assesses the nature of the client's problem. Of special interest are the conditions under which the problems occur, responses in the environment that are evoked by the applicant, and his means of coping with the problem. The worker also evaluates the barriers and resources for change in the individual and the environment as a basis for goal setting. This information is obtained from the client, family members, and significant others.

The worker's goals and purposes for the group provide a general guide for group composition—the reason the group has been established and what it expects to accomplish. In making up the group, the worker seeks individuals who will have maximum impact on each other. The group must be capable of developing appropriate levels of cohesiveness, solidarity, and mutuality, and viable internal structures.

An important principle in this approach is the setting of specific goals expressed in precise, operational terms. Formulated by the worker in conjunction with the client, they consist of a specification of the state or condition which the individual should achieve by the end of treatment. By using these goals as a base, a contract or set of agreements between worker and group members regarding the problems to be dealt with is established. In contrast to a legal document, the contract in group work can be modified during the life of the group by both the members and the worker.

Principal Interventions and Strategies

The worker is viewed as a change agent who by the very nature of his position intervenes at the individual, group, and larger social system levels to achieve individual treatment goals. The means of influence utilized are direct, indirect, and/or extra direct. Using a direct means of influence, the worker effects change through immediate interaction with a group member. In this manner, he may serve as central person—the object of identification and drives; symbol and spokesman—the agent of legitimate norms and values; motivator-stimulator—the definer of individual goals and tasks; and executive—the controller of membership roles.[33]   Using an indirect means of influence, the worker induces change by creating or modifying group conditions to help the members meet their goals. Such means include limiting the size of the group and admitting members who demonstrate certain behaviors in the group. Extra direct means of influence refer to the worker intervening in social systems outside the group that have impact on the client.

The worker intervenes in order to achieve individual treatment goals. He must possess a strategy of intervention that makes use of every potential resource.

Not only must he know where he wants to go (treatment outcomes) but he must formulate approaches and techniques taking advantage of every legitimate way to achieve these ends. Besides his concern for the group's composition, the worker is concerned also with the group's purpose on major activities. Getting groups "off to a good start," assuming that a well-initiated group can move along successfully with occasional assistance, is not enough. The worker must be concerned with every point in the group's movement and must participate to guide it in desired directions.[34]

The group structure, such as communication, power, and roles, can support or hinder the client and worker in attaining their goals. The worker may develop, maintain, or modify these patterns to attain the instrumental and treatment goals of the group through the use of program activities such as games, behavioral modification, problem-solving and conflict resolution, and changes in composition.

From its inception, the preventative and rehabilitative approach has focused on the use of the group as a means of influencing client behavior so as to improve the client's social functioning and reduce dysfunctional behaviors. In recent years, there has been increased emphasis on assisting clients to change their reaction to their social situation and on helping them develop ways of changing their environment more directly. In discussing this form of intervention, Vinter and Galinsky suggest such worker activity as manipulation of the social or physical situation, education of others, interpretation, evaluation, and co-optation.[35]

Interactionist Approach

The interactionist approach (or reciprocal model) evolved from the early writings of Grace Coyle, Helen U. Phillips, and, in recent years, William Schwartz. It suggests a helping process that is intended to serve both the individual and society. It presupposes an organic, systemic, "symbiotic" relationship between the individual and society which becomes the center of social work attention. It also assumes a reciprocal relationship between the group and the individual, with the group worker serving as a mediator between the two. In this role, the social worker's responsibility is to correct and to prevent imbalances in the relationship, a responsibility that includes rehabilitation, provision of service, and preventative work.

Function and Focus

Unlike the prevention and rehabilitative approach, the interactionist approach does not begin with an a priori prescription or desired outcome. It does, however, seek an ideal group state, namely, a system of mutual aid whereby members help each other with common tasks. Emphasis is placed on engagement in the process of interpersonal relations, with the members calling on each other in their own or common cause. The individual is viewed primarily in terms of his motivation and capacity for reciprocity. Attention is therefore directed toward the relational aspects of behavior as determined by the present reality of the group system. Understanding of the individual is bounded by the social context in which he, the group, and the worker interact. It is assumed that people create many helping relationships in addition to and concurrent with the one formed with the worker, thus providing shared leadership between the leader and participants.

Assessment and Group Formation

Diagnostic consideration or structural descriptions of the individual are not regarded as important predictors of behavior in the group and do not serve as a basis for selecting the membership. Instead, assessment is directed at the individual's current functioning in the group. Before the first meeting, the worker uses any information he has to develop a feel for the way members may act and react both individually and as a group. This "preliminary empathy" is referred to as the "tuning in" process and takes into consideration how the clients may perceive him, feelings about being in the group, and fears of self-disclosure.

Composition does not play an important part in the interactionist approach. In its place is emphasis on developing consensus in the early phase of the group between what the client needs and what the agency can offer. The worker helps the individuals consider what it is they are seeking and whether or not the agency and the worker can actually be of assistance. If there is consensus, ground rules and procedures are designed to move the group members as quickly as possible to a collaborative and independent style of problem-solving. The worker seeks feedback from the individuals and encourages specificity in their communications. He makes a "demand for work" in which he challenges the members to "move through their timidity to the words and feelings they need to express in order to accept their problems and aspirations without coloring them in euphemisms."[36] Later, he will monitor the terms of the contract and perhaps have occasion to ask both group and agency to renegotiate, as they pass through the various stages of work.

Pervading the interactionist approach is a series of principles that involve the worker's sensitivity to the clients' personal struggles, particularly as they become part of the group. In the early phases, the worker uses empathy, skill, and generates from his own imagination the feelings and color of the member's experience.

It is something like the Stanislavskian effort to help actors create a new experience by using both their knowledge and their feelings, their observations and their instincts. The worker's exercise in preliminary empathy demands a similar ability to connect his thoughts and his emotions as he readies himself for his opening moves with the clients.[37]

Principal Interventions and Strategies

Schwartz describes five major tasks to which the worker addresses himself in the group situation:

1. The task of searching out the common ground between the client's perception of his own needs and the aspects of social demand with which he is faced.

2. The tasks of detecting and challenging the obstacles which obscure the common ground and frustrate the efforts of people to identify their own self-interests with that of "significant others."

3. The task of contributing data/ideas, facts and value concepts which are not available to the client and which may prove useful to him in attempting to cope with that part of social reality which is involved in the problems on which he is working.

4. The task of "lending a vision" to the client in which the worker both reveals himself as one whose own hopes and aspirations are strongly invested in the interaction between people and society and projects a deep feeling for that which represents individual well being and the social good.

5. The task of defining the requirements and the limits of the situation in which the client-worker system is set. These rules and boundaries establish the context for the "working contract" which binds the client and the agency to each other and which creates the conditions under which both client and worker assume their respective functions.[38]

The image of the worker projected by this approach is that of mediator or enabler of the convergence between client need and agency service. In this position he is influencing and is being influenced by both systems. Leadership is not limited to the activities of the worker, but is shared with the members. Noting the complexity of this position for a worker trained to work with clients in a one to one situation, Schwartz writes:

The caseworker first experiences this, "there are so many of them and only one of me." From both sides of the relationship interesting things begin to happen: the worker moves—a little reluctantly at first—to share his authority and to learn to live with a "diluted" control over the events of the helping process; and the client's battle with authority is markedly affected as he learns that his feelings about dependency and strength are part of the human condition and not necessarily a unique and personal flaw.[39]

This "all in the same boat" dynamic is an important ingredient in the development of a sense of mutual aid within the group.[40]

The ending phase is seen as a significant part of the helping process in that it can evoke powerful feeling in both the client and the worker. The participants may wish to evade their feelings of anger and the experience brought about by the separation process. The worker calls attention to the imminence of the ending, and watches and reaches for the cues that emerge—sometimes in devious forms. The worker as a member of the group involves himself closely in the separation experience, sharing his own experience while retaining his function and authority within the system.

An important aspect of the interactionist approach is the theme of intimacy which is linked to the value of mutual aid. The worker strives to help the participants talk to each other in a purposeful way, but, more importantly, to invest in each other. This aspect requires the expression of feelings and the discussion of issues that are genuinely significant within the participant's life. Without this honesty, there is no real investment but rather false consensus, charades, and games designed to produce the illusion of work without anything being risked in the process.

Developmental Approach

The developmental approach as described by Emanuel Tropp is closely related to the interactionist approach. Based on developmental, phenomenological, and humanistic underpinnings, the group is viewed as a microcosm of society wherein people help each other to grow and develop. With an emphasis on natural growth processes, especially at the group level, individuals are helped to recognize and build on their strengths whether they are in trouble or whether they are striving for self-actualization.

Function and Focus

The development theme underscores social work's goal of enhancing social functioning through the restoration of impaired functioning, and preventing impaired functioning and/or development toward optimal functioning. The group is seen as a vehicle by which the individual can realize his potential for self-awareness, self-evaluation, and self-activation. The basic elements of socially functional behavior are effectiveness in task performance, responsibility to others, and satisfaction of self. Phenomenological and humanistic themes underlie the developmental approach. The phenomenological theme relates to current individual and group behavior. The realities of the group situation "are guides to perceiving and evaluating what is happening. These realities start with the purpose of the group (why it was formed), the function (what it aims to do), and the structure (how it is set up to achieve the desired ends)."[41] The life of the group is thought of as an ongoing series of engagements with group tasks. The group confronts each task and then has to struggle with the conflict that this confrontation generates. Social behavior within the group is viewed primarily in terms of its conscious component rather than unconscious forces.

The humanistic motif has to do with the worker's functions and relations with the group. The worker is seen as sharing one major characteristic with a "real person" in which he is open, empathic, and genuine. The group offers the members an experience in free human communication—spontaneous, natural, relaxed, and unpredictable. It gives people the chance to be authentically themselves.

Assessment and Group Formation

Pregroup assessment is not viewed as an important variable in the developmental approach. Prior to the group's formation, the worker seeks information as to the significant core of commonality prospective members have and as to whether the individual will be harmful or harmed by the experience. Throughout the life of the group, individual and group behavior is continuously assessed.

It is an assessment of what concern the members have *in common*, based on how they describe, evaluate, and respond to their own and others' experiences in coping. This process becomes translated into a clear set of practitioner functions, which now become formulated as *perceiving, evaluating, and acting* in relation to the group as a whole and to individual members. But the behaviors on which the leader's assessment is based are the common experiences of the group as it works to achieve its goal.[42]

Besides assessing the activity of the various members in the group, the worker considers the activities of the group as a whole. This assessment is conducted in relation to the group's developmental stages, and the worker uses this information to assist members in resolving interactional difficulties.

Principal Interventions and Strategies

When the group is formed, the worker and the members come to an agreement about its purpose, function, and structure. In the beginning, the worker assists the members to become oriented to the group situation and to deal with their personal uncertainties, fears, and anticipation. He does so by clarifying his role in the group and by facilitating task selection and identification.

As the group progresses into a middle stage and demonstrates more open expression, greater involvement, and increased acceptance of the value of the experiences, the worker clarifies tasks completed and those still to be accomplished and facilitates the group's ability to do for itself. In the ending stage, the worker assists the group to complete tasks, evaluate growth and areas needing more work, and helps them look ahead to the future. Criteria for evaluating a group's performance center around accomplishing the group's purposes and specific goals selected for those purposes, getting optimum results in quality and quantity, using time and effort in a productive way, and obtaining active group participation. In addition, an effective group is one that shows responsiveness, openness, and responsibility. The worker enhances and facilitates the group's performance by stimulating, modeling, setting limits, and supporting responsible behavior.

The essence of this strongly group-oriented model of practice that facilitates the member's growth is engagement of the group with its tasks and engagement of the members with the group in undertaking the tasks. The social demands of common goal achievement provide a learning laboratory for each member. With the worker's guidance, the members have the opportunity to learn about themselves, for example, their strengths, weaknesses, and effective and noneffective forms of communication. As learning occurs, new behaviors and skills are subsequently transferred to the client's life outside the group.

The group and the worker jointly choose the goals and program content for each session. The general range of activity will depend upon the group's purpose and function. For example, in a counseling group, the range would cover the many possible concerns of the participants, while in an activity group, the possibilities might include athletics, cultural and community programs, and social events. In making the decision, the worker facilitates the group by seeking ideas from the members through free expression, consideration of alternative solutions, and the possible effect of action and inaction. Once a decision is made, the worker assists the group to organize for action and to carry out their decision in a responsible way.

Interventive behaviors utilized by the worker are based on his experience with the members in the group rather than on his knowledge of how the members operate outside the group. This here and now strategy gives each member the opportunity to start fresh without having to live up to the preconceived expectations of others. By dealing with the member on a current reality basis, the worker places emphasis on what the members have in common and relates to them on the basis of events within the group.

Social Goals Approach

This approach is not identified with a single formulation or a central theoretician, but is in fact a model that has its origins in the earliest traditions of group work practice. Closely resembling the community organization method of social work, this approach attempts to deal with those problems that are related to the social order and the social value orientation in small groups. Historically, youth service agencies, settlements, and Jewish community centers relied on this approach in developing group services.

Function and Focus

Key concepts are "social consciousness" and "social responsibility," with the group worker creating a broader base of knowledgeable and skilled citizenry. There is an assumption that a unity exists between social action and psychological health. Each individual is seen as potentially capable of some form of meaningful participation in the mainstream of society, and every group as possessing a potential for affecting social change.

The worker is viewed as an "influence" person with responsibility for the cultivation of social consciousness in groups. While he does not articulate a particular view, he does seek to inculcate a value system. He personifies the values of social responsibility and serves as a role-model for the client, stimulating and reinforcing modes of conduct appropriate to active citizenship.

The social goals approach envisions group work services at a community level and the agency as an integral part of the neighborhood. Though it does not set up priorities for services, priorities develop out of the needs of the community at any one given time. The agency becomes the vehicle through which members may acquire skills and knowledge for community change.

This approach is based on the premise that the individual and his environment are inseparable and that the social group worker works toward the enhancement of social functioning of the individual, of the group, and of the society. More specifically:

The socially mature individual in our culture is socialized into a democratic society with democratic values. The democratic tradition in social group work is both ethically and therapeutically sound. The individual in the patient group as well as the developmental group should learn, for example, to participate in shaping the world around him.

Social action is inherent in social group work. The level and form it takes must be appropriate to the setting and to the members' level. The value of group experience in environmental change as a means of socializing and enhancing of the individual and his world are equally important in all group settings.[43]

The interrelation of the individual and his social environment necessitates that the worker expand his role rather than limit it to working with small groups. Some broader functions would include conscious use of total agency milieu to facilitate social functioning and working with small groups, as well as large groups of various kinds. The worker uses one-to-one relationships and contacts which may have important effects on particular individuals with certain problems at a particular time.

The group process according to the social goals approach lies at the center of social group work practice. The worker's function is to facilitate the process and to free the group members and the group process itself to bring about change. In this position, the worker may be more or less active at a given time as a means of enhancing the group's development.

Assessment and Group Formation

Although no specific techniques for assessment are indicated, theories of planned change, especially from community organization practice, provide a framework. The worker first attempts to understand "the normative behaviors manifested in the group as representative of the life-style of the community and its subcultures." With this knowledge as a background, he is able to formulate an individual assessment with respect to self-image, identity, social skills, knowledge of environmental resources, resistances, and leadership potential.

Group goals are the product of a collaborative effort by both worker and the group members. The very process of arriving at the goals, as well as the goals themselves, enhances the functioning of the individual and the group as a whole. The more specific and better understood, the more easily the goals can be attained. Similarly, the agency and the worker have to make their goals and objectives explicit. It is important that over the life of the group, the goals be reevaluated so as to meet the changing needs of the clients.

Principal Interventions and Strategies

In recent years, the concept of the community has been expanded to include mental hospitals. Jacobs utilized the social goals model as a part of treatment at Camarillo State Hospital.[44] In a similar vein, Reid found the approach to be an effective element within the therapeutic milieu of the Menninger Clinic.[45] In both situations, the authors show how important it is for the patients to go beyond themselves and the egocentricity of the counseling experience and to participate with others in a common cause.

To deal with the external environment of the group, the social goals approach, according to Papell and Rothman, has generated a significant body of principles designed to activate the group in relation to agency and community.

Clarification of agency policy, positive use of limitations, identification
with agency goals, determination of appropriate issues for collective
action and the weighting of alternatives for action and their consequences
are all familiar principles heavily relied on in the social goals model.
Furthermore, assessment and implementation with regard to the individual
do not have to await intensive study of each member. The worker's assessment is first directed toward understanding normative behaviors manifested in the group as representative of the life style of the community
and its sub-cultures.[46]

The worker's intervention is directed toward helping the group
to achieve its goals and to enable the group to achieve its full
potential for action. To accomplish this end the worker
proposes alternatives for action, mediates between the group
and the agency or community, and intervenes in the group and
community in the interest of achieving group goals. In addition,
he may stress democratic participation, the sharing of leadership activities, and the development of consensus.

RECENT THEORETICAL INPUTS

During the early years of social group work in the United
States, relatively few individuals worked with groups. Any
writing and research on groups, helping skills, and methods was
done by a handful of practitioners and academicians who were
struggling with this newfound way of helping children and
adults grow. Sociologists and psychologists writing on groups
were viewed as companions in the search for knowledge and
understanding.

In comparison, the 1960s and 1970s were marked by a
knowledge explosion in social work and the social sciences.
Hundreds of books pertaining to groups as a helping process
were published, and scores of new journals were established
throughout the country specifically focused on working with
groups. Groups became fashionable and an established part of
psychology, psychiatry, education, nursing, and occupational
therapy. As a result, a multitude of approaches not specifically
tied to any particular discipline or profession, for example,

transactional analysis, Gestalt counseling, and encounter groups, emerged.

A change also occurred in what was to be thought of as non-verbal methods in working with groups. Early group workers used such activities as folk dancing, arts and crafts, clubs, and games as tools in pursuing the objectives of the social group work process. Wilson and Ryland in their book *Social Group Work Practice* (1949) entitled the second half of the book "Analysis of Program Media" and went into a thorough exposition of program content and underlying values.[47] In recent years, nonverbal activities have come to be associated with the encounter movement and include such exercises as body lifting, "trust falls," "blindwalks," and beating on pillows.

As social science knowledge has increased, social workers have hungrily adapted it for use with individuals, families, small groups, and communities. Of particular importance to social workers working with groups have been role theory, existentialism and humanism, systems theory, and socio-behavioral theory. Elements of these theories are visible within the various approaches to group work that are presently being utilized.

Role Theory

Role theory has been most visible in the prevention and rehabilitative and the developmental approaches in social group work. The term *role* refers to the individual's social status and behaviors accompanying this status. Of special importance are the individual's social functioning and adaptation to society. How a particular role is carried out is influenced by the person's past experiences, the expectations others have of him, and the rewards and punishments linked to the behaviors that make up the role. Roles are reciprocal in that they prescribe not only the expected behaviors of a person but also the behaviors of others to him. Small groups often require members to play many roles, whereas in larger groups there is greater functional delineation. The smaller group, because of its informal structure, can usually operate without a large number of well-defined roles.

The larger group, on the other hand, without defined functions and appropriate roles would evolve to a point of incessant conflict.

The construct of role has implications for assessment and intervention. As part of the assessment process, the worker evaluates the client's definition of appropriate role behavior, transactions and communications with significant others, and the role expectations others have of him. Interpretation of this information is viewed in light of the client's ethnic group, religion, and socioeconomic class. In gathering information during the early stages of the social study phase, a role analysis serves as an efficient way of locating the person-situation strengths as well as deficiencies, because as the worker focuses on role expectations, role reciprocity, and role complementarity, he avoids the danger of an exclusive concern with clinical pathology.[48]

The group provides a vehicle for assessing the participants' role functioning. It is assumed that many of the behaviors and roles the person demonstrates outside the group will be replicated within the group. As a "living laboratory," the worker is in a position to observe certain actions and reactions as they occur. He is also in a strategic position to influence the member's performance of roles within the group. He may help the members better carry out their responsibilities, examine difficulties in resolving group-related tasks, or transfer knowledge and skills learned inside the group to situations outside the group.

Existentialism and Humanism

In the last ten years, the medical model in general and the study-diagnosis-treatment approach in particular have come under attack for failure to view the client as an individual with special needs, weaknesses, strengths, and concerns. It is argued that man is more than an organism comparable to rats, pigeons, and monkeys; more than a communication system; and more than a computer. It is also felt that one does not have to know the facts of a problem before a cure or resolution can be found.

Concurrent to this attack has been a move toward a more humanistic approach in social work. Based on the writings of Victor Frankl, Rollo May, Gordon Allport, and Abraham Maslow, this approach operates on the beliefs that (1) man has the potential freedom to make responsible choices, although this freedom may be impaired by inner conflicts or blockages in development; (2) man can be helped to find meaning in life through the liberation of his inner strengths; (3) dignity is inherent in the human condition; (4) man is a being in the process of becoming; and (5) with help, man may move to a higher level of functioning.

According to this approach, the worker shares one overriding characteristic with the client, that is, the common human condition. No matter how great the differences between the worker and client, their common humanity creates a link of life experiences. The worker engages in an I-Thou rather than a subject-object or an I-It relationship with the client. The goal of the helping process is the client's achievement of a firm sense of wholeness and fuller experiencing of freedom and autonomy with social awareness and social responsibility. This goal fits in with social group work's early interest in the socialization of the individual and its roots in adult education, progressive education, recreation, and the social settlements. With an emphasis on the natural development process, people are helped to recognize and build on their strengths whether they are in trouble or whether they are striving for self-actualization.

An important element of the existential and humanistic approach is the importance of genuineness on the part of the worker. Various writers, including Emanuel Tropp, Alan Klein, and Kenneth Reid, have noted that when the worker is willing to be open and honest he is at a tremendous advantage in that the interaction, as perceived by the clients, is uncomplicated, straightforward, and usually more meaningful. He enters into the relationship with the group without presenting a front or facade. The feelings he is experiencing are available to him, and he is able to communicate them when appropriate. As part of this openness, the worker may himself disclose some of his own struggles, disillusionments, concerns, and fears.

From the existential and humanistic position, the worker has no prescription of how the client should live. He sees his task as that of an enabler who has knowledge and skills to assist in the unlocking process that will allow the client to resume a more positive form of growth. The worker perceives his skills as being those of empathy, understanding, appreciation for individual beings and their struggles, and an open honesty that offers the possibility of genuine dialogue.

Systems Theory

Over the past ten years, the systems approach has become a significant part of social work practice, particularly group work. Writers such as William Schwartz and Alan Klein have underscored its importance, and it serves as one of the basic elements in the interactionist approach. While not a theory as such, it is more correctly a framework of concepts for describing and analyzing systems. Its usefulness lies in understanding the interrelatedness between various systems. A system, defined as a complex set of elements or components, is directly or indirectly related to a network, such that each component is related to some other in a more or less stable way within any particular period of time. Systems analysis is a descriptive device for identifying the interdependency of parts of a system and the interrelatedness between systems. It also provides a means of locating tensions and ascertaining how they operate.

According to Schwartz, the function of social work in general and group work in particular is to mediate the transactions between people and the systems in which they carry on their relationships within society—the family, peer group, social agency, neighborhood, job, and others.[49] In this role, the worker has two interrelated responsibilities: he must help each individual negotiate the system immediately crucial to his problem, and he must help the system reach out to incorporate the client, deliver its services, and thus carry out its function in the community.

By charting a system, the worker can find problems in process, structure, or in the state of the component parts. He can use this information to assist the group to come to grips with its malfunction. The analysis also allows the group worker to select the most feasible point of entry within the system or subsystems. As one variable within the system is influenced, there will be a change in other variables.[46]

The worker can facilitate a continuing introduction of various stimuli into the group, a process that necessitates constant adjustment. He can help to regulate the tension levels so that they will be optimum for the maintenance of the group and meet the needs of the participants. He can facilitate communication within the group and its surroundings, and he can help provide the linkage to a number of other systems. For the group to be truly adaptive, it must be sensitive to changes in itself and in the environment, it must be willing and able to adjust values, norms, and goals, and it must have some way of perpetuating that which is nutritive and growth inducing.

Socio-Behavioral Theory

The infusion of socio-behavioral theory and techniques into social work practice came at a time when the more traditional practice theories were coming under attack. Critics, questioning whether such approaches as insight therapy were effective or relevant, pressed for techniques that were based substantially on empirical research. While the research in the area of group work and socio-behavioral theory tends to be sparse, a growing number of studies suggest that the two in combination can serve as a powerful force in bringing about change.

Treatment consists of modifying maladaptive and undesirable behaviors and increasing desirable behaviors. The worker uses four fundamental procedures in this process: he identifies the problem situation and specifies the relevant behaviors that are to be changed; he determines the reinforcers that maintain the undesirable behaviors and the reinforcers that may be manipulated to change it; he programs reinforcement schedules; and he provides training for behavioral deficits where they exist so that the desired behaviors necessary for problem-solving are acquired. Of the various approaches presently utilized in social group work, the preventative and rehabilitative approach best lends itself to the use of behavior modification. Rose writes:

For this reason I draw on the concepts of Vinter and his problem-solving goal oriented model of group treatment. He proposes careful assessment not only of the problem of each client in the group but also of social conditions and psychological attributes which might hinder or facilitate treatment. On the basis of this assessment the client is assigned to a group of individuals sufficiently dissimilar to be able to help one another but sufficiently similar to communicate with each other. Also, on the basis of the assessment tentative treatment goals are formulated with the client, and group goals are developed with all group members.[51]

By using behavior modification within the group, the emphasis becomes that of solving the problem(s) of concern to the client. In contrast to other approaches, the goal of treatment is that of resolving a specific problem rather than learning to be a good member or having a good group experience. Aspects of the group's process such as group cohesion, effective communication, and democratic decision-making become relevant only to the extent that they facilitate the achievement of the specific treatment goals, which are related to desired individual behavior outside the group.

Small Group Theory

Over the years, group workers have looked to sociologists, psychologists, educators, and psychiatrists for practice knowledge as to the dynamics of groups. Since 1955, a growing quantity of empirical research on groups has been generated by individuals trained in social group work. Some were doctoral students seeking a joint degree in the social sciences, while others were practitioners trying to understand the groups with which they were working. The research tended to be practice oriented, done with the intent of deepening and making more effective the service provided to people in groups and assisting workers be more deliberate, rather than haphazard, in their effort to create and work with groups. Concepts of group development, leadership, interaction, worker interventions, and group processes have all been targets of research and experimentation. Knowledge derived from small group research has found its way into practice approaches. One example of this is the growing awareness of the recurrent phases and cycles that occur in a small group's development. Sarri and Galinsky, after reviewing the literature on group development, identified seven stages that groups generally go through. From this they established a series of strategies available to the worker in assisting the group achieve its purpose.[52] Similarly, Garland, Jones, and Kolodny made an analysis of theories of group development and devised a developmental approach of their own. This approach, referred to as the *Boston* or *process model*, is based on the premise that groups move through definable stages much in the same way as living organisms. The sequence begins with a preaffiliation state and continues through stages of power and control, intimacy, differentiation, and separation.[53]

Knowledge about small group theory, as it relates to social work with groups, serves as the foundation for a growing number of books. Hartford's *Groups in Social Work* (1972), systematically draws together small group theory, research findings, and practice experience.[54] *Contemporary Approaches to Group Treatment*, (1975) by Feldman and Wodarski, provides a comprehensive overview of the most currently used group treatment methods along with available research data that supports these methods.[55] *Group Theory for Social Workers*, (1977) by Heap, summarizes basic group theory and introduces a series of concepts and propositions on small group theory for the practitioner.[56] Another book, written in 1979, was Shulman's *The Skills of Helping Individuals and Groups;* it was based on a four year study into the helping process. Shulman identifies basic skills, techniques and concepts perceived by workers and clients as being helpful.[57]

Although the number of books on small group theory, particularly as it relates to social work, have increased, the number of journal articles have decreased. Tropp, in reviewing articles listed under the heading "group work" in *Abstracts for Social Workers* between 1965 and 1976 found a sharp downward trend in articles specific to group work, while the number of articles on other types of groups such as group therapy and sensitivity training remained constant. The peak years for publication of group work articles were from 1970 to 1973 with approximately ten or eleven such articles each year. Between 1974 and 1976 there was an annual total of six.[58] In a similar review of all issues of the central professional journal *Social Work* since its inception in 1956, Tropp found that in the first seven years there was an average of one or two group work articles per issue.[59] After 1963, however, this dropped to about one out of every six issues. With the appearance of the journal *Social Work With Groups* in the spring of 1978, there may be a reverse in this trend with more articles published that link small group theory with practice knowledge.

NOTES

1. President Lyndon B. Johnson, Message on Poverty, March 16, 1964.

2. John Kenneth Galbraith, *The Affluent Society* (Boston: Houghton Mifflin Co., 1958), p. 253.

3. U.S., Department of Commerce, Bureau of the Census, "Characteristics of the Low-Income Population: 1973," *Population Reports*, Series P-60, July 1974.

4. Frances Piven and Richard Cloward, "Eroding Welfare Rights," *The Civil Liberties Review* 1, No. 2 (Winter-Spring 1974): 41-51.

5. Council on Social Work Education, Annual Statistical Report reported in the *Encyclopedia of Social Work*, 17 (New York: NASW, 1977), p. 1669.

6. Charles F. Grosser, "Community Development Programs Serving the Poor," *Social Work* 10, No. 3 (July 1965): 15-21.

7. Helen Harris Perlman, "Social Work Method: A Review of the Past Decade," *Social Work* 10, No. 4 (October 1965): 168.

8. H. Meyer, E. Borgatta, and W. Jones, *Girls at Vocational High* (New York: Russell Sage Foundation, 1965).

9. Willard C. Richan and Allan R. Mendelsohn, *Social Work: The Unloved Profession* (New York: New Viewpoints, 1973), p. 6.

10. Jesse Steiner, *Community Organization: A Study of Its Theory and Practice* (New York: Century, 1930), p. 99.

11. Bessie A. McClenahan, *Organizing the Community: A Review of Practical Principles* (New York: Century, 1925).

12. Eduard Lindeman, *The Community, An Introduction to the Study of Community Leadership and Organization* (New York: Association Press, 1921).

13. Steiner, *Community Organization*, p. 150.

14. Robert Lane, "The Field of Community Organization," in *Proceedings of the National Conference of Social Work, 1939* (New York: Columbia University Press, 1939), pp. 496-97.

15. Earle E. Eubank, *The Concepts of Sociology* (Boston: D.C. Health and Co., 1932), p. 163.

16. W. I. Newstetter, "The Social Intergroup Work Process," *Proceedings of the National Conference of Social Work, 1947* (New York: Columbia University Press, 1947), pp. 205-17. Newstetter had experimented with the concept several years before he presented this paper.

17. Charles Grosser, "The Legacy of the Federal Comprehensive Projects for Community Organization," Twenty-fifth Annual Program Meeting, Council on Social Work Education, 1967, p. 2.

18. Jack Rothman, "Three Models of Community Organization Practice," *Social Work Practice, 1968* (New York: Columbia University Press, 1968).

19. Roland L. Warren, *The Community in America* (Chicago: Rand McNally and Co., 1963).

20. Saul D. Alinsky, *Reveille for Radicals* (Chicago: University of Chicago Press, 1946).

21. "The Practice of Social Group Work"—Commission on Practice, 1955-1958 (New York: Group Work Section, NASW, 1957; Summary 1958).

22. Margaret E. Hartford (ed.), *Working Papers Toward a Frame of Reference for Social Group Work—1959-1963* (New York: NASW, 1964).

23. Ibid., p. 8.

24. Ibid., p. 9.

25. William Schwartz, "Analysis of Papers Presented on Working Definitions of Group Work Practice," in Margaret E. Hartford (ed.), *Working Papers Toward a Frame of Reference for Social Group Work—1959-1963"* (New York: NASW, 1964), pp. 59-61.

26. Beulah Rothman and Catherine Papell, "Social Group Work Models: Possession and Heritage," *Education for Social Work* 2 (Fall 1966): 66-77.

27. Charles Garvin and Paul Glasser, "Social Group Work: The Preventative and Rehabilitative Approach," *Encyclopedia of Social Work* (New York: NASW, 1971), pp. 1263-1272.

28. Emanuel Tropp, "Social Group Work: The Developmental Approach," *Encyclopedia of Social Work* (New York: NASW, 1971), pp. 1246-1252.

29. William Schwartz, "Social Group Work: The Interactionist Approach," *Encyclopedia of Social Work* (New York: NASW, 1971), pp. 1252-1263.

30. Robert W. Roberts and Helen Northen (eds.), *Theories of Social Work with Groups* (New York: Columbia University Press, 1976), p. 371.

31. Paul H. Glasser and Charles D. Garvin, "An Organizational Model," in Robert W. Roberts and Helen Northen (eds.), *Theories of Social Work with Groups* (New York: Columbia University Press, 1976), p. 80.

32. Robert D. Vinter, "An Approach to Group Work Practice," in Paul Glasser, Rosemary Sarri, and Robert Vinter (eds.), *Individual Change Through Small Groups* (New York: The Free Press, 1974), p. 4.

33. Garvin and Glasser, "Social Group Work," p. 1269.

34. Robert Vinter, "The Essential Components of Social Group Work Practice," in Paul Glasser, Rosemary Sarri, and Robert Vinter (eds.), *Individual Change Through Small Groups* (New York: The Free Press, 1974), p. 16.

35. Robert D. Vinter and Maeda J. Galinsky, "Extragroup Relations and Approaches," in Paul Glasser, Rosemary Sarri, and Robert Vinter (eds.), *Individual Change Through Small Groups* (New York: The Free Press, 1974), p. 287.

36. William Schwartz, "Between Client and System: The Mediating Function," in Robert W. Roberts and Helen Northen (eds.), *Theories of Social Work with Groups* (New York: Columbia University Press, 1976), p. 190.

37. Ibid., p. 188.

38. William Schwartz, "The Social Worker in the Group," *New Perspectives on Services to Groups* (New York: NASW, 1961), p. 7.

39. William Schwartz and Serapio R. Zalba (eds.), *The Practice of Group Work* (New York: Columbia University Press, 1971), p. 11.

40. Ibid., p. 12.

41. Tropp, "Social Group Work," p. 1248.

42. Emanuel Tropp, "A Developmental Theory," in Robert W. Roberts and Helen Northen (eds.), *Theories of Social Work with Groups* (New York: Columbia University Press, 1976), p. 218.

43. Mildred Sirls, Jack Rubinstein, Erma Meyerson, and Alan Klein, "Social Group Work Practice Elaborated: A Statement of Position," Unpublished position paper, University of Pittsburgh, Graduate School of Social Work, April 1964.

44. Joseph D. Jacobs, "Social Action as Therapy in a Mental Hospital," *Social Work* 9, No. 1 (January 1964): 54-61.

45. Kenneth E. Reid, "Social Group Work Enhances Milieu Therapy," *Hospital and Community Psychiatry* 19, No. 1 (January 1968): 50-53.

46. Rothman and Papell, *Social Group Work Models*, p. 69.

47. Gertrude Wilson and Gladys Ryland, *Social Group Work Practice* (New York: Houghton Mifflin Co., 1949).

48. Herbert S. Strean, "Role Theory," in Francis Turner (ed.), *Social Work Treatment: Interlocking Theoretical Approaches* (New York: The Free Press, 1974), p. 329.

49. Roberts and Northen, eds., *Theories of Social Work with Groups*, p. 181.

50. Alan F. Klein, *Effective Group Work: An Introduction to Principle and Method* (New York: Association Press, 1972), p. 129.

51. Sheldon Rose, *Treating Children in Groups* (San Francisco: Jossey-Bass, 1974), p. 8.

52. Rosemary C. Sarri and Maeda J. Galinsky, "A Conceptual Framework for Group Development," in Robert Vinter (ed.), *Readings in Group Work Practice*, (Ann Arbor, Michigan: Campus Publisher, 1967), pp. 72-94.

53. James A. Garland, Hubert E. Jones and Ralph L. Kolodny, "A Model for Stages of Development in Social Work Groups," in Saul Bernstein (ed.), *Explorations in Group Work* (Mass.: Boston University School of Social Work, 1973), pp. 17-71.

54. Margaret E. Hartford, *Groups in Social Work* (New York: Columbia University Press, 1972).

55. Ronald A. Feldman and John Wodarski, *Contemporary Approaches to Group Treatment* (San Francisco: Jossey-Bass, 1975).

56. Kenneth Heap, *Group Theory for Social Workers* (Oxford: Pergamon Press, 1977).

57. Lawrence Shulman, *The Skills of Helping Individuals and Groups*, (Itasca, Illinois: F. E. Peacock, 1979).

58. Emanuel Tropp, "What Ever Happened to Group Work," *Social Work With Groups*, 1, No. 1 (Spring 1978), p. 90.

59. Ibid., pp. 90-1.

Chapter 7

THE PAST AS PROLOGUE

Group work was practiced long before it was defined. In
England, it developed at a time when the country was going
through the tremendous changes produced by the Industrial
Revolution. During the first quarter of the nineteenth century,
most Englishmen had been connected with agriculture; within
a generation a majority of the population had moved to the
cities where they were engaged in industry. This shift in life-
style brought with it a new set of problems for the individual,
the family, and the community as a whole. Traditional family
patterns were breaking down, there was greater unemployment, and crime was on the increase. England gave an outward
picture of national greatness and imperial power, but behind
this lay a welter of social problems affecting a substantial
number of the population living in conditions of squalor,
poverty and frequent unemployment. This widespread poverty
was in glaring contrast with the overall increase in the nation's
wealth, most of which was possessed by a small minority of
the population. The contrast between poverty and riches led
social reform and political thinkers to seriously question the
organization of a society which allowed this state of affairs
to exist.

A large percent of the English population living in urban
areas was dependent for its livelihood on an industrial system that manufactured for home and overseas markets. The
workers, both skilled and unskilled, were at the mercy of the
alternating slump and boom that affected the economy. After
the 1850s there was a demand by social investigators and reformers for England to break away from the laissez-faire
philosophy, and called for measures to reduce poverty, sickness,

and unemployment among the underprivileged. Organizations began to evolve made up of young men and women and committed to the formation of the kingdom of God on earth. The evangelistic motive served as the base for many of the early organizations, including the Boys' Brigade, the Y's, and the settlements. These organizations were founded by men and women who wanted to influence the lives of others in a positive way, such as saving souls, educating the poor, and providing safe and moral forms of recreation for impoverished children. Individuals such as Canon Barnett, William Smith, Emma Robarts, and Mary Jane Kinnaird, felt it was both their mission and duty to win men and women to the faith.

These organizations were not based solely on the humanitarian or religious impulse: the motive of protecting property was an equally important factor in their origin. It was hoped that by drawing young people together into clubs and organizations, it would strengthen their character and reduce delinquency and crime. While there is little evidence that early group work actually did reduce the problem, farmers and urban residents felt greater security seeing young people under the leadership of an adult. Some organizations such as the Scouts and the Boys' Brigade offered special attractions that other groups could not. Members of these two groups could wear uniforms, parade, and play at being soldiers, and so children willingly participated, despite these organizations' authoritarian approach. Other movements, especially in the latter half of the nineteenth century, offered gymnasiums, sports, outings, and camping.

The group service organizations at the turn of the century were oriented toward the pursuit of knowledge, patriotic duty, self-help and mutual aid, spiritual awakening, recreation and education. No one organization followed any one theme exclusively but instead tended to focus on all of them to some degree. The Ragged Schools and the Mechanics Institutes emphasized the pursuit of knowledge out of a concern that reading, writing, and learning should not be restricted to the upper classes but rather should be possessed by all free men. Those who felt education of the lower classes was more dangerous than their remaining in ignorance, reacted to the idea of educating the masses with both alarm and contempt. Organizations such as the Scouts stressed patriotism, military preparedness, and active participation in community life. Frequently underlying this patriotism was a strong nationalistic orientation based on the principle of Social Darwinism and imperialism. Certainly the background of those who founded the Scouts was instrumental in establishing the ideology of the organization. For example, two-thirds of the leadership of the British Boy Scouts were or had been military officers.

The theme of self-help and mutual aid was a constant in nearly all group service agencies in England during the nineteenth century. Leaders in these organizations felt that small groups, such as Scout patrols, or larger groups, such as the friendly societies, could and should take care of their members and not look to "outsiders" to do it for them. This theme was also exemplified in the settlement movement where it was believed that people would not radically change or improve by having things done for them. Linked to this was the belief in the direct influence of people living and sharing their lives and their ideas on some common ground.

The theme of recreation came at a time when leisure-time pursuits and recreation in general were becoming part of the life of all classes, and not just the middle and upper classes. Generations of working boys had grown up to accept from early childhood the formula that a workingman's life was eating, drinking, sleeping, and working. Organizations such as the boys' clubs provided outlets for young men to "play" and to involve themselves in healthy physical activities.

The Industrial Revolution in America also brought far reaching social and cultural changes to urban areas. Cities grew at a phenomenal rate and were subject to the many dislocations caused by economic expansion. In the four decades surrounding the Civil War, the population of American cities rose at the rate of 4 percent per decade; and by 1880 over a quarter of the nation's people lived in urban areas. By 1900, 40 percent of the American people lived in such metropolitan centers as New York, Chicago, Philadelphia, and Detroit.

As industries developed and factories were built, they were

manned by individuals willing to work for low wages, under
difficult and unsafe conditions. The average work week was
little less than 60 hours and the average wage for skilled workers
was about twenty cents an hour, and for an unskilled worker
just half that amount. Annual wages for the factory worker
came to an average of $400 to $500 from which a working
family saved an average of $30 after spending nearly half the
remainder for food, another quarter on rent, and the balance
on fuel, light, and clothing.

The economic revolution that resulted from the Industrial
Revolution created conditions in which competition and
business flourished. With this came the doctrine of laissez-faire,
which sharply limited what the government could do to solve
social and economic problems. The philosophy of Charles
Darwin, as interpreted by Herbert Spencer and William Graham
Sumner, provided the intellectual base for this new competitive
order. Translated into economic and social terms, Darwinian
theory brought science to the support of predatory capitalism
and justified poverty and slums. It was argued that these conditions were natural for the unfit, who, because of lack of thrift
and industry, had not survived the economic struggle. Any
governmental effort to relieve poverty would be a perversion
of the law of nature.

During the 1860-1899 period, groups were considered by
educators and settlement leaders to be a means by which
numbers of people could find an outlet for improving conditions in their lives. In contrast to the methodological and
goal-oriented nature of early casework, group work was an
opportunistic program with no acknowledged set of methods.
Group work, based in local neighborhoods and providing
activities to meet local needs, focused primarily on action and
gave little attention to theory. The use of groups was highly
visible in both settlement houses and youth service agencies.
The settlement, unlike the Charity Organization Society, did
not distinguish between giver and receiver. The early settlement
leaders believed that social problems stemmed more from the
neighborhood or community than from the individual; the

individual was seen as the victim of destructive social conditions and forces. It was assumed that the individual "victim" could be helped to bring about constructive change in his environment if he banded together with other "victims." This banding together was encouraged and supported by the settlers who became part of the neighborhood.

Public recreation centers were nonexistent in the 1890s and in many neighborhoods, the settlement was the focal point for recreation. Besides gymnasiums, playgrounds, and gamerooms, social clubs were introduced as a way of helping individuals make constructive use of their leisure time. Although these clubs were mainly social, they often provided impetus to vocational and educational ambitions and helped many of the members learn the new ways of the American community.

The youth service agencies such as the Scouts and the Ys were stimulated by the growing mechanization of industry and were considered a means of molding youth into productive citizens. A majority of these organizations were geared to either boys or girls in preadolescence and early adolescence, and they rewarded such personal virtues as honesty, loyalty, and integrity. Most of these agencies relied heavily on competition and ritual to motivate their programs. In many respects, they were protective associations created as a response to city life in an industrial and urbanized society. These organizations ranged themselves against mobility and rootlessness, delinquency and crime, and the inability of a transient and disorganized population to take action in its own behalf. The major thrust of these early group service agencies was toward the normal rather than the maladjusted, and they stressed development of the "whole" person.

The concerns underlying the early work with groups were a decrease in opportunity for satisfying social needs and a decrease in social control. These decreases, resulting in part from the change in family, neighborhood, and village life, could be compensated for by the conscious organization of groups around a particular interest. The varied activities of group life could help develop emotionally sound personalities as well as produce satisfactory social relationships and the means for passing on social patterns. While both the settlement and youth service agencies employed some paid staff from the onset, they were almost exclusively dependent on volunteers. Generally, these volunteer leaders were college-educated, middle-class adults, recognized as being of good character. It was hoped that, through their personalities and life-style, they would set examples that the members would emulate.

The youth service agencies, the social settlements, the adult education movement, the recreation movement, and eventually progressive education all assumed a stance of social responsibility in a competitive order and a personal, cultural identity in an impersonal culture. They stressed the need for individualizing, for collective security, and for the equalization of political and economic power. All of these movements and agencies saw the group as a means of socializing the individual and of maintaining a democratic society. The use of the small group as a potent force in socializing the individual was most obvious in the "character-building" programs, where desirable personal characteristics were made known via slogans, awards, and rituals and with a variety of inducements. Honesty, loyalty, patriotism, courtesy, reverence, graciousness, dependability, and health of body, mind, and spirit were set forth in alluring pledges and were reinforced during impressive ceremonies.

In the 1930s, there was less emphasis on the use of slogans and virtue and a move toward concepts such as social adjustment, security of personality, capacity for self-maintenance, acceptance of responsibility, and emotional security. These newer objectives grew out of an increased understanding of the dynamics of personality and behavior as gleaned by the social and medical sciences, and from the experiences and observations of group workers in various agencies. The most notable contributions in these areas, by Cooley, Mead, Simmel, Durkheim, and Dewey, brought about more than a change in wording: they directed the group worker away from symptomatic behavior to a deeper appreciation and understanding of personality in action. This change produced a new way of utilizing activities and programs. Heretofore, group workers had thought of activities as ends in themselves. Sports, aesthetic pursuits, social recreation, and the like were for enjoyment and were vehicles for making use of one's leisure time. By the 1930s, it was realized that not only the activity or the subject alone was important, but also the human relations in which the activity was set. The experience in and through the group began to emerge as a significant part of the group work process.

The emphasis on use of the group as a means of socializing the individual continued into the 1950s and was most observable in such youth developmental agencies as the Ys and the Scouts, where the primary objective remains socialization. These agencies maintained that group experience benefited the individual by developing potential that might not otherwise achieve fulfillment. The theme of socialization of the individual also insured the preservation of social values dominant within the culture and enhanced the human resources of a democratic society.

The concept of the group as a means of maintaining a democratic society was closely intertwined with the use of the group as a means of socialization. From the beginning group work was interested in the use of group experience as a preparation for responsible participation in the democratic process. This interest manifested itself in several ways. First, it was thought that experience in the small, intimate, self-governing group found in a club would help develop common goals and foster the creation and acceptance of self-imposed authority in the acquisition of leadership skills. Second, it was felt that if the worker introduced social issues as discussion topics during group sessions, members could discuss the issues and be better informed. Third, the group was seen as a way of dealing with neighborhood tensions, especially in interracial or interethnic group situations.

For those concerned by the emergence of a mass society and the problems of urbanization, as were Follett, Lindeman, and Mayo, the group could be used to conserve humanistic values. Small groups that were part of or linked to larger social units were viewed by these social scientists as providing opportunities for collective decision-making and individual participation.

Through the group, the individual would have a vehicle for articulating his concerns and decentralizing the decision-making process.

The importance of the notion that the group is a means of maintaining a democratic society had declined over the years. The "Definition of the Function of the Group Worker" (1949) contains several phrases that refer to the worker directing his energies toward the improvement of society. By 1962, however, this idea was more muted and no longer central. "Working Papers Toward A Frame of Reference for Social Group Work Practice" makes only one leading reference to "group life as experience in developing a sense of responsibility for active citizenship, and for improving the nature of participation in social action."[1] Still, practitioners in settlement houses and other agencies directly concerned with disadvantaged segments of the urban population prized the concept very highly. By the 1950s, the definition of community was expanded to include mental hospitals, treatment facilities, and correctional institutions. Social group workers in these settings stressed client participation in decision-making, the development of the client's leadership skills, and social action as a way of bringing about change.

Until the late 1930s, there was general agreement that the chief aim of group work was the development and adjustment of the individual through voluntary group association and activity. Such development was seen as occurring, with the assistance of a trained worker, primarily out of the interplay of personalities in group situations and out of the activities making up the program. The objective was the development of socially desirable attitudes within the individual. "Socially desirable" was understood to cover a wide range, from the development of tolerance of people from other cultural backgrounds to the promotion of socialization within the community. By 1938, discussions began as to whether group work should be aimed at individuals requiring corrective or therapeutic treatment. Many argued that group work should be concerned mainly with education and prevention rather than with therapeutic goals. World War II in many ways settled the issue. Group work began to be used in military and veterans' hospitals and, soon after, became a part of the services of child guidance clinics, state hospitals, and private hospitals. Initially, the worker was part of the treatment team in which his observations of the client's behavior were used for diagnostic purposes. As workers became more skilled, and through the writings of Redl, Lewin, Moreno, Konopka, and Slavson their roles changed from being gatherers of information to therapists.

Since the mid 1960s, it has been evident that there are several forms of social group work and not just one. These include the interactionist approach, the social goals approach, the developmental approach, and the preventative and rehabilitative approach. Each, in its own way, is a permutation of the socialization, treatment, and maintenance of a democratic society theme. The theme of socialization is most apparent in the interactionist and developmental approaches wherein the group is viewed as a vehicle by which the individual can realize his potential for self-awareness, self-activation, and self-valuation. By building on strengths, the worker enables the group members to face life situations, stresses, and difficult developmental stages. The ideal group state occurs when a system of mutual aid emerges in which the members can call on each other in their own or a common cause. It is assumed that people most effectively enhance their social functioning through group experiences in which the members share a common goal. As the members seek to achieve this common goal, they develop skills in problem-solving, decision-making, and leadership.

The theme of maintaining a democratic society is highly visible in the social action and interactionist approaches. Concepts such as social consciousness and social responsibility serve as the foundation of these approaches with the overall goal being that of creating active, well-informed, and responsible citizens. Through collective action, citizens are encouraged to challenge the obstacles that prevent them from living fulfilled and meaningful lives. The social goals approach regards the individual as being in need of opportunity and assistance in revitalizing his drive toward others in a common cause and in converting self-seeking into social contributions. Every group is thought to possess the potential for effecting social change. The worker, through his interaction with the individual members and the group as a whole, moves toward uncovering this strength in the group, with social action the desired outcome.

The theme of treatment or correction is most apparent in the preventative and rehabilitative approach. This social group work model establishes the treatment of individuals as the central function of both group work and social work. The group is viewed as a tool or context for treatment of the individual. Diagnostic goals, along with group goals, are developed for each individual. The worker is viewed as a change agent who uses a problem-solving approach, sequentially phasing his activities in the tradition of study, diagnosis, and treatment. In this role, he is characteristically directive and assumes a position of clinical preeminence and authority. He exercises his authority by controlling membership, screening activities against his own professional objectives, assigning tasks and roles, and defining group purposes so that they are consistent with the several treatment goals established for the individual members.

Despite influences from such roots as recreation, education, and the youth service agencies, the historical impetus of group work was toward an identification with social work as a profession and with social welfare as a field of service. By their very nature, group workers reflected concern with social conditions and their effects on people. Even though they drew inspiration from educational theory, psychiatric findings, and small group research, many saw these developments as instruments to be used in achieving social objectives. The fact that a substantial number of the early group work programs were sponsored and financed by many of the same funding sources as social casework programs also served to draw group work toward social work. The relationship between these various efforts took on greater importance and meaning during the 1929 depression, as they came together around common problems and clientele. Each recognized that the other had valuable knowledge and skill that could be used to reduce suffering and meet human needs.

The alliance of group work with social work had implications for both parties. It served to expand the scope of social work itself, bringing it back to the earlier and broader conception of its role and function. It brought sociological thinking into a profession that had almost totally come to view man and human behavior in individualistic terms. It brought to social work a recognition of its lack of commitment to social reform. It reintroduced to social work the "normal" client, something that had become completely antipathetic to the development of social work as a therapeutic profession. For group work, it gave professional identification and status to a collection of individuals of various backgrounds working in diverse fields. It gave promise of a clearer and more distinct sense of function and focus, something that many group workers lacked. The merger also led to a more conscious method of working, supervising, and recording, and it stimulated a greater awareness of basic concepts of human behavior.

From a negative standpoint, group work quickly embraced, as had casework before it, the Freudian explanation of human behavior to the exclusion of other explanations and approaches. The alliance lessened much of the spirit in inquiry that had been a part of early group work. Perhaps most significant was a decrease in the emphasis that group workers placed on social action. Ironically, while group work was to make social action more visible within the profession of social work, group workers generally became less involved in social action.

THE FUTURE

In studying the roots and branches of any subject, one cannot help but wonder about the future. Certainly, as information on the development of the use of groups in social work has been compiled, analyzed, and synthesized, the question of the future has arisen. Specifically, what form and function will group work take in the decades to come and how will it be different from what has evolved to date? Of course, no accurate answer to this question is possible. We may consider trends and social indicators, but in the final analysis our own imagination can be as accurate. Toffler, in his book *Future Shock*, writes that

"in dealing with the future . . . it is more important to be imaginative and insightful than to be one hundred percent right."[2]
With this idea in mind, the following postulations are offered
with regard to the future:

(1) The group work method will remain an important part
of social welfare in general and social work in particular. From
its early beginnings in the settlements and youth service agencies, it has served as an effective vehicle for socializing individuals, maintaining a democratic society, and preventing and
treating behaviors considered deviant by society. Over the
years, group work has been modified to fit the needs of the
particular period in history, with certain elements accentuated
and others receiving less emphasis. As society changes, group
work will adjust to meet the changes.

(2) Despite attempts to develop a homogeneous method or
approach to the use of groups in social work, a number of
different approaches will prevail. Historically, there has never
been a single method of group work practiced by a majority
of those working with groups. Perhaps it is not necessary to
find an approach that can be agreed upon, but it is more
important that it be recognized that diverse problems, clientele,
and settings require different approaches and that those working with groups need to be comfortable with these approaches
and able to use them where appropriate.

(3) As social work moves toward the generalist approach and
broadens the students' repertoire of skills to work with individuals, families, and small groups, knowledge and skills that have
been peculiar to social group work will be lost. Despite the
knowledge explosion in the helping professions, the length of
professional education has remained constant. Information that
was once considered essential to group workers, such as pro-
gramming, may become a luxury that we can no longer afford
to teach in a graduate program.

(4) There will be a greater move toward the use of the group
as a means of treatment. Until the 1940s, the group workers'
clients were "normal" personalities, and emphasis was on developing character and strengthening personality. In the postwar years, there was increased emphasis on working with

individuals who were emotionally or physically impaired; those who acted out against the community and its institutions, for example, delinquents; school behavior problems; and those who withdrew from participation in the "establishment," for example, alcoholics and drug addicts. This trend will be reinforced through the availability and use of tax-supported funds for professional positions and the expansion of the job market in clinical and treatment settings.

(5) Possibly as a result of this greater emphasis on treatment, there will be a continued move away from the goal of maintaining a democratic society. While the needs that brought this goal to the attention of early workers has not diminished, interest by social agencies has decreased. In addition, community organization has absorbed many of the individuals who in the past would have been drawn to social group work.

(6) Finally, there will be development of more peer helping groups and mutual aid systems. The initial thrust of this concept comes from nonprofessional sources such as ex-patient clubs, Mothers Anonymous (for mothers who abuse their children), Synanon, Weight Watchers, Burns Recovered, and Recovery, Inc. In part, these groups have developed as a response to professionalism and the rigid helping roles to which they have adhered in the past. They have also grown out of a recognition by the members that helping has benefits not only for the person being helped, but also for the helper.

Toffler takes this expansion of groups another step by suggesting that temporary organizations need to be provided for people who happen to be passing through similar life experiences or transitions. These groups would be established for families about to lose a parent or a spouse, for those about to gain a child, for men and women preparing to change occupations or to retire—for anyone, in other words, who faces an important life change. Some of these groups might meet for several months, while others might meet for only a single session, or long enough to help the person with his transitional difficulties.[3]

By helping the client with some intrapsychic conflict in his painful past, the worker will help him focus on his personal objectives and plan practical strategies for future use in the new life situation. Like the Peace Corps, which uses "anticipatory guidance" in preparing a volunteer for the problems he will face overseas, the temporary organization will serve as a vehicle to make the transition easier.

NOTES

1. Margaret Hartford (ed.), *Working Papers Toward a Frame of Reference for Social Group Work—1959-1963* (New York: NASW, 1964.)

2. Alvin Toffler, *Future Shock* (New York: Bantam Books, 1970), p. 6.

3. Ibid., p. 383.

APPENDIX I

Approximate Beginning Dates of Organizations Contributing to the Development of Work with Groups in Great Britain

Friendly Societies	1634
Sunday School Movement	1786
Mechanics Institutes	1823
Ragged Schools	1830
YMCA	1844
Boys' Clubs	1858
YWCA	1876
Boys' Brigade	1880
Toynbee Hall	1884
Church Lads' Brigade	1891
Boys Scouts	1907
Girl Guides	1909

It is important for the reader to note that each of these organizations had informal precursors.

APPENDIX II

Dates of National Organization of Youth Service Programs in the United States

B'nai B'rith	1851
YMCA (of the U.S.)	1866
Girls' Friendly Society	1877
International Society of Christian Endeavor	1881
Epworth League	1889
United Boys' Brigades	1894
YWCA National Board	1906
Boys' Clubs of America	1906
Boy Scouts of America	1910
Campfire Girls	1912
Boy Rangers of America	1913
Pathfinders of America	1914
4-H	1914
Catholic Boys' Brigade	1916
Jewish Welfare Board	1917
Junior Achievement	1919
Order of DeMolay	1919
Catholic Youth Organization	1930

SELECTED BIBLIOGRAPHY

Adams, Jane. *The Spirit of Youth and the City Streets.* New York: Macmillan Co., 1909.

———. *Twenty Years at Hull House.* New York: Macmillan Co., 1926.

Aldridge, Gordon J. "Program in a Camp for Emotionally Disturbed Boys." *The Group* 14, No. 2 (December 1953): 13-18.

American Association of Group Workers. "Definition of the Function of the Group Worker." (Mimeographed)

Atkinson, R. K., and Vincent, George E. *The Boys' Club.* New York: Association Press, 1939.

Baden-Powell, Robert. *Scouting for Boys.* London: 1909.

Barnett, Henrietta. *Canon Barnett, His Life, Work, and Friends.* Vol. 1. London: John Murray, 1918.

Bernheimer, Charles S., and Cohen, Jacob M. *Boys' Clubs.* Baltimore: Lord Baltimore Press, 1914.

Binfield, Clyde. *George Williams and the Y.M.C.A.* London: Heinemann, 1973.

Bowman, LeRoy L. "Application of Progressive Education to Group Work," in Joshua Leiberman (ed.), *New Trends in Group Work.* New York: Association Press, 1939, pp. 118-22.

———. "Dictatorship, Democracy, and Group Work in America." *Proceedings of the National Conference of Social Work, 1935.* Chicago: University of Chicago Press, 1935, pp. 382-92.

Boyd, Neva. "Group Work Experiments in State Institutions in Illinois." *Proceedings of the National Conference of Social Work, 1935.* Chicago: University of Chicago Press, 1935, pp. 339-52.

Bradford, Leland P. "Human Relations Training at the First National Training Laboratory in Group Development." *The Group* 10, No. 2 (January 1948): 4-10.

Bremner, Robert H. *From the Depths: The Discovery of Poverty in the United States.* New York: New York University Press, 1964.

Bright, Sally. "Letting the Public in on Group Work Objectives." *The Group* (October 1948): 10-15.

Bruckner, William. "Group Work Commitment to Social Responsibility." *Proceedings of the National Conference of Social Work, 1952.* New York: Columbia University Press, 1952, p. 560.

Bryson, Lyman. *Adult Education.* New York: American Book Co., 1936.

Burns, Mary E. "The Historical Development of Casework Supervision in the Professional Literature." Ph.D. dissertation, School of Social Service Administration, University of Chicago, 1958.

Butler, George. *Introduction to Community Recreation.* New York: McGraw-Hill, 1940.

Case, Victoria, and Case, Robert O. *We Called It Culture: The Story of Chautauqua.* Garden City, N.Y.: Doubleday and Co., 1948.

Cohen, Nathan E. "Body of Knowledge Basic to Group Work." *Toward Professional Standards.* New York: Association Press, 1947, p. 8.

————. *Social Work in the American Tradition.* New York: Dryden Press, 1958.

Cooley, Charles Horton. *Social Organization.* New York: Schocken Books, 1943.

Coyle, Grace L. *Group Experience and Democratic Values.* New York: Woman's Press, 1947.

————. *Group Work and American Youth: A Guide to the Practice of Leadership.* New York: Harper and Brothers, 1948.

————. "Group Work and Social Change." *Proceedings of the National Conference of Social Work, 1935.* Chicago: University of Chicago Press, 1935, p. 393.

————. "Group Work: A Method in Recreation." *The Group* (April 1947): 3-6.

————. "Group Work in Recreation." *Proceedings of the National Conference of Social Work, 1947.* New York: Columbia University Press, 1947, pp. 203-8.

————. "On Becoming Professional." *Toward Professional Standards.* New York: Association Press, 1947, p. 1.

————. "Social Group Work." *Social Work Yearbook, 1954.* New York: Russell Sage Foundation, 1954, Vol. 12, pp. 481-486.

Davis, Allen F. *Spearheads for Reform: The Social Settlements and the Progressive Movement, 1880-1914.* New York: Oxford University Press, 1967.

Devine, Edward T. *When Social Work Was Young.* New York: Macmillan Co., 1939.

Dewey, John. *Experience and Nature.* Chicago: Open Court Publishing Co., 1925.

DuVall, Everett. *Personality and Social Group Work.* New York: Association Press, 1943.

Eager, W. McG. *Making Men: A History of Boys' Clubs and Related Movements in Great Britain.* London: University of London Press, 1953.

Education for Social Work. Reprinted from *Report of the Commissioner of Education for the Year Ended June 30, 1915.* Washington, D.C.: U.S. Government Printing Office, 1915, pp. 345-48.

Ephraim, Miriam R. "Introduction." *The Group* 10, No. 2 (January 1948): 3.

Eubank, Earle E. *The Concepts of Sociology.* Boston: D. C. Heath and Co., 1932.

Fisher, Raymond. "Contributions of Group Work in Psychiatric Hospitals." *The Group* 12, No. 1 (November 1949): 3-11.

Follett, Mary Parker. *The New State.* New York: Longmans, Green, 1920.

Garvin, Charles, and Glasser, Paul. "Social Group Work: The Preventative and Rehabilitative Approach." *Encyclopedia of Social Work.* New York: NASW, 1971.

Gillis, John R. *Youth and History: Tradition and Change in European Age Relations 1770-Present.* New York: Academic Press, 1974.

Glasser, Paul, Sarri, Rosemary, and Vinter, Robert. *Individual Change Through Small Groups.* New York: The Free Press, 1974.

Gosden, P. H. J. H. *Self-Help: Voluntary Associations in the 19th Century.* London: B. T. Balsford, 1973.

Grusd, Edward E. *B'nai B'rith: The Story of a Covenant.* New York: Appleton-Century, 1966.

Hacker, Louis M. *The World of Andrew Carnegie 1865-1901.* Philadelphia: J. B. Lippincott, 1968.

Hale, Nathan, Jr. *Freud and the Americans: Beginnings of Psychoanalysis in the United States 1876-1917.* New York: Oxford University Press, 1971.

Hamilton, Alice. *Exploring the Dangerous Trades: The Autobiography of Alice Hamilton, M.D.* Boston: Little Brown and Co., 1943.

Harrison, Harry, and Detzer, K. *Culture Under Canvas: The Story of Tent Chautauqua.* New York: Hasting House, 1958.

Hartford, Margaret E. *Groups in Social Work.* New York: Columbia University Press, 1971.

————. (ed.). *Working Papers Toward a Frame of Reference for Social Group Work—1959-1963.* New York: NASW, 1964.

Hartshorne, Hugh. "Objectives of Group Work." *Group Work, 1939.* New York: Association Press, 1939, p. 39.

Hayes, Samuel P. *The Response to Industrialism, 1885-1914.* Chicago: University of Chicago Press, 1957.

Hibbert, Francis A. *The Influence and Development of English Gilds.* (First published in 1891) New York: Augustus M. Kelly, 1970.

Hofstadter, Richard. *The Age of Reform: From Bryan to F.D.R.* New York: Vintage Books, 1955.

Holden, Arthur. *The Settlement Idea: A Vision of Social Justice.* New York: Macmillan Co., 1922.

Hopkins, Charles H. *The History of the Y.M.C.A. in North America.* New York: Association Press, 1951.

Hudson, J. W. *The History of Adult Education.* (Initially published by Longman, Brown, Green and Longman, Poternoster Row, 1851.) New York: Augustus M. Kelly, 1969.

Hunter, Robert (ed.). *Poverty.* New York: Macmillan Co., 1907.

Hurlbutt, Mary E. "The Pugsley Award." *Proceedings of the National Conference of Social Work, 1935.* Chicago: University of Chicago Press, 1935, p. vii.

Jacobs, Joseph D. "Social Action as Therapy in a Mental Hospital." *Social Work* 9, No. 1 (January 1964): 54-61.

Kaiser, Clara. "Social Group Work Practice and Social Responsibility." *Proceedings of the National Conference of Social Work, 1952.* New York: Columbia University Press, 1952, pp. 52-58.

Kerr, Rose. *Story of the Girl Guides.* London: Girl Guides Association, 1932.

———. *The Story of a Million Girls.* London: Girl Guides Association, 1941.

Kilpatrick, W. H. *Group Education for a Democracy.* New York: Association Press, 1940.

Klein, Alan F. *Effective Group Work: An Introduction to Principle and Method.* New York: Association Press, 1972.

Klein, Philip. "Social Work." *Encyclopedia of the Social Sciences.* New York: Macmillan Co., 1934, Vol. 14, p. 169.

———. *Society, Democracy, and the Group.* New York: Morrow, 1953.

Konopka, Gisela. *Group Work in the Institution: A Modern Challenge* New York: Association Press, 1954.

———. "Similarities and Differences Between Group Work and Group Therapy." Report of the Group Therapy Committee, AAGW. (Mimeographed) ST-451-8.

———. *Social Group Work: A Helping Process.* Englewood Cliffs, N.J.: Prentice-Hall, 1963.

———. *Therapeutic Group Work with Children.* Minneapolis, Minn.: University of Minnesota Press, 1949.

———. "Therapy Through Group Work." *Toward Professional Standards.* New York: Association Press, 1947, pp. 140-146.

Lane, Robert. "The Field of Community Organization." *Proceedings of the National Conference of Social Work, 1939* New York: Columbia University Press, 1939.

Lee, Joseph. *Constructive and Preventive Philanthropy.* New York: Macmillan Co., 1906.

Levy, Charles S. "From Education to Practice in Social Group Work." *Journal of Jewish Communal Service* (Winter 1958): 175-80.

Lewin, Kurt, Lippitt, Ronald, and White, R. "Patterns of Aggressive Behavior in Experimentally Created 'Social Climates.' " *Journal of Social Psychology* 10 (1939); 271-99.

Lieberman, Joshua (ed.). *New Trends in Group Work.* New York: Association Press, 1938.

Lindeman, Eduard. *The Community, An Introduction to the Study of Community Leadership and Organization.* New York: Association Press, 1921.

——. *The Meaning of Adult Education.* New York: New Republic, 1926.

——. "The Roots of Democratic Culture." *The Group* (1939): 1-6.

List, Ely. *Juliette Low and the Girl Scouts.* New York: Girl Scouts of America, 1960.

Lustman, Claire R. "Group Work Within a Medical Setting." Paper presented at the National Conference of Social Work, Atlantic City, N.J., May 1950.

Maloney, Sara. "Development of Group Work Education in Social Work Schools in the U.S." Ph.D. dissertation, Western Reserve University, 1963.

Mayo, Elton. *The Social Problems of an Industrial Civilization.* Andover, Mass.: Andover Press, 1945.

McCaskill, Joseph. *Theory and Practice of Group Work.* New York: Association Press, 1930.

McClenahan, Bessie A. *Organizing the Community: A Review of Practical Principles.* New York: Century, 1925.

Meier, Elizabeth G. *History of the New York School of Social Work.* New York: Columbia University Press, 1954.

Menninger, William C. "Psychiatric Social Work in the Army and Its Implications for Civilian Social Work." *Proceedings of the National Conference of Social Work, 1945* New York: Columbia University Press, 1945, pp. 13-92.

Meyer, H., Borgatta, E., and Jones, W. *Girls at Vocational High.* New York: Russell Sage Foundation, 1965.

Middleman, Ruth R. *The Non-Verbal Method in Working with Groups.* New York: Association Press, 1968.

Morrison, Theodore. *Chautauqua: A Center for Education, Religion and the Arts.* Chicago: University of Chicago Press, 1974.

Murphy, Marjorie. *The Social Group Work Method in Social Work Education.* Curriculum Study XI. New York: Council on Social Work Education, 1959.

Neely, Ann Elizabeth. "Current Practices and Problems in Professional Education for Group Work," in Harry R. Eby (ed.), *Main Currents in*

Group Work Thought: Proceedings of the A.A.S.G.W. 1940 New York: Association Press, 1941, p. 58.

Neumeyer, Martin H., and Neumeyer, Esther S. *Leisure and Recreation.* New York: A. S. Barnes and Co., 1936.

Newstetter, W. I. "The Social Intergroup Work Process." *Proceedings of the National Conference of Social Work, 1947* New York: Columbia University Press, 1947.

———. "What Is Social Group Work." *Proceedings of the National Conference of Social Work, 1935.* Chicago: University of Chicago Press, 1935, pp. 291-99.

Northen, Helen. *Social Work with Groups.* New York: Columbia University Press, 1969.

Oursler, Will. *The Boy Scout Story.* Garden City, N.Y.: Doubleday and Co., 1955.

Phillips, Helen U. *Essentials of Social Group Work Skill.* New York: Association Press, 1957.

Piven, Frances, and Cloward, Richard. "Eroding Welfare Rights," *The Civil Liberties Review* 1, No. 2 (Winter-Spring, 1974).

Rabinowitz, Benjamin. *The Young Men's Hebrew Association 1854-1913.* New York: National Jewish Welfare Board, 1948.

Reck, Franklin M. *The 4-H Story: A History of 4-H Club Work.* Ames, Iowa: Iowa State College Press, 1951.

Redl, Fritz. "Diagnostic Group Work." *American Journal of Orthopsychiatry* 14 (January 1944): 53-67.

Reid, Kenneth E. "Social Group Work Enhances Milieu Therapy." *Hospital and Community Psychiatry* 19, No. 1 (January 1968): 50-53.

Rice, Anna V. *A History of the World's Young Women's Christian Association.* New York: Parish Press, 1947.

Richan, Willard C., and Mendelsohn, Allan R. *Social Work: The Unloved Profession.* New York: New Viewpoints, 1973.

Richmond, Mary. *Social Diagnosis.* New York: Russell Sage Foundation, 1917.

———. "Some Next Steps in Social Treatment." Reprint in *The Long View.* New York: Russell Sage Foundation, 1930, pp. 487-88.

Roberts, Robert W., and Helen Northen (eds.). *Theories of Social Work with Groups.* New York: Columbia University Press, 1976.

Rogers, Ethel. *Sebago-Wohelo.* Battle Creek, Mich.: Good Health Publishing Co., 1915.

Romney, G. Ott. "The Field of Recreation." *Proceedings of the National Conference of Social Work, 1947.* New York: Columbia University Press, 1947, pp. 196-201.

Ross, Edward A. *Social Control: A Survey of the Foundation of Order.* New York: Macmillan Co., 1920.

Rothman, Beulah, and Papell, Catherine. "Social Group Work Models: Possession and Heritage." *Education for Social Work* 2 (Fall 1966): 66-77.

Rowe, Helen. "Report of the Central Committee." *Toward Professional Standards.* New York: Association Press, 1947, p. 169.

Ryland, Gladys. *Employment Responsibilities of Social Work Graduates.* New York: Council on Social Work Education, 1958.

School of Applied Social Sciences: A Graduate Professional School of Western Reserve University in the City of Cleveland, 1916-1917. Western Reserve University Annual, 1917.

Schwartz, William. "Implications of the Present Scene for Social Group Work Practice." *Proceedings of the National Conference of Social Work, 1955.* New York: Columbia University Press, 1955, 103-8.

———. "Social Group Work: The Interactionist Approach." *Encyclopedia of Social Work.* New York: NASW, 1971.

———, and Zalba, Serapio R. (eds.). *The Practice of Group Work.* New York: Columbia University Press, 1971.

Simon, Paul (ed.). *Play and Game Theory in Group Work: A Collection of Papers of Neva Leona Boyd.* Chicago: University of Illinois, Jane Addams School of Social Work, 1971.

Sims, Mary S. *The Natural History of a Social Institution—The Young Women's Christian Association.* New York: Woman's Press, 1935.

Slavson, S. R. *Introduction to Group Therapy.* New York: Commonwealth Fund, 1943.

Smith, Anne. "Group Play in a Hospital Environment." *Proceedings of the National Conference of Social Work, 1935.* Chicago: University of Chicago Press, 1935, pp. 346-52.

Sorenson, Roy. "Case Work and Group Work Integration: Its Implication for Community Planning." *Proceedings of the National Conference of Social Work, 1935.* Chicago: University of Chicago Press, 1935, pp. 311-22.

Springhall, John. *Youth, Empire and Society: British Youth Movements, 1883-1940.* London: Croom Helm, 1977.

Steiner, Jesse. *Community Organization: A Study of Its Theory and Practice.* New York: Century, 1930.

Strauss, Anselm (ed.). *George Herbert Mead on Social Psychology.* Chicago: University of Chicago Press, 1964.

Sullivan, Dorothy (ed.). *The Practice of Group Work.* New York: Association Press, 1941.

Swift, Arthur. "The Essential of Training for Group Leadership." *Proceedings of the National Conference of Social Work, 1935.* Chicago: University of Chicago Press, 1935, pp. 365-73.

Tead, Ordway. *The Art of Leadership.* New York: McGraw-Hill, 1935.

Trecker, Harleigh B. *Foundation and Frontiers.* New York: Whiteside, Morrow, 1955.
———. *Social Group Work: Principles and Practice.* New York: Woman's Press, 1948.
Trolander, Judith. *Settlement Houses and the Great Depression.* Detroit, Mich.: Wayne State University Press, 1975, p. 149.
Tropp, Emanuel. *A Humanistic Foundation for Group Work Practice.* 2d ed. New York: Selected Academic Readings, 1971.
———. "Social Group Work: The Developmental Approach." *Encyclopedia of Social Work.* New York: NASW, 1971.
U.S., Department of Agriculture, Misc. Circ. 72. "A Decade of Negro Extension Work, 1914-24." 1925.
U.S., Department of Commerce, Bureau of the Census. Characteristics of Low Income Population, 1973. *Population Reports.* Series P-60, July 1974.
Vincent, John H. *The Chautauqua Movement.* (First published in 1885.) Freeport, N.Y.: Books for Libraries Press, 1971.
Vinter, Robert D. (ed.). *Readings in Group Work.* Ann Arbor, Mich.: Campus Press, 1967.
Warren, Roland L. *The Community in America.* Chicago: Rand McNally and Co., 1963.
Watson, Frank. *The Charity Organization Movement in the United States: A Study in American Philanthropy.* New York: Macmillan Co., 1922.
Westlake, H. F. *The Parish Gilds of Mediaeval England.* London: Society for Promoting Christian Knowledge, 1919.
Williamson, Margaretta. *Social Worker in Group Work.* New York: Harper and Brothers, 1929.
Wilson, Elizabeth. *Fifty Years of Association Work Among Young Women, 1866-1916.* New York: National Board of the YWCA, 1916.
Wilson, Gertrude. "Human Needs Pertinent to Group Work Services." *Proceedings of the National Conference of Social Work, 1942.* New York: Columbia University Press, 1942.
———. "Trends in Professional Education." *Toward Professional Standards.* New York: Association Press, 1947, p. 33.
———, and Ryland, Gladys. *Social Group Work Practice.* New York: Houghton Mifflin Co., 1949.
Wolff, Kurt H. (ed. and trans.). *The Sociology of Georg Simmel.* New York: The Free Press, 1950.
Woodroffe, Kathleen. *From Charity to Social Work in England and the United States.* Toronto: University of Toronto Press, 1962.
Woods, Robert A., and Kennedy, Albert J. *The Settlement Horizon: A National Estimate.* New York: Russell Sage Foundation, 1922.
Young, A. F., and Ashton, E. T. T. *British Social Work in the Nineteenth Century.* London: Routledge and Kegan Paul, 1956.

INDEX

About the Author

KENNETH E. REID is associate professor of Social Work at Western Michigan University in Kalamazoo. His articles have appeared in journals such as *Social Work Education*, *Social Casework*, and the *Journal of Social Welfare*.